Gardens in the Wasteland

Dissertationes Theologicae Holmienses
Dissertations from Stockholm School of Theology
www.ehs.se/dth

Editors:
Joel Halldorf
Jonas Ideström
Thomas Kazen
Samuel Rubenson
Susanne Wigorts Yngvesson

No. 6

Björn Asserhed

Gardens in the Wasteland

Christian Formation in Three
Swedish Church Plants

WIPF & STOCK · Eugene, Oregon

Gardens in the Wasteland: Christian Formation in Three Swedish Church Plants

Dissertation presented at University College Stockholm to be publicly examined in Room 219–220 at Åkeshovsvägen 29, Bromma, February 7, 2024, at 13:00, for the degree of Doctor of Philosophy in Theology (Practical Theology with Church History: Practical Theology). The examination will be held in English.

Faculty examiner: Pete Ward, Professor of Practical Theology, Durham University.
Supervisor: Joel Halldorf, Professor of Church History, University College Stockholm.
Assistant supervisor: Stefan Paas, Professor of Missiology and Intercultural Theology at Vrije Universiteit Amsterdam & Professor of Missiology at Theologische Universiteit Utrecht.

Abstract

Gardens in the Wasteland is an ethnographic study of Christian formation within three Swedish church plants working against a backdrop of advanced secularisation. The thesis analyses the formative practices employed by these church plants with the intention of forming persons towards a lived Christian identity. Employing a situated learning theory framework, it traces the formative trajectories and negotiations that emerge from these shared practices, and also examines the articulations of callings and intentions within these church plants.

The findings reveal that the establishment of a church plant often stems from a sense of place-oriented calling that encompasses a vision of vibrant Christian life and community. These church plants cultivate formative practices – aimed at certain *teloi* – that guide individuals on their journeys towards a lived Christian identity. Through participation in these practices, individuals align themselves with the church plant's vision of Christian life. This identity formation process is not static but rather involves ongoing negotiations, both on a personal and community level, as individuals grapple with the meaning of Christian identity and faith amidst an increasingly secularised society.

Trädgårdar i ödemarken: Kristen formation i tre svenska församlingsplanteringar

Akademisk avhandling presenterad vid Enskilda Högskolan Stockholm för disputation i sal 219–220, Åkeshovsvägen 29, Bromma, 7 februari 2024 kl. 13.00, för graden teologie doktor i Praktisk teologi med kyrkohistoria med inriktning mot praktisk teologi. Disputationen kommer att äga rum på engelska.

Opponent: Pete Ward, professor i praktisk teologi, Durham University.
Handledare: Joel Halldorf, professor i kyrkohistoria, Enskilda Högskolan Stockholm.
Bitr. handledare: Stefan Paas, professor i missionsvetenskap och interkulturell teologi vid Vrije Universiteit Amsterdam och professor i missionsvetenskap vid Theologische Universiteit Utrecht.

Sammanfattning

Trädgårdar i ödemarken är en etnografisk studie av kristen formation i tre svenska församlingsplanteringar som befinner sig i ett sammanhang präglad av långt utvecklad sekularisering. Avhandlingen analyserar de formativa praktiker som används av dessa planteringar med intentionen att forma personer mot en levd kristen identitet. Genom att använda situerat lärande som teoretisk ram, spårar avhandlingen de formativa livsbanor och förhandlingar som uppstår i dessa praktiker. Studien undersöker också hur kallelser och intentioner artikuleras i församlingsplanteringarna.

Resultaten visar att etableringen av en församlingsplantering ofta startar i erfarenheten av en kallelse som omfattar en vision av ett kristet liv och en levande gemenskap på en specifik plats. Dessa planteringar skapar formativa praktiker med specifika *teloi* som vägleder individer på deras livsbanor mot en levd kristen identitet. Genom att delta i dessa praktiker anpassar sig individer till församlingsplanteringens vision av det kristna livet. Denna identitetsformation är inte statisk utan medför kontinuerliga förhandlingar om innebörden av kristen tro och identitet. Denna förhandling sker både på individuell och på gemenskapsnivå, i kontexten av ett alltmer sekulariserat samhälle.

Enskilda Högskolan Stockholm

Enskilda Högskolan Stockholm erbjuder utbildningsprogram i mänskliga rättigheter och demokrati, samt i teologi/religionsvetenskap. Högskolan grundades 1993 genom en sammanslagning av utbildningsinstitutioner med rötter från 1866, hette tidigare Teologiska högskolan, Stockholm, och har tre avdelningar: Avdelningen för mänskliga rättigheter och demokrati, Avdelningen för religionsvetenskap och teologi, samt Avdelningen för östkyrkliga studier. Forskarutbildningen i Praktisk teologi med kyrkohistoria bedrivs inom inriktningarna Praktisk teologi respektive Kyrkohistoria. Utbildningen fokuserar på den kristna kyrkans utveckling och den kristna trons praktiska gestaltning, i ett konstruktivt samspel mellan empiriska metoder och teori. Utbildningen innefattar bland annat historiska, hermeneutiska, filosofiska, teologiska, sociologiska och etnologiska perspektiv.

University College Stockholm

University College Stockholm offers programmes in Human Rights and Democracy and in Theology/Religious Studies. The university college was founded in 1993 through a merger of educational institutions with roots dating back to 1866, is also known as Stockholm School of Theology, and has three departments: the Department of Human Rights and Democracy, the Department of Religious Studies and Theology, and the Department of Eastern Christian Studies. The doctoral programme in Practical Theology with Church History provides specialisations in Practical Theology and Church History respectively. It focuses on the development of the Christian church and practical expressions of Christian faith, in a constructive interplay between empirical methods and theory. The programme includes historical, hermeneutical, philosophical, theological, sociological, and ethnological perspectives.

Wipf and Stock Publishers
199 W 8th Ave, Suite 3
Eugene, OR 97401

Gardens in the Wasteland
Christian Formation in Three Swedish Churches
By Asserhed, Björn
Copyright © 2024 by Asserhed, Björn All rights reserved.
Softcover ISBN-13: 979-8-3852-5397-5
Hardcover ISBN-13: 979-8-3852-5398-2
eBook ISBN-13: 979-8-3852-5399-9
Publication date 5/16/2025
Previously published by Enskilda Högskolan Stockholm, 2024

This edition is a scanned facsimile of the original edition published in 2024.

Preface

In the autumn of 2018, just as I was embarking on doctoral studies, I went to lunch with a friend who happens to be a church planter. Curious for his opinion – and perhaps seeking some inspiration myself – I asked him what issues he thought needed more academic attention. "What church planting methods actually work in secular Sweden?" he responded instantly. Clearly, this was something he had given much thought. While I appreciated his answer, the more I thought about it, the more questions it raised. Could we even speak about methods in this context? And what does "working" mean in this context? Working for whom, at the expense of what, and how should we measure it?

From that day, I have had a split vision of the task at hand. I wanted my thesis to provide church planting practitioners with valuable insights for reflecting on their practices. At the same time, I hope to contribute to the academic discourse by bringing the church planting practice into the conversation. Of course, meeting the academic requirements and conventions might be valuable for myself and other researchers, but that does not necessarily mean that the practitioners themselves will benefit from the research. However, at its best, practical theology can empower the church to engage in theological reflection for discernment in its daily undertakings and in fulfilling its missional calling. I hope that this thesis will provide some guidance and inspiration as to how this reflection can be done and what it could involve. I will leave it to the reader to decide whether I have succeeded in realising this split vision.

As with most meaningful things in life, this thesis is the result of a community. It is a material artefact that involves conversations, interactions, and contributions by many people. While I take full responsibility for the contents of the final product, I want to mention a number of those who, in different ways, have played a part in shaping it.

First and foremost, I want to thank my supervisor, Joel Halldorf, who has provided excellent advice and support along the way and who never hesitated to walk the extra mile when needed. I also want to thank Stefan Paas, my assistant supervisor, who gave the project an expert "outsider's perspective" from Amsterdam.

Over the years, I have been grateful to be part of a doctoral band of brothers and sisters in the *Church and Society* research school in Stockholm: Jonas Ideström, Sune Fahlgren, Tone Stangeland Kaufman, Daniel Strömner, Ellen Vingren, Joel Appelfeldt, Pernilla Myrelid, Hanna Alenius, Simon Hallonsten, Elin Lockneus, Torbjörn Toll, and Anki Falk. You have invested time and energy in my texts, helped me sharpen my arguments, and made me a better theologian.

I also want to mention Mattias Neve, Philipp Bartholomä, Roland Spjuth, and Fredrik Wenell, all of whom have provided critique in the most positive sense of the word. A special thanks to Carl Johan and Linda Berglund, who have offered both fellowship and an extra bed in Stockholm – with breakfast included. Thanks to Victoria Strelchuk and David Michael, who have provided excellent assistance with the English language.

I have received generous financial contributions from *Stockholms Kristliga Ynglingaförening*, *Helge Ax:son Johnsons stiftelse*, and *C.E. Wikströms minnesfond*, which has helped considerably in making this project possible. For that support, I am very grateful.

Over the course of this almost six-year-long project, I have had the honour of serving as a pastor in Finspångs Missionsförsamling and Equmeniakyrkan Linköping. I have also had the joy of returning to Norrköping Vineyard, which I had a part in planting 30 years ago. To those congregations: Thank You! You have all been part of my journey.

This thesis would not have been possible to write without the three church plants in the study. Thank you for trusting me and for opening your homes, your lives, and communities for me. The time I spent with you has been most valuable to me, both academically and personally. In many respects, this book is written for you.

Finally, I want to thank my parents, and my family – Lina, my wife, and our children Hanna, Jona, Daniel, and Elias. Thank you for your love, patience, and encouragement. You are my joy!

Norrköping, Advent 2023
Björn Asserhed

Contents

Preface 7

Contents 9

Tables and Figures 15

1. Christian Formation in "The Wasteland" 17
1.1 Introduction 19
    Research Problem 20
    Research on Christian Formation 20
    Research Questions 23
1.2 Christian Formation and Church Plants in Secular Sweden 25
    Christian Formation 26
1.3 Practical Theology: Discerning Theology in the Lived 43
    Practical Theology, Learning and Formation 44
    Discerning Theology in Practice 46
    Researching Lived Theology 47
    Reflexivity: Personal Engagement in the Research Context 49
    Disposition and reading guide 51

2. Research on Christian Formation 53
2.1 Callings and Intentions in Christian Formation 53
2.2 Practices of Christian Formation 57
    Formation Through Liturgical Practices 58
    Formation in Missional Situations 59
2.3 Christian Formation as Identity Formation 62
2.4 Christian Formation as Negotiation of Faith and Culture 65
2.5 Conclusion 69

3. Methods and Methodology 73
3.1 An Ethnographic Study With an Abductive Approach 73
    The Abductive Conversation Between Theory and Contexts *74*
    Focused Theological Ethnography *75*
3.2 Ethical Considerations and the Question of Positionality 78
3.3 Selection and Material 81
3.4 Analysis and Presentation 84
3.5 Research in a Pandemic Situation 86
3.6 Introducing the Church Plants 87

4. A Theoretical Understanding of Christian Formation 89
4.1 Christian Formation, Learning and Practice 89
    Learning and Practice *90*
4.2 Situated Learning Theory 93
    Learning as Changed Participation *95*
    Critique of Situated Learning Theory *96*
    Participation in the Community of Practice *97*
    Trajectories *99*
    Negotiation of Meaning *100*
    Conclusion *101*
4.3 Analysing Christian Formation from a Practice Perspective 104
    The Use of Theory in the Analysis Chapters *105*

5. The Calling to Christian Formation 107
5.1 The Calling to Industrial City 108
    Identity and Intention *109*
    The Significance of Place *112*
    Pro-Social Action *116*
    Calling: Forming Fishermen *121*
5.2 The Calling to Cathedral City 121
    Identity and Intention *122*
    The Significance of Place *125*
    Pro-Social Action *130*
    Calling: Forming Faithful Neighbours *131*
5.3 The Calling to Harbour City 132
    Identity and Intention *132*
    The Significance of Place *136*
    Pro-Social Action *139*

Calling: Forming Good Samaritans *142*
5.4 Conclusion *142*

6. Formative Practices **145**
6.1 Analysing Practices of Christian Formation 145
    Landscape of Practices *146*
    Traditions of Formation *147*
6.2 The Revival Meeting Practice in Industrial City 149
    Flow of Sub-Practices *150*
    The Revival Meeting as Formation *156*
6.3 The Small Group Practice in Cathedral City 158
    Intentional Habits *159*
    Flow of Sub-Practices *160*
    The Small Group as Formation *164*
6.4 The Apprenticing Practice in Harbour City 166
    The Social Ministry Context *167*
    Implementations of the Practice of Apprenticeship *168*
    Practice Tool *173*
    Apprenticeship as Formation *175*
6.5 Conclusion 176

7. Trajectories of Formation **179**
7.1 Formation in Communities 179
7.2 Analysing Practice Trajectories 180
7.3 Industrial City 182
    Trajectorial Analysis *187*
    Summary *188*
7.4 Cathedral City 189
    Personal Trajectories *189*
    Trajectorial Analysis *194*
    Summary *195*
7.5 Harbour City 195
    Personal Trajectories *196*
    Trajectorial Analysis *200*
7.6 Conclusion 202

8. Negotiating Secular Culture **205**
8.1 Culture, Tradition, and Negotiation 206
    Culture and Consensus *206*

    Tradition 207
8.2 Negotiating Secular Perceptions 209
    The Spiritual Poverty of Sweden 209
    The Church as Questioned or Ignored 210
    Lack of Knowledge and Tolerance 211
8.3 Adaptability: Negotiating Relevance 212
    Unique Church Expressions 212
    Lifestyle Symbols 213
8.4 Integrity: Negotiating Individualism 215
    Sexual Morals 216
    Diversity 218
    Summary 220
8.5 Sustainability: Negotiating Performance Culture 221
    Culture of Performance 221
    Summary 224
8.6 Resilience: Negotiating Power 224
    Democratic Structures 225
    Challenged Leadership 225
    Summary 227
8.7 Conclusion 227

9. Conclusions and Discussion 229
9.1 Summary of Results 229
    Callings and Intentions 229
    Formative Practices 230
    Formative Trajectories 232
    Negotiation of Secular Culture 233
9.2 Agency: From Calling to Practice 234
    God, Calling, and Ecclesial Agency 234
    Re-inventing Practices of Christian Formation 236
9.3 Participation: From Periphery to Centre 237
    Modes of Participation 237
    Levels of Formative Engagement 239
9.4 Telos: From Secular to Christian Formation 241
    Missional Contextualisation 244
9.5 Reflections on Theory and Methodology 246
    Ethnography, Situated Learning, and Theological Discernment 246
    Research in the Pandemic 248

9.6 Conclusion 249

10. Theology for New Gardens in the Wasteland 251
10.1 Experiential Faith 251
    Experience of God 251
10.2 Modern Technology and Practices of Christian Formation 253
10.3 Ecclesiology 254
    The Significance of Calling 255
    Liquid Ecclesiology 255
10.4 Ministry 257
    Serving the Neighbour 258
    Being Holy 258
10.5 Discernment 260
    Missional Discernment 260
    The Garden as a Discernment Model 261
10.6 Epilogue: Growing Gardens of Christian Formation 263

Appendix I: Interview Guide: Participant 265

Appendix II: Interview Guide: Leader 267

Appendix III: Group Interview Guide 269

Bibliography 271

Index of Biblical Literature 281

Index of Authors 283

Index of Subjects 287

Tables and Figures

Tables
Table 1:   Observed gatherings and interviews in the three research contexts.
Table 2:   Theoretical concepts in relation to research questions and their location in the thesis.
Table 3:   Callings of the church plants.
Table 4:   The landscape of practices of the church plants.
Table 5:   A summary of the formative practices in the church plants.
Table 6:   Tangen's identification themes with related practices.

Figures
Figure 1:   The abductive interplay of theoretical levels and material in qualitative research.
Figure 2:   Map made by the planters in Industrial City, showing the city as they see it. Text in Swedish: "So that people will get to know Jesus and become his disciples"
Figure 3:   Wenger's different types of trajectories in the communities of practice.
Figure 4:   Trajectories in participation and engagement of persons in Industrial City.
Figure 5:   Trajectories in participation and engagement of persons in Cathedral City.
Figure 6:   Trajectories in participation and engagement of persons in Harbour City.
Figure 7:   Engagement modes in communities of formative practice.

1. Christian Formation in "The Wasteland"

The formation of Christian faith is closely linked to the cultural situation of the churches. This includes their understanding of society, for how they view society impacts their core practices. A century ago, T.S. Eliot (1888–1965) described the industrialised city of London in the wake of World War I as a wasteland: "The dead tree gives no shelter, the cricket no relief, And the dry stone no sound of water".[1] This is a landscape of fragmented relationships, a place of death and decay, where days pass without meaning. It is not far-fetched to assume that Eliot, who converted to Catholicism a few years after writing the poem, was inspired by the imagery of a desolate wilderness drawn by the psalmist:

> They wandered in the wilderness in a solitary way; they found no city to dwell in. Hungry and thirsty, their soul fainted in them. Then they cried unto the Lord in their trouble, and he delivered them out of their distresses. And he led them forth by the right way, that they might go to a city of habitation. Oh that men would praise the Lord for his goodness, and for his wonderful works to the children of men! For he satisfieth the longing soul, and filleth the hungry soul with goodness.
>
> (Ps 107:4–9 KJV)

Wasteland is also the metaphor used by a Swedish pastor to describe the state of the Swedish society of today. What this pastor, an informant in this study, is trying to convey by this image is that new life is needed in the dry and barren spiritual desert of secular culture. And this, she tells us, is achieved by planting new church communities in Swedish cities.[2]

What this informant might view as new life is conceptualised in this thesis as Christian formation, that is, social practices that intend to shape Christian faith

---

[1] T. S. Eliot (2021), *The Waste Land*, Berkeley, California: Mint Editions, p 1.
[2] The thesis uses the definition by Stefan Paas and Marry Schoemaker: "the creation of new Christian communities for missionary reasons" in Stefan Paas and Schoemaker, Marry (2018), "Crisis and resilience among church planters in Europe", *Mission Studies*, 35 (3), p 366.

and lived Christian identity.[3] However, modern secularisation presents challenges to traditional models of Christian formation. To begin with, both the separation of church and state and the independence of societal institutions from the church allow people to form identities outside the traditional religious mindset. Formative institutions such as schools and universities are separated from the church. The church has lost its role as the provider of societal legitimation with the formative power "to discipline the beliefs and behaviour" in society[4] and also as the provider of moral narrative.[5] Most independent societal institutions develop their own logic with little regard for religious norms and narratives. Growing demands of professionalism and rationalism leave little room for transcendence.[6] As common life no longer operates with references to God or faith, religion has lost much of its formative power in the wider society and is now relegated to the private sphere.[7] When the monopoly of institutional religion is broken, the church becomes an institution for people with a special interest in religion, and the congregations present their unique offerings in the marketplace of culture, religion and spirituality.[8]

However, a world of options can also challenge individuals and communities and foster creativity among religious providers. When being a Christian is no longer a cultural given, the development of Christian faith demands an active choice on the individual's part.[9] It no longer occurs through state-governed

---

[3] This definition is further developed on p 26.

[4] Grace Davie (2014), "Managing Pluralism: The European Case", *Society*, 51 (6), 613–22, p 615.

[5] Charles Taylor (2007), *A Secular Age*, Cambridge, Massachusetts: Harvard University Press, p 475. Taylor describes the culture of authenticity as: "the understanding of life which emerges with the Romantic expressivism of the late-eighteenth century, that each one of us has his/ her own way of realizing our humanity, and that it is important to find and live out one's own, as against surrendering to conformity with a model imposed on us from outside, by society, or the previous generation, or religious or political authority".

[6] E.g. Bryan R. Wilson (2016), *Religion in Secular Society: Fifty Years On*, Oxford: Oxford University Press.

[7] José Casanova (1994), *Public Religions in the Modern World*, Chicago: University of Chicago Press, p 40: "Religion was progressively forced to withdraw from the modern secular state and the modern capitalist economy and to find refuge in the newly found private sphere. Like modern science, capitalist markets and modern state bureaucracies manage to function 'as if' God would not exist".

[8] Taylor (2007). According to Taylor, belief in God, today, is "understood to be one option among others, and frequently not the easiest to embrace" (p 3).

[9] Stefan Paas (2011), "Post-Christian, Post-Christendom, and Post-Modern Europe: Towards the Interaction of Missiology and the Social Sciences", *Mission Studies*, 28 (1), 3–25. The article gives a good summary of the different theories of secularisation.

institutions and involves the whole population. Instead, churches need to take this responsibility themselves.

Many churches in Sweden have struggled with diminishing membership for decades. Baptisms decline in number, and many congregations have a sense of being lost. While the cultural changes provoke different responses, most churches are affected by what sociologists call "detraditionalisation". Paul Heelas and Linda Woodhead define this as a weakening of tradition, the sacralisation of the self, individualisation, the instrumentalisation of religion, and a move towards universalism that emphasises commonality among the different religions.[10] This weakening of both a distinct collective identity and tradition also takes place within churches and can then be described as "internal secularisation".[11]

In contrast, a burgeoning church-planting movement is hoping to engage contemporary urban culture in innovative ways in order to renew the churches and cities. They want to emphasise the distinctiveness of the Christian faith in a way that addresses contemporary challenges. The question is whether these newly planted churches represent new gardens starting to grow in the secular wasteland.

This thesis in the field of practical theology presents ethnographic research on Christian formation in secular culture. By looking closely at the formative practices of new churches and their relation to the broader Swedish culture, I hope to understand how people can be formed as Christians in secular societies.[12]

1.1 Introduction

In this section, I will articulate the specific problem this thesis will address and provide an overview of the most significant perspectives in the current research that

---

[10] Linda Woodhead and Heelas, Paul (2000), *Religion in Modern Times*, Hoboken, New Jersey: Wiley-Blackwell, p 344.

[11] Pink Dandelion (2019), *The Cultivation of Conformity*, Oxfordshire: Routledge, p 144. Dandelion points to the loss of religious language, a self-defined cosmology and morals, and a tradition narrative. Cf. Karol Jasiński (2021), "The Internal Secularisation of Religion", Collectanea Theologica, 91 (4), 95–111. Jasiński points to different effects on religion from internal secularisation: degradation of religion (as explained by Dandelion), critique and cleansing of religion from unhealthy patterns, and rediscovery of the true nature of religion.

[12] John D. Boy (2015), *Blessed Disruption: Culture and Urban Space in a European Church Planting Network*, New York: City University of New York. Boy finds that studying church planting is an apt way to explore the interplay between religion and secular society as the church plants exploit and engage contemporary urban culture in innovative ways, rather than opposing it.

are relevant to the study. From there, I will move to the research questions and the structure of the thesis.

Research Problem

In practical theology, few studies investigate formative practices in missional situations. While missional practices such as church planting and evangelism are increasingly being studied, minimal attention has been paid to Christian formation within the context of missional practices.[13]

The particular problem that this study delves into regards Christian formation in a situation of advanced secularisation, where churches feel the need to change their approach to Christian formation. Churches, as minorities, struggle to find language and practices that are both faithfully Christian and, at the same time, culturally relevant. As a result, churches need to adapt to this atmosphere by innovating and evolving. This thesis studies Christian formation as a set of social practices employed to shape Christian faith and lived Christian identity. Church planting is a missional strategy to address the loss of Christian formation, and it has emerged as a significant movement within the free church movement in Sweden. Since church plants are geared to address questions posed by the changing conditions, they provide useful contexts for studying Christian formation in secular societies.[14]

Research on Christian Formation

Practical theology studies the practices of the church, but missional practices are often neglected due to unfortunate boundaries between theological fields.[15]

---

[13] As described in the following section, Philip Wall's and Karl Inge Tangen's studies could be considered exceptions to this lack of attention on missional practices. Another exception can be found in Dwight Zscheile (2012), *Cultivating Sent Communities: Missional Spiritual Formation*, Grand Rapids, Michigan: Eerdmans.

[14] Boy (2015), p 2.

[15] One recent example of this is found in Pete Ward and Tveitereid, Knut (2022), *The Wiley Blackwell Companion to Theology and Qualitative Research*, London: John Wiley & Sons. The study of missions or subjects of evangelisation is almost totally absent. Another example is Bonnie J. Miller-McLemore (2014), *The Wiley Blackwell Companion to Practical Theology*, London: John Wiley & Sons. This book contains one chapter on how evangelism is taught in theological seminaries. The two extensive volumes on practical theology only mention church planting in passing. One exception to this is Pete Ward, who raises missional issues when it comes to church approaches to culture. Pete Ward (2008), *Participation and Mediation: A Practical Theology for the Liquid Church*, London: SCM, p 52. Ward finds the relationship between practical theology and missiology to be "blurred". While there is a growing sensibility to context and contextualisation in practical theology, these issues have historically been studied in missiology.

1.1 Introduction

Hence, church planting, which is essential to the formation of the church, is studied as a theme within missiology. Christian formation, similarly, is often located in the field of religious education.[16] I find this to be a bit unfortunate. The study of lived practices of Christian formation within church plants is an area that demands attention in a changing landscape that has not been addressed in the field of practical theology. Church plants are fruitful contexts for research since they intend to be innovative when it comes to finding new practices for formation. In the following summary of research, the most relevant studies in neighbouring fields are mentioned:

Richard R. Osmer finds a particular missional identity in the vocation of some Christian leaders.[17] This identity is shaped by the calling to live in a constructive tension between being true to community identity and being relevant in the culture. Missional communities have different identities, intentions and practices, leading to different teloi.[18] But across these differences, the *telos* (Greek, "ultimate goal", plural *teloi*) of Christian formation is described as Christ-likeness or union with Christ.[19] In his studies, Andrew Root emphasises the need for openness to divine action in this formation.[20]

The secular context of the West is described as a challenge for Christian communities by Fredrik Wenell, who suggests that Christians in Sweden are experiencing a diaspora situation.[21] Stefan Paas and Philip Bartholomä argue that newcomers in church plants hold sensibilities, feelings and questions that need to be considered in Christian formation.[22] Both Anna Strhan and Jessica Moberg describe

---

[16] E.g. Jeff Astley (2017), "The Naming of Parts: Faith, Formation, Development and Education", in Stuart-Buttle, Ros and Shortt, John (eds.), *Christian Faith, Formation and Education* (New York: Springer), 13–28.

[17] Richard R. Osmer (2012), "Formation in the Missional Church: Building Deep Connections between Ministries of Upbuilding and Sending", in Zscheile, Dwight (ed.), *Cultivating Sent Communities: Missional Spiritual Formation* (Grand Rapids, Michigan: Eerdmans), 29–55, p 50–51.

[18] Christopher B. James (2018), *Church Planting in Post-Christian Soil*, Oxford: Oxford University Press.

[19] Osmer (2012), p 52; Andrew Root (2017a), *Faith Formation in a Secular Age*, Ada, Michigan: Baker Academic, p 130.

[20] Andrew Root (2017b), "Faith Formation in a Secular Age", *Word & World*, 37 (2), 128–41.

[21] Fredrik Wenell (2015), *Omvändelsens skillnad: En diasporateologisk granskning av frikyrklig ungdomskultur i folkkyrka och folkhem*, Uppsala: Uppsala University. Wenell leans on the theology of John Howard Yoder.

[22] Stefan Paas and Bartholomä, Philipp (2020), "The Missional Future of Free Churches in a Secular Context: A German Case Study", *Journal of Empirical Theology*, 33 (2), 157–77.

how formation involves the negotiation of cultural issues on an individual and a church community level.[23] Moberg discovers the presence of a "therapeutic authenticity" in the Neo-charismatic church in Stockholm.[24] In a recent study by Mattias Neve on Emerging Church communities in Sweden, relationality and authenticity are cited as important values in the innovation paradigm of church planting and as reasons for people to join a new church.[25]

One of the most important recent studies on Christian formation was conducted by Karl Inge Tangen, who sees ten factors necessary for participants to be able to grow in identification with the church community and its faith in London and Copenhagen.[26] Tangen describes the life stories of individuals joining the new churches and finds that in addition to a sense of involvement in the God-sized drama, close community, places to engage in ministry, and supportive leadership were some of the most important factors for identification with the particular churches.

The missional strategy of planting churches as a response to the secular challenge is somewhat successful.[27] According to Stefan Paas and Alrik Vos, one of the reasons for this might be that church plant leaders and communities have a stronger missional mindset than many old churches.[28] The article doesn't explain how the missional mindset translates into developing and deepening Christian faith and practices over time.

---

[23] Anna Strhan (2015), *Aliens and Strangers*, Oxford: Oxford University Press; Jessica Moberg (2013), *Piety, Intimacy and Mobility*, Huddinge: Södertörns högskola. In their respective studies, Strhan and Moberg both point to the negotiation between Christian faith practices and secular culture, in London and Stockholm.

[24] Moberg (2013).

[25] Mattias Neve (2021), *In Pursuit of Proximity: A Missiological Study of Four 'Emerging church' Communities in Sweden*, Amsterdam: Vrije Universitet; Johannes Vålandsmyr (2014), Hvorfor og hvordan plante menighet i Norge? et kvalitativt studie av misjonsteologiske begrunnelser og misjonsstrategiske modeller for menighetsplanting, Stavanger: Misjonshøgskolen. Regarding the innovative "new churches" paradigm, see Stefan Paas (2016), *Church Planting in the Secular West*, Grand Rapids, Michigan: Eerdmans.

[26] Karl Inge Tangen (2012), *Ecclesial Identification Beyond Late Modern Individualism*, Leiden: Brill. This study was conducted using one church in Copenhagen and one in London.

[27] E.g. Stefan Paas (2018), "A Case Study of Church Growth by Church Planting in Germany: Are They Connected", *International Bulletin of Mission Research*, 42 (1), 40–54.

[28] Stefan Paas and Vos, Alrik (2016), "Church Planting and Church Growth in Western Europe: An Analysis", *International Bulletin of Mission Research*, 40 (3), 243–52; Paas (2016). Paas gives three motives for, or paradigms of, church planting, one being the need for innovation of "new churches", that is, churches that are compatible with the secular environment of the West.

In his research on Fresh Expressions[29] in the UK, Philip Wall emphasises the need for a theologically reflected practice of Christian formation. He finds that an entirely instruction-oriented pedagogy that relies on words rather than practices and on monologue rather than dialogue has limited value.[30] A conclusion of this is that Church planters' understandings of learning and formation have consequences for formative practices.

Despite the works referenced above, it is still the case that there is a lack of research on Christian formation in the field of practical theology, particularly in terms of missional situations, such as church plants, and the attendant formative trajectories in religious communities and cultural negotiation within the secular context.[31] This is particularly true for the Swedish context, where empirical research on church plants is sparse.[32] In this thesis, I aim to investigate Christian formation by looking closely at three church plants in Sweden. I hope to be able to contribute to a deeper understanding of the negotiations that are part of the formative practices in secular culture and to show how individuals' formative trajectories develop within the missional situations that the church plants represent.

Research Questions

This study investigates what Christian formation looks like in the context of advanced secularisation in missional situations. This investigation is conducted with the help of the following sub-questions:

1. How are the callings and intentions of the church plants articulated, and what do the callings and intentions mean for Christian formation?

---

[29] Fresh Expressions is a missional initiative originally formed in the Church of England. The initiative was a response to the report Church of England Mission and Public Affairs Council (2004), *Mission-shaped Church*, London: Church House. Today, Fresh Expressions is a cross-denominational international movement with the goal of forming new communities of faith that connect with people who usually don't go to church.

[30] Philip Roger Wall (2014), *Salvation and the School of Christ – A Theological-ethnographic Exploration of the Relationship Between Soteriology, Missiology and Pedagogy in Fresh Expressions of Church*, London: King's College; Knut Tveitereid (2015), *Pragmatics of Discipleship*, Bergen: NLA University College. Tveitereid finds evidence of a clearly pragmatic language on discipleship in Norwegian Christian youth organizations.

[31] A more thorough discussion of previous research is presented in the following chapter.

[32] Peter Svanberg (1999), *Church Planting in Sweden in the 21st Century: A Model for New Methodist Churches*, Asbury Seminary; Neve (2021).

2. What practices of Christian formation are present in the church plant communities?
3. How are people formed towards a lived Christian identity in the church plant communities?
4. What cultural tensions do the church plants negotiate, and what do the negotiations mean for Christian formation?

From January 2020 to June 2021, I performed field studies in three church plants in three mid-sized cities in Sweden. The thesis has a descriptive and interpretative approach, describing what is going on in terms of formative practices in church planting and interpreting the ongoings using an understanding of Christian formation from the perspective of practice theory.[33] To that end, I use ethnographic methods (interviews and observations) to study how people are formed as Christians in church plants.

As the research questions indicate, the thesis is primarily concerned with formative practices. This means that the study concerns both social and individual aspects.[34] In each of the three church plants of the study, I will investigate one main formative practice significant to how persons are formed towards a lived Christian identity. In the analysis, the following concepts are central.[35]

- *Lived identity:* I use this concept tentatively to mean a person's self-perception as a performed, socially grounded reality. In other words, the lived identity changes through participation in social formative practices. Christian formation intends to foster a Christian identity that is not only a label but is also – and more importantly – enacted in and through social practice.[36]

---

[33] This broadly reflects the first three tasks of practical theology proposed by Richard R. Osmer (2008), *Practical Theology: An Introduction*, Grand Rapids, Michigan: Eerdmans. He presents four questions: "what is going on?" (the descriptive-empirical task of priestly listening), "why is this going on (the interpretative task of sagely wisdom), "what should be going on?" (the normative-evaluative task of prophetic discernment), and "how should we move on from here?" (the pragmatic-strategic task of servant leadership).

[34] Paul Hager, Lee, Alison, and Reich, Ann (2012), "Problematising Practice, Reconceptualising Learning and Imagining Change", in Hager, Paul, Lee, Alison, and Reich, Ann (eds.), *Practice, Learning and Change* (New York: Springer), 1–16.

[35] The concepts and their backgrounds are further developed in the chapter on situated learning theory, p 89.

[36] This understanding will be developed later using situated learning theory. A lived perspective of what it means to be Christian can be seen in the liturgical understanding of James K.A.

- *Calling:* This refers to a sense of clarity of purpose and personal mission leading to action with a pro-social intention.[37] The callings to plant churches in appointed places represent different visions of lived Christian identity.
- *Trajectories (of lived identity) towards community telos:* Trajectories represent movements of participation and engagement between the centre and periphery in the formative practice communities.
- *Negotiation (of lived identity) between telos and secular culture:* The communities negotiate what it means to be Christians in a secular context. Negotiation is the process of meaning-making in which individuals participate in the community. This negotiation is analysed with a view to the secular context in which the churches are planted, and the identities formed and lived therein.[38]

1.2 Christian Formation and Church Plants in Secular Sweden

In this section, I will introduce the research object, the research domain and the research context. Initially, I will define what Christian Formation means in the thesis. Furthermore, Sweden as a secular cultural context will be described, followed by an introduction to church plants as the domain of the study.

Smith and Debra Dean Murphy: You become Christian by making liturgical participation a regular habit.

[37] A.R. Elangovan, Pinder, Craig C., and McLean, Murdith (2010), "Callings and Organizational Behavior", *Journal of Vocational Behavior*, 76 (3), 428–40. The authors define calling as "a course of action in pursuit of pro-social intentions embodying the convergence of an individual's sense of what he or she would like to do, should do, and actually does". They describe the Christian roots of the term and suggest a typology of religious versus secular, occupation-related versus non-occupation related. In the case of church planters, the calling is clearly religious but could be described both as occupational and not strictly occupational. However, what is clear is that there is a sense of clarity of purpose and personal mission leading to action with a pro-social intention.

[38] Describing the societal context in which the churches are planted as secular is a simplification in this thesis. Societies are multilayered with diverse cultures, meanings and views of life. Similarly, the church-planting communities are regarded as unequivocally Christian even though the persons, culture and practices which constitute the communities also carry more or less reflected secular understandings. The relationship between the church-planting communities and society is complex, changing and subject to negotiation. This simplification is made to emphasise the argument of formation towards the Christian faith versus a secular view of life.

Christian Formation

In this thesis project, I initially chose the term "discipleship", often used by church communities, to describe processes of growing in faith. Using this term, however, is not without its complications. As Knut Tveitereid points out, the term is ambiguous, and there is no consensus on its meaning among those who use it. For instance, "discipleship" can be used in reference to ideals, personal development, mystical union with Christ, a certain movement or spirituality, or to Jesus' twelve disciples.[39] The term is too imprecise to describe the particular phenomena of my investigation. Therefore, I turned to "Christian formation" instead.

But how is the concept of Christian formation used in theological research? It is quite clear that Christian formation is seen as having a goal, a telos. As we will note, this can involve being taught and "traditioned" into the Christian faith, being attuned to new attitudes and behaviour, or being united with Christ. Also, the formation has a locus – an actual place and a socio-cultural setting where this happens. Finally, how does Christian formation come about? Some refer to the individual process, others emphasise formation in and through a community, and yet others consider the formation within the larger cultural setting.

Jeff Astley defines the concept in the following way:

> ...all the processes of teaching and/or learning that help to shape a learner in a tradition and its beliefs, experiences and practices, in a way that leads to the learner's acceptance of that tradition in her thinking, valuing, feeling and perceiving, and her dispositions to act and experience, *together with her appraisal of the tradition's merits and faults*.[40]

In Astley's definition, the individual learner is in focus. The person is shaped by the *acceptance* of a faith tradition while simultaneously assessing this tradition and internalising it. Christian formation is a process that supports this shaping. Wendi Sargeant, who researches emerging churches in Australia, adds a dual-integrative perspective of individuals being formed by the community and how the community is formed by the individuals. She points to the formation of identity, theology, and character in this process:

---

[39] Tveitereid (2015). Cf. Christopher Beard (2015), "Missional Discipleship: Discerning Spiritual-formation Practices and Goals within the Missional Movement", *Missiology: An International Review*, 43 (2), 175–94. Beard addresses the loss of "conceptual clarity due to terminological imprecision" regarding the term discipleship. He proposes "missional discipleship" as "the experiential process of identity formation which results in a disciple who exhibits tangible evidence of mission, community, and obedience in his or her life" (p. 175). This, interestingly, resonates rather well with my understanding of Christian formation in this thesis.

[40] Astley (2017), p 22, authors emphasis.

> Christian formation is concerned with the way in which individuals and communities perceive themselves and their life, their attitude towards others, and how their vision and values are shaped by their understanding of God, of themselves and of God's people. Christian formation involves the development of character as individuals and as the Christian church – the Body of Christ.[41]

Sargeant describes Christian formation as a life-long process that involves all aspects of life and is empowered by the Holy Spirit, who forms the individual and community "into alignment with God's will as one participates in the Christian story".[42] Likewise, Andrew Root emphasises the role of the Holy Spirit in the Christian community. The telos of Christian formation is the mystical union with Christ, which meets challenges in a secular setting:

> We struggle with faith-formation processes (and so many are impotent) because they are disconnected from the experience of divine action itself. We confirm that divine action is implausible when our imagination for faith formation can be constructed outside the mystery of divine action itself. We then live with a divide. We turn the processes of faith formation over to a hyper-pragmatism that creates methods and models without consideration of the shape of the divine action.[43]

James K.A Smith starts his "cultural liturgies" project by addressing the issue of Christian formation as "a formation of desires and imagination that creates a certain kind of person who is part of a certain kind of people".[44] He argues that the overly cognitive orientation of religious education and discipleship in the churches has proven inadequate as it fails to consider the situatedness in a community with a certain vision, a telos.[45] Smith mainly places the formation of Christians in the liturgical practice of the gathered church and describes how the liturgical practices of the gathered people of God precede the theoretical reflection:

> Before Christians had systematic theologies and worldviews, they were singing hymns and psalms, saying prayers, celebrating the Eucharist, sharing their property, and becoming a people marked by a desire for God's coming kingdom – a desire that constituted them as a peculiar people in the present.[46]

---

[41] Wendi Anne Sargeant (2011), *Christian Education and the Emerging Church*, New York: Pickwick Publications, p 104.

[42] Sargeant (2011), p 104.

[43] Root (2017a), p 156.

[44] James K. A. Smith (2009), *Desiring the Kingdom: Worship, Worldview and Cultural Formation*, Grand Rapids, Michigan: Baker Academic, p 29.

[45] Smith (2009), p 29.

[46] Smith (2009), p 139. Cf. Debra Dean Murphy (2001), "Worship as Catechesis: Knowledge, Desire, and Christian Formation", *Theology Today*, 58 (3), 321–32. Murphy similarly argues that

In Smith's evocative description of the liturgy, there is a movement that starts with a calling from God to gather as one broken and graced eschatological community. The participants learn the language of the kingdom of God through the body – knees, eyes, ears, tongues, hands – in singing, praying, giving, and confessing. They are, through baptism, initiated into a new story and experience a radical reordering of the social world in Christ. Scripture and the sermon practice re-narrate the world in which they live. The gathered people of God experience the Eucharistic practice, which is a gracious communion with a forgiving God and a communal supper at the same time. And finally, the liturgical community is sent out from the liturgical space as signs of a new kingdom and as "cultural labourers" challenged to change the world to which they are sent:[47]

> I suggest that the range of Christian practices "beyond Sunday" are best understood as extensions of the liturgical practices of gathered worship; they are important and formative because (and insofar as) they draw on the formative power of specifically liturgical practices.[48]

As this thesis investigates Christian formation in missional situations, the note about Christian formation "beyond Sunday" deserves further reflection. Smith dismisses the idea of separation of mission and liturgy. He states that the church worships *for* the mission, gathers *for* sending, and centres itself on the practices of the body of Christ *for* the sake of the world. Nevertheless, according to Smith, the liturgy of the gathered in the church is the *locus* of Christian formation. In the gathering and sending movements, which Smith refers to as the centripetal and centrifugal teloi, the gathering is still primary.[49]

---

liturgical worship is what forms a person towards being Christian. It is impossible to get hold of this knowledge in mind and body except by participating and doing. It is, at its core, a corporeal and performative form of knowledge: "to admit the intimate connection between knowledge and action, between learning and bodily practice, is to recognize that, for Christians, worship is the site at which our formation and education are initiated and completed [...] What we do, how we act, in the liturgical assembly shapes us in particular and powerful ways and is both formative of identity and catechetical in the most basic sense"., p 324.

[47] Smith (2009), pp 155–214.
[48] Smith (2009), p 212.
[49] James K. A. Smith (2013), *Imagining the Kingdom: How Worship Works*, Grand Rapids, Michigan: Baker Academic. In a conversation with Smith (April 2018), I asked him about how he would approach formation through missional practices. In response, he emphasized liturgy as mission and liturgy for mission, which is close to how he unpacks the relationship between mission and liturgy in his writings. For further reading on how his thoughts play out in missional practice, he suggested Rutba-House (ed.) (2005), *School(s) for Conversion: 12 Marks of a New*

When defining *spiritual formation*, another way of speaking about Christian formation, Dwight J. Zscheile describes it as an intentional communal process guided by the Holy Spirit "for the sake of the world".[50] This last phrase points out the missional characteristic of this formation. It is not only a matter of individual or even communal change but a change towards ministry in the world. In other words, the telos of Christian formation involves mission.

William R. McAlpine has addressed the issue of missional engagement in relation to space, building a cultural theology that fosters an appreciation of church buildings as missional liturgical spaces. By acknowledging the meaning of space for mission, he points to an important issue in the missional discussion.

> My contention is that [...] one cannot engage in ritual in a vacuum; nor can ritual be effectively conducted in spaces that distract from a meaningful ritualistic experience, even though other legitimate purposes may be served. It is likely inconceivable for many to imagine participating in the Eucharist or conducting a Bar Mitzvah at a rock concert or in a station in the London Underground. Sacred place constitute an essential component of ritual; they impart meaning, and they do matter.[51]

Like James K.A. Smith, McAlpine points to the liturgy and the church building as the natural locus of Christian formation. Some proponents of Missional theology challenge this theology in favour of an emphasis on building relationships rather than church buildings.[52] Darrell L. Guder distinguishes between the church as a place and the church as a people. He strongly suggests the latter and describes the church as a community, servant and messenger sent to represent the reign of God as opposed to a vendor of religion in a place set apart for liturgy.[53] This difference is often described as an attractional versus a missional model. Alan Hirsch argues that,

---

Monasticism, Eugene, Oregon: Cascade Books. This book could be considered a manifesto for the New Monasticism movement.

[50] Dwight Zscheile (2012), "A Missional Theology of Spiritual Formation", in Zscheile, Dwight (ed.), *Cultivating Sent Communities: Missional Spiritual Formation* (Grand Rapids, Michigan: Eerdmans), 1–28, p 7.

[51] William R. McAlpine (2011), *Sacred Space for the Missional Church*, Eugene, Oregon: Wipf and Stock, p 172.

[52] Cornelius J.P. Niemandt (2012), "Trends in Missional Ecclesiology", *HTS Teologiese Studies / Theological Studies*, 68 (1), 1–9; Beard (2015).

[53] Daniel L. Guder and Barrett, Lois (1998), *Missional Church: A Vision for the Sending of the Church in North America*, Grand Rapids, Michigan: Eerdmans. Gudder is far from the only voice in the missional movement that suggests the abandonment of traditional church buildings in favour of evangelisation and discipleship.

[...]the attractional model of drawing people into church programs commonly used by the Western church have given the impression that the church has "become both a consumable and a service provider, a vendor of religious goods and services".[54]

In the missional movement, there have been attempts to correct the attractional model"[55] When speaking of missional situations in this thesis, I acknowledge the shift of perspective represented by missional arguments. While having some form of liturgical life, the three church plants in this study intentionally gather at places without traditional liturgical references and cite missional reasons for doing so.

James K.A Smith's definition of Christian formation deepens the discussion of secular cultural teloi in contrast to Christian formation. Secularisation, according to Smith, has its own cathedrals of learning (universities), mission and evangelisation (marketing), and sacrifices (military), and the individual in a secular society might experience transcendence through shopping. By having distinctly different goals – and "rituals of ultimate concern" – than Christian formative practices, secular culture performs mis-formation of individuals and communities, to which the church needs to provide counter-formation.[56]

In this thesis, I lean on a practice understanding of Christian formation, which involves individual, socially situated, and spatially located formation in secular culture. In short, Christian formation is social practices with the intention of leading to Christian faith and lived Christian identity. What I mean by having a practice perspective will be further described later in this chapter and in the chapter on situated learning theory (Chapter 4).

Sweden as a Secular Context

Sweden is considered one of the most secularised countries in the world. World Values Survey grades Sweden as one of the least traditionalistic and most self-expressive countries.[57] Religion as a bearer of tradition has a diminishing impact on Swedish culture. Sweden, which often tends to view itself as having a balanced position on most issues, in this case, seems quite extreme. Professor Katarina Westerlund describes the place of religion in Swedish culture in the following way:

---

[54] Beard (2015); Alan Hirsch (2006), *The Forgotten Ways*, Grand Rapids, Michigan: Brazos Press. Beard (p 180) is citing Hirsch (p 44).

[55] My intention is not to give a full account of the missional movement or the discussion on missional versus attractional church, but to point to two different mindsets that affect practices of Christian formation.

[56] Smith (2009), p 88.

[57] https://www.worldvaluessurvey.org.

1.2 Christian Formation and Church Plants in Secular Sweden

As a result of widespread secularization and the declining participation in church activities, knowledge about religion and spirituality is now generally low in Sweden. People are becoming less religious, and remain unconnected with faith or world-view communities. To be active in a church and practise institutional religion in such a society is even rarer and might be regarded as somewhat awkward or stupid.[58]

While the number of church members is relatively high, the number of active church-goers and practitioners is much lower. In 2022, just above 50% of the Swedish population – 5.6 million members out of 10.5 million citizens – were members of the former state church, the Church of Sweden (In 1930, that figure was 99.3%).[59] There are approximately 100,000 Catholics, 100,000 Orthodox and 100,000 Muslims and between 200,000 and 400,000 members in the free churches.[60] Few, about 15% of the population, can be considered entirely secularised in belief and practice. Most Swedes believe in "something" and appreciate the religious rites of the church; 36% call this something God – but 12% have prayed to this God in the last year.[61] Between 1988 and 2019, persons who attended a church service at least once a year dropped from 31% to 19%. The number who attended at least once a month dropped from 10% to 7%.[62] Sociologist Grace Davie has described this Scandinavian phenomenon as "belonging without believing", and this double-sided image raises the question of what we mean when speaking about Sweden as secular.[63]

Historically, a stronger uniformity of religion and culture characterised post-reformation Sweden. The church was part of the government apparatus, keeping

---

[58] Katarina Westerlund (2021), "'And the Word Was Made Flesh?' – Exploring Young People's Situated Learning in Leadership and Spirituality in a Secular Context", *Journal of Youth and Theology*, 2021 1–23, p 4, with reference to David Thurfjell (2015), *Det gudlösa folket*, Stockholm: Norstedts.

[59] Thurfjell (2015). https://www.scb.se/hitta-statistik/sverige-i-siffror/manniskorna-i-sverige/sveriges-befolkning/ [4 Sept 2023]. https://www.svenskakyrkan.se/statistik [4 Sept 2023]. In 1930, most free church members were still formal members of the state church. This is not the case after 2000.

[60] Thurfjell (2015), p 21. Thurfjell estimates as many as 400,000 members in free churches. Øyvind Tholvsen (2021), *Frikyrkoundersökningen – En rapport om frikyrkornas utveckling i Sverige 2000–2020*, Sveriges Frikyrkosamråd. Tholvsen claims that there were 219,000 members in 2201 local free churches at the end of 2020, representing 2.1% of the population.

[61] Thurfjell (2015), p 29. Marcus Weissenbilder (2020), *Svenska religionstrender*, Göteborg: SOM-institutet.

[62] Weissenbilder (2020).

[63] Grace Davie (2007), *The Sociology of Religion*, Thousand Oaks, California: sage. Cf. Thurfjell (2015), p 22.

registers of all citizens and entrusted with safeguarding their faith.[64] Small religious gatherings and conventicles outside the state church's control were prohibited between 1726 and 1858 to deter growing pietistic influences.

The late 19th century to early 20th century saw the rise of the free church movement, along with the temperance and labour movements, all of which contributed significantly to the democratisation and modernisation of Sweden.[65] The introduction of democratic practices in these movements, for example, granting each member of a free church congregation the right to vote, opened for alternative and independent churches in Swedish society. Lawfully leaving the state church was not possible until 1860, and before 1951, secession was only granted to members of designated faith denominations.

The church was separated from the state in 2000. However, laws still regulate the Church of Sweden, and political parties are involved in the democratic assembly governing the church.[66] In other words, the differentiation between state and church is not complete.

Several studies indicate tension in the relationship between the Swedish state, majority culture, and free churches. Even during the religious freedom reforms of the 19th century, scepticism towards religion outside the state church persisted in many parts of society. Linnea Lundgren notes that, from the state's perspective, a shift from deliberation to recognition was fully realised only in the 1970s. Minority groups, such as free churches, were granted the same rights to develop their own cultural and religious life as independent denominations parallel to the state church. But after 2000, there was another shift towards the priority of Civic religion:

---

[64] Lars Trägårdh (2014), "Statist Individualism: The Swedish Theory of Love and Its Lutheran Imprint", in Halldorf, Joel and Wenell, Fredrik (eds.), *Between the State and the Eucharist: Free Church Theology in Conversation with William T. Cavanaugh* (Eugene, Oregon: Wipf and Stock), 13–38. Trägårdh stresses the importance of the strong tradition of law in Sweden, even before the Reformation.

[65] For more on this, see Harry Lenhammar (1999), *Sveriges kyrkohistoria: Individualismens och upplysningens tid*, eds. Lenhammar, Harry and Wernolf, Inga, Stockholm: Verbum; Anders Jarlert (2001), *Sveriges kyrkohistoria: Romantikens och liberalismens tid*, eds. Jarlert, Anders and Wernolf, Inga, Stockholm: Verbum Harry Lenhammar describes the gradual disintegration of religious uniformity in Sweden through pietist influences (pp 32–77). Anders Jarlert writes about the revival movement and the emergence of the Swedish free churches. Especially the abolition of laws regulated conventicles (pp 148–174).

[66] Thurfjell (2015). Cf. Swedish Law (1998:1591, §4): "The congregation's basic task is to celebrate worship, conduct education and perform diaconia and mission". (my translation). The church is to be Evangelical-Lutheran, democratically governed, and have a nationwide presence.

1.2 Christian Formation and Church Plants in Secular Sweden

However, the desire to prevent and control minority religious communities became more evident around the turn of the century when new discussions emerged regarding how to limit the impact of certain minority religious communities who, for example, promoted conflicting values to society at large.[67]

This shift, where "emphasis was on shared moral standards and common values", resulted in the exclusion of religious perspectives and stronger control of religious minority groups.[68] According to Lundgren, the state policies were enacted to foster social coherence, and in turn, resulted in demands of conformity and compliance being placed on religious minorities. Today, while many acknowledge the resources that religion brings to society, religion is increasingly considered a risk in Swedish society.[69] She finds that the Swedish state increasingly takes the role of the protector of the individual from religious minority groups:

> [M]inority religious communities who did not seem to share the same values as the wider society, i.e., that did not promote the autonomy of the individual but rather promoted communitarian virtues and a narrow community where the individual was connected to his or her communal obligations rather than to society at large, were seen as deeply problematic.[70]

In other words, the state considers alternative formative teloi as potential threats to society. Historians Lars Trägårdh and Henrik Berggren have shown that civil society generally has a downplayed role in Sweden. In Germany, there is an emphasis on the relationship between family and state, and the United States encourage the relationship between individual and family.[71] However, the social contract in Sweden stresses the relationship between the individual and the state and gives less attention to civil society, according to Trägårdh and Susanne Wallman Lundåsen:

> In sharp contrast to Continental Europe, the social contract on which the welfare state was built is one between the individual and the state at the expense of the family and the intermediary institutions of civil society, such as the churches, and private and voluntary charity organizations. Many of the latter are associated not first and foremost with pluralism and freedom, but with demeaning private charity, unequal patriarchal relations and informal abuses or uses of power. In Sweden, the state is thus conceived as the

---

[67] Linnea Lundgren (2021), *A Risk or a Resource? A Study of the Swedish State's Shifting Perception and Handling of Minority Religious Communities between 1952–2019*, Ersta Sköndal Bräcke Högskola, p 320.
[68] Lundgren (2021), p 323.
[69] Lundgren (2021), p 332.
[70] Lundgren (2021), p 329.
[71] Henrik Berggren and Trägårdh, Lars (2009), *Är svensken människa? Gemenskap och oberoende i det moderna Sverige*, Stockholm: Norstedts; Trägårdh (2014).

liberator of the individual from such ties of dependency, an order of things I have termed "statist individualism".[72]

This means that the space in which religious minority groups, such as church plants, can shape faith and build a common life according to their own traditions must be negotiated in Sweden.[73] Karin Kittelmann Flensner has shown how this pressure to comply with secular norms plays out in Swedish schools:

> The secularist discourse was hegemonic in the [Religious Education] classroom, which meant that positions perceived to be outside that norm appeared as abnormal and deviant. When the secularist discourse became hegemonic, religion and faith were associated with out-dated irrational and unintelligent attitudes.[74]

Kittelmann Flensner's ethnographic study is interesting because it offers insight into what it "feels like" to be religious in a public school context characterised by advanced secularity and, at times, an insensitivity towards religion. When religious identity is considered a feature of others only, religion becomes a separate function rather than part of what it means to be human.[75] Maria Zackariasson concludes that free churches play the role of the other in Sweden: "The religiousness associated with the free churches thus contributes to establishing them as different or

---

[72] Susanne Wallman Lundåsen and Trägårdh, Lars (2013), "Social Trust and Religion in Sweden: Theological Belief Versus Social Organization", *Religion and Civil Society in Europe* (Dordrecht: Springer Netherlands), 109–24. Neither I nor the authors intend to say that one of these three models is better than the other. Historical developments in different Western countries have led to different trade-offs between groups in societies. I do intend, though, to problematise some taken-for-granted views in Sweden about the presence of a unique tolerance for deviants.

[73] In studying an interesting case of "religion-making" in the dealings between The Missionary Church of Kopimism (who believe that copying information is a sacred virtue) and the Swedish government, Per-Erik Nilsson and Enkvist, Victoria (2016), "Techniques of Religion-making in Sweden: The Case of the Missionary Church of Kopimism", *Critical Research on Religion*, 4 (2), 141–55. The authors follow how the state regulates religion through a bureaucratic exercise of sovereign power over the religious. By staking the conditions for being granted the status of a religious community, the state becomes an active agent in shaping the structure, message, and followers. As a result, the Kopimism faith community itself had to negotiate its formation within discursive boundaries set up by the state. While not taking a stand in the actual case as to whether Kopimism can be seen as a religion, Nilsson and Enkvist conclude that the neutrality of the state is undermined in this kind of "religion-making".

[74] Karin Kittelmann Flensner (2015), *Religious Education in Contemporary Pluralistic Sweden*, Göteborg: Götebrog University.

[75] Thurfjell (2015), p 50.

diverging, in relation to the image of Sweden as a highly secularised country".[76] One historical reason for this, according to David Thurfjell, was a two-way pull from revivalist Christianity, represented by the free churches on the one hand and influential secular critics on the other, which has alienated the Christian identity in Sweden.

While these studies are helpful in describing changes and problematising the conditions in Swedish society connected to secularisation, a definition of the concept is needed. Secularisation can be broken down into the processes of differentiation, rationalisation, privatisation and pluralisation. Rather than using a single definition, I acknowledge the complexity of the term by referring to these processes. In different ways, these processes provide conditions for forming an identity as a Christian:

- *Differentiation*: The separation of church and state and the independence of societal institutions leads to a loss of a common moral narrative.[77]
- *Rationalisation:* A science and evidence-based rationality leads to demands for professionalism and rationalism within churches.[78]
- *Privatisation:* Voices in society avoid religious references as religion is relegated to the private sphere.[79] The church becomes an institution for people with a special interest in religion, and faith is an individual choice.
- *Pluralisation:* The existential sphere presents the individual with a plethora of options for beliefs and practices. Congregations present

---

[76] Maria Zackariasson (2012), "Coming from the Outside. Learning and Experiences among Youths from Non-religious Families in Christian Youth Organisations", *Learning, Culture and Social Interaction*, 1 (3–4), 249–58, p 5.

[77] Davie (2014), p 615. Taylor (2007), p 475. Thurfjell (2015), p 37. The theory of differentiation suggests that as the strength of the general institutional cohesion in society is weakened, the church's influence decreases. The church institution and traditions are not employed to the same degree, and society becomes post-Christian.

[78] E.g. Wilson (2016).

[79] Casanova (1994). "Religion was progressively forced to withdraw from the modern secular state and the modern capitalist economy and to find refuge in the newly found private sphere. Like modern science, capitalist markets and modern state bureaucracies manage to function 'as if' God would not exist" (p 40).

their unique offerings in the marketplace of culture, religion, and spirituality.[80]

While the processes are hard to distinguish, privatisation and pluralisation highly affect the relationship between the individual and the church community. Likewise, the relationship between the church community and society at large is affected by differentiation, rationalisation, and pluralisation. Thus, these processes affect Christian formation.

Secularisation has occurred over an extended period.[81] According to Charles Taylor, deep shifts in Western imagination lie beneath these changes. A romanticism of authenticity has played a crucial role since the 1960s.[82] He describes the culture of authenticity as,

---

[80] Taylor (2007). According to Taylor, belief in God today, is "understood to be one option among others, and frequently not the easiest to embrace"(p 3).

[81] A broader discussion on theories of secularisation is beyond the scope of this thesis. Secularisation theory emerged during the nineteenth and twentieth Centuries as a result of achievements by Max Weber, Emile Durkheim, Karl Marx and others. (Pippa Norris and Inglehart, Ronald [2011], *Sacred and Secular: Religion and Politics Worldwide*, Cambridge: Cambridge University Press). Two of the main theses of this theory are the differentiation thesis, claiming that religion develops as an autonomous sphere – independent from politics, science and economy – and thus loses influence and finally disappears. The other, privatisation thesis means that religion is mainly an expression of the subjective with little or no impact on institutional life (Ola Sigurdson [2009]. *Det postsekulära tillståndet - religion, modernitet, politik*, Göteborg: Glänta). Charles Wright Mills articulates the idea of the inevitable secularisation of Western society: "Once the world was filled with the sacred – in thought, practice, and institutional form. After the Reformation and the Renaissance, the forces of modernization swept across the globe, and secularization, a corollary historical process, loosened the dominance of the sacred. In due course, the sacred shall disappear altogether except, possibly, in the private realm". (C. Wright Mills [1959], *The Sociological Imagination*, Oxford: Oxford University Press, pp 32–33). Some fifty years later, in "Secularization – In defence of an unfashionable theory", Steve Bruce, working from a substantialist understanding of religion rather than a functional one, concludes that secularisation theory is right when looking at the numbers and the influence of religion in both eastern and western part of Europe – Europeans are secular in practice. Peter Berger, once a proponent of the theory of secularisation, later argues that: "Secularization theory, based on the idea that modernity necessarily brings about a decline of religion, has for a time served as a paradigm for the study of religion. It can no longer be maintained in the face of the empirical evidence". (Peter L. Berger (2014), *The Many Altars of Modernity*, Berlin: De Gruyter, p ix.). Berger explains his former stance as a misinterpretation of the empirical evidence. Pluralism shouldn't be interpreted as secularism. Grace Davie describes the secularism debate as multi-dimensional and ongoing (Davie [2007]).

[82] Cf. Root (2017a), p 17. Trägårdh (2014). Trägårdh, likewise, points to Sweden in the 1960s, where churches and other bodies were increasingly viewed as problematic obstacles standing between the state and the individual.

1.2 Christian Formation and Church Plants in Secular Sweden

the understanding of life which emerges with the Romantic expressivism of the late-eighteenth century, that each one of us has his/ her own way of realizing our humanity, and that it is important to find and live out one's own, as against surrendering to conformity with a model imposed on us from outside, by society, or the previous generation, or religious or political authority.[83]

Before "The Secular Age", as he calls the present condition, the self was porous to cosmic realities, and the question was not of God's existence but rather one's own relation to this God. God was the one setting moral standards for society, and there was a shared understanding of what was right and wrong. In the immanent frame – the present view of things – God has been removed from the moral equation and, in some sense, replaced by authenticity. Accordingly, the individual becomes the source of morality. This approach gives the human being a greater sense of agency and potentially makes her morally responsible, not to God, but to her fellow humans and herself. But it also creates a sense of existential loneliness, as there is no ultimate Other to which one can relate[84]

When society is no longer constructing a common life dominated by one religious view, all religions are relativised. Luke Bretherton makes a helpful distinction between *secularity* and *secularism*. Secularity means that society is still open to transcendent claims. Secularism, on the other hand, is a temporal view of modernity that postulates the disappearance of religion as humanity progressively moves towards human autonomy, economic growth and social cohesion. Here, religion is tolerated only insofar as it contributes to these modern goods. Otherwise, it is considered anti-modern or reactionary.[85] The space in which churches operate in the West is continuously negotiated between these two versions of secular culture.

---

[83] Taylor (2007), p 475.

[84] This is obviously a very short summary of Taylor's very long presentation of the Age of Authenticity, using expressions like expressive individualism, buffered self, the Nova effect, etc. See Taylor (2007) and James K. A. Smith (2014), *How (Not) to Be Secular*, Grand Rapids, Michigan: Eerdmans; Root (2017a) for good summaries. For a study that relates Swedish evangelicalism to Charles Taylor's theory of modernity, see Joel Halldorf (2012), *Av denna världen? Emil Gustafson, moderniteten och den evangelikala väckelsen*, Skellefteå: Artos.

[85] Luke Bretherton (2019), *Christ and the Common Life*, Grand Rapids, Michigan: Eerdmans, p 229. In Bretherton's description, secularity is a necessary road to Christian co-existence with others in society and could be seen as a part of the Christian mission. In contrast, secularism, for religious groups, could mean demands of conformation to beliefs, views and teloi that exclude large parts of religion. When the church no longer provides the narrative framework for the common life, it doesn't mean that all narratives have equal standing but that all other narratives are subjugated to modern secularism.

It is fair to assume that Christian formation takes different shapes depending on which view is operative in the cultural context.

By comparing the results of similar studies, we can better understand the processes and reasons why people move towards and away from the Christian faith and identity. Soul Searching by Christian Smith and Melinda Lundquist Denton describes the faith of young Americans. They found that while teenagers are generally positive towards religion, they generally hold pluralistic and individualistic views about religious truth – "everyone makes their own way to the meaning of life". This means that evangelism and recruiting others to your own faith community is seen as questionable behaviour and that religion is usually relegated to the private sphere. The book is known for introducing *Moralistic Therapeutic Deism* (MTD). This faith is moralistic in the sense that "God wants people to be good, nice, and fair to each other, as taught in the Bible and by most world religions".[86] Good people are rewarded by going to heaven when they die. According to MTD, the therapeutically oriented goal of life is "to be happy and to feel good about oneself".[87] Whatever religion you choose, the important thing is that it gives you the means to deal with problems and helps you feel good. After creating the world, the god of MTD is not very engaged in the creation. This deistic god does not ask for devotion or obedience but is, rather, a "divine butler" who helps you solve problems. MTD is not a religion in itself, though the authors describe it as a parasitic faith that lives on other religions.[88]

Andersson, Spjuth, and Wenell invoke the concept of MTD when they discuss the Swedish situation against the background provided by Charles Taylor. The authors find that young Swedes are similar – but not the same – as their American counterparts.[89] There are similarities in relation to the therapeutic approach to faith insofar as the teenagers in their study relate to a God that gives them inner peace, accepts them as they are, and makes them feel positive about themselves. Also, they motivate their faith with moral arguments. In following Jesus, they become good and loving persons. However, they don't share the deistic view of God

---

[86] Christian Smith and Lundquist Denton, Melinda (2009), *Soul Searching: The Religious and Spiritual Lives of American Teenagers*, Oxford: University Press, p 162.

[87] Smith and Lundquist Denton (2009), p 162.

[88] Smith and Lundquist Denton (2009), p 166.

[89] Greger Andersson, Spjuth, Roland, and Wenell, Fredrik (2017), "Unga i karismatiska och evangelikala kyrkor resonerar om sin tro", *Scandinavian journal for leadership & theology*, (4), 1–22. The research is performed among youth in evangelical charismatically-minded churches in Sweden.

that characterizes teenagers in the U.S. Instead, they believe in an active God who sees them and answers their prayers.

The young Swedes describe contemporary society as loveless and performance-oriented, feeling accepted only according to their advantages and achievements. At the same time, they express an appreciation of the general value rhetoric of the culture, like the importance of love and accepting everyone as they are, as well as the significance of personal well-being and caring for those in need. They often experience prejudices against them as Christians and feel they are perceived as boring and intolerant.

Furthermore, the study shows that for adolescents, church means "community", but Andersson, Spjuth, and Wenell note that they lack a deeper reflection on how the community could host the "accept everyone as they are" and simultaneously offer formation towards mature, loving Jesus-follower-ship. This inability to express important features of the Christian faith is also present in the Swedish study. Further, young Christians rarely use Christian concepts or refer to the Bible when speaking about their faith but rather use ordinary language. This indicates an increasing religious illiteracy in Sweden, according to the authors.

This wider social context provides background to the negotiations in the practices of the church plant communities. Christian formation is not something that takes place in the church alone. While the churches are active in this, the churchgoers live their lives in a society affected by secularisation. This is why looking at the negotiation of cultural issues and formative trajectories is critical to understanding Christian formation. To flourish in the secular wasteland, the new church plants need to renegotiate how the Christian faith can be lived in the contemporary situation.

Church Plants as Labs for Re-Innovation of Christian Formation

Forming new church communities for the sake of mission is something that has mainly occurred in free churches in Sweden. From circa 1850 to 1930, the Swedish free churches emerged in a messy situation, with bad harvests, poverty, emigration, industrialisation, and revival. Thousands of local congregations united in different denominations and associations. The free churches emerged in opposition to the Swedish state church with convictions as their *raison d'être*.[90] This led to new ways

---

[90] Philipp Bartholomä (2015), "The Ecclesiological Self and the Other: Concepts of Social Identity and Their Implications for Free Churches in Secular Europe", *Ecclesial Practices*, 2, 156–76 discusses the change that is needed in the free church movement in Germany to no longer

of organising church life and mission and new religious practices that became patterns in the evangelical revival. These new practices included the revival meeting, the conventicle, and urban social ministry – all of these continue, as we shall see, to play an important part today.[91]

A century ago, the motive for planting churches was mainly to seek a more faithful expression of the church than what the Swedish state church provided. Today, church planting is mainly about reaching more people, as church pews are sparsely populated, or finding new and creative ways of authentically being church.[92] The fact that the growth of the older free churches ended 70–80 years ago is an important background for recent developments in the Swedish ecumenical church-planting endeavour. Since the mid-twentieth century, these denominations have seen a decline in membership. This has caused former rivals to unite in new constellations. For example, the United Methodist Church in Sweden, Baptist Union of Sweden, and Mission Covenant Church merged as the Uniting Church in Sweden in 2011.

The joint initiative in 2018 called *Vidare* (which can be translated as "Moving on") set the goal of planting more churches in 2025 than are closed down that year.[93] The formation of this strategic alliance shows that, since the early 1990s, the reasons for and the way of speaking about church planting in Sweden has changed from being mainly about church splits due to congregational conflicts to an increasingly strategic and ecumenical endeavour.[94] During the past two decades, more than 450 churches and missional initiatives have been started, and the

---

identify itself in opposition to state church, but from its own vision. The former state church, Church of Sweden, is today formally a free church itself, but still describes itself as a territorial church in its regulating documents (Kyrkoordningen).

[91] Cf. Carola Nordbäck (2014), "Trons mötesplatser – Ett kyrko- och väckelsehistoriskt perspektiv", in Amundsen, Arne Bugge (ed.), *Vekkelsens møtesteder* (Lund: Lunds universitet), 9–52. Nordbäck uses a perspective of practice traditions in analysing the pietistic revival meeting as such within the Church of Sweden. For a further discussion of different kinds of gatherings within Swedish evangelicalism, see also Halldorf (2012), p 269–279.

[92] Paas (2016).

[93] The churches and organisations behind this initiative are the Evangelical Free Church, Uniting Church in Sweden, EFS (part of Church of Sweden), Vineyard Sweden, Swedish Mission Alliance, the Swedish Pentecostal movement, Seventh-day Adventist Church in Sweden and mission organisations Operation Mobilization and Go Out Mission.

[94] The practice of planting churches is still to some degree debated in Sweden, other terms are also used, for example *församlingsgrundande* (the founding of local churches) or *nystart* (starting new local churches), parallel to *omstart* (restarting an existing church).

churches and denominations are collaborating around church-planting efforts in Sweden.[95]

Stefan Paas and Mary Schoemaker define church planting as "the creation of new Christian communities for missionary reasons".[96] This is the definition used in this thesis, and it captures what is significant in the process in a way that makes sense to insiders and outsiders. Ott and Wilson's definition captures something of an insider's view. Church planting is, they write, "that ministry which through evangelism and discipleship establishes reproducing kingdom communities of believers in Jesus Christ, who are committed to fulfilling biblical purposes under local spiritual leaders".[97] According to the *Mission-shaped Churches* report presented by the Church of England, church planting is best thought of as a verb, not a noun. It is "the process by which a seed of the life and message of Jesus embodied by a community of Christians is immersed for mission reasons in a particular cultural or geographic context".[98] This contextualised embodiment of the life and message of Jesus is recognised as an emerging church.

At this point, it is worth clarifying the terminology around church planting and how I use it in this thesis. I distinguish between church plants, new churches, and established churches. The act of church planting aims to establish a new church. Before it can be considered a church, it is a church plant – a church in becoming. Depending on the ecclesiology, goals, and planting methods, the transition from plant to church occurs at different times. This could be likened to garden work; "planting" means putting seeds in the soil with the intention of having a fully grown flower, bush, or tree. Getting to a healthy, mature plant will require a lot of time and work, but once the seed has been planted, the essential work is done before the first shoots have broken through the soil. I study formative practices in church plants, which means that they are not yet recognised as new churches by themselves or their denominations. The first few years are interesting

---

[95] Jonas Melin, Svanberg, Peter, and Wellstam, Julia (2020), *Vi planterar nya församlingar*, Evangelie förlag. According to Tholvsen (2021) at least 471 churches were planted in 2000–2020, while during the same time, 1127 churches have been closed. Svanberg (1999). Svanberg, in a DMin dissertation on church planting in Sweden, identifies three of 34 church plants started between 1992–96, that report a relatively high number of new converts. Of the three churches (Stockholm Karisma Center, Mötesplatsen, Örebro and Tomaskyrkan, Stockholm) only one exists today.

[96] Paas and Schoemaker (2018), p 366.

[97] Craig Ott and Wilson, Gene (2011), *Global Church Planting*, Ada, Michigan: Baker Academic, p 8.

[98] Mission and Public Affairs Council (2004), p 32.

since they bear particular possibilities and challenges. To be the first ten people differs significantly from being the last ten in the church before it closes – sadly a common experience of many parishioners in Sweden today. Planting a church raises the immediate need to be relevant in the cultural context. Therefore, the interplay between church and society in church plants reveals the conditions for religious life in the wasteland.

In a recent analysis of Swedish church-planting narratives, I conclude that church planting could be understood as "mission through community". This means that the community itself is a relational vehicle to reach new people, address their needs, and be an alternative worshipping community. The planters in the study underline the importance of close relationships in the communities. Churches are planted in different ways – as projects of evangelism or worship services for a specific group, area or culture – with the hope that they will become independent church communities. To achieve this, Swedish church planters tend to use different strategies: going public to gather big meetings, forming a network of small groups, or going person to person to slowly build a community. Public gatherings are culturally adapted to reach young people without knowledge of the church, gospel, or liturgy. The language and music are often contemporary, and the message consists of an uncomplicated and engaging presentation of Jesus. In many cases, the experience of calling to plant a church is linked to a particular place, but sometimes, a church is strategically planted in an area in response to changing demographics. Planters stress the importance of being locally grounded in the work of planting. Some planters find that the building where the church plant meets is an essential way of communicating the church's identity.[99]

Stefan Paas uses the terminology of "better churches", "more churches", and "new churches" in describing the different logics behind the church planting

---

[99] Björn Asserhed (2020), *Församling som mission*, Stockholm: Vidare. Cf. Michael Moynagh (2012), *Church for Every Context: An Introduction to Theology and Practice*, Norwich: Hymns Ancient and Modern Ltd, pp 201–205. Michael Moynagh describes church planting as a practice of "birthing" a church. He proposes two models of the church-planting practice that he calls the "worship-first journey", which focuses on the worship meeting and inviting people to join a small group and the "serving-first journey", which means finding ways of serving the people in the community and making contact with them. There are many similar descriptions of these models. Steve Nicholson and Bailey, Jeff (1999), *Coaching Church Planters*, Association of Vineyard Churches, refers to similar models as "inside-out" and "outside-in". Aubrey Malphurs (2004), *Planting Growing Churches for the 21st Century: A Comprehensive Guide for New Churches and Those Desiring Renewal*, Ada, MI, US: Baker Books, calls them "hot-start" and "cold-start". In Asserhed (2020), I refer to "start big", and "small group building" and add the "one-to-one" model.

practice.¹⁰⁰ In the *better churches* paradigm, church planting is a response to a situation where the present church is perceived as inadequate due to false teaching or inadequate praxis. In this situation, planting new churches is done in opposition or protest to the old church. There is a felt need for reforms to adjust the current path. The *more churches* paradigm rests on the evangelistic motivation to reach more people with the Christian message. Church planting is described as the most effective method of evangelism. Church plants, it is said in this paradigm, grow faster than established churches and extend the range of options for religiously interested people.¹⁰¹ In the *new churches* paradigm, church planting is a kind of ecclesial innovation that relates to the churches' need to be relevant in a changing and fragmented culture and builds on a theology of cultural pluralism.¹⁰² This is the most prominent motive in the church plants of this study. Being innovative is not only a necessity for a declining church but, according to Andreas Reckwitz, a part of urban Western culture:

> Creative work, innovative organization, self-developing individuals and creative cities are all participants in a comprehensive, concerted cultural effort to produce novelty on a permanent basis, feeding the desire for the creation and perception of novel and original objects, events and identities.¹⁰³

While this is the most prominent motive in the church plants of this study, other examples can be found outside of Sweden. For instance, the Emerging Church movement and Fresh Expressions in the UK are two important examples of the new paradigm of church planting.

1.3 Practical Theology: Discerning Theology in the Lived

In this section, I locate this study of Christian formation in the field of practical theology and its methods.

---

¹⁰⁰ Paas (2016), p 50.
¹⁰¹ Donald A. McGavran (1990), *Understanding Church Growth*, Grand Rapids, Michigan: Eerdmans. See Paas (2016) for a presentation and critical treatment of these ideas.
¹⁰² I would argue that, at least in Sweden, a prevailing pluralism has been an important reason for a change of perspective towards church planting. Instead of seeing new ecclesial expressions as threatening, harmful or heretic, the general argument among church planters is that different expressions of church are needed to reach different people. E.g. Melin et al. (2020).
¹⁰³ Andreas Reckwitz (2017), *The Invention of Creativity: Modern Society and the Culture of the New*, Cambridge: Polity, p 3–4.

Practical Theology, Learning and Formation

Practical theology directs attention to what is going on in practice. In this thesis, formative practices in church plants are at the centre of attention. Practice as a theoretical concept holds together different aspects of doing and reflection in a particular context.[104] Practical theology also involves discerning voices of theology in a situation.[105] What is performed in practice could be found to differ from, or even contradict, what is explicitly stated as belief.[106] The tension is embedded in practice and opens up spaces for theological interpretations and reflections.

The split between what is deemed as theoretical – the cognitive and abstract – and the practical – the social and material – is a well-known feature of modernity that, according to Bonnie Miller-McLemore, is still present in theological reflection of Christian formation. In discussing the relentlessness of the modern split and the politics of knowledge, she finds that "[d]espite all that practical theologians have accomplished in advancing the cause of practice [...] the very categories we seek to unsettle, those of theory and practice, continue to entrap us".[107] Practical theology needs to be able to hold these aspects together.

Christian formation in the West has relied on an overly cognitive understanding of education, leading to a head-knowledge Christianity.[108] "What if education [...] is not primarily about the absorption of ideas and information, but the

---

[104] Hager et al. (2012).

[105] Helen Cameron et al. (2010), *Talking about God in Practice*, Norwich: Hymns Ancient and Modern Ltd. The approach of the ARCS team (Action Research Church and Society) involves the distinction of four voices of theology: the theology expressed implicitly in practices (operant voice), the theology articulated explicitly by practitioners (espoused voice), theological traditions (normative voice), and academic theology (formal voice).

[106] Sven-Erik Brodd approaches this problem as "implicit" theology acknowledging that "[i]n practice there are hidden ecclesiologies that are operative and contribute to the understanding of the churches". Sven-Erik Brodd (2015), "Ecclesiology under Construction", in Fahlgren, Sune and Idestrom, Jonas (eds.), *Ecclesiology in the Trenches* (Eugene, Oregon: Wipf and Stock), 1–28.

[107] Bonnie J. Miller-McLemore (2016), "The Theory-Practice Binary and the Politics of Practical Knowledge", in Mercer, Joyce A. and Miller-McLemore, Bonnie J. (eds.), *Conundrums in Practical Theology* (Leiden: Brill), 190–218, p 190. This is not a problem in theology alone, cf. Joseph A Raelin (2007), "Toward an Epistemology of Practice", *Academy of Management Learning & Education*, 6 (4), 495–519.

[108] An interesting parallel to the head-knowledge image sketched by Smith is the ecclesiological "head-footing" character suggested by Jan Eckerdal (2012), *Folkkyrkans kropp: Einar Billings ecklesiologi i postsekulär belysning*, Skellefteå: Artos. Small Children draw the Cephalopod, a head with feet and limbs attached to it. Eckerdal finds in the theology of the Swedish bishop and theologian Einar Billing (1871–1939) an asocial ecclesiology where all members are connected directly to the head – Christ (p 278).

formation of hearts and desires?" James K.A. Smith asks in his trilogy on cultural liturgies.[109] It follows that formation is not limited to values, information and worldviews but involves all things in life. Debra Dean Murphy goes as far as to say that the "schooling" model of modern pedagogy, which emphasises the classroom as the site for lecturing using an instructional model and an abstract curriculum, is a "strategy for avoiding our own conversion":[110]

> As long as our understanding of what it means to know and learn remains wedded to the modern fiction of the cool, clinically detached observer and to a view of the end of knowledge as the technical mastery of information, we fail to recognize that to learn, to know, is to be transformed – it is to implicate our selves, our very bodies in the actions and practices of learning and coming to know.[111]

However, the theorising of practice seems to be an inherent contradiction and could end up being just theoretical. Pete Ward advises against turning practice into a theory as it risks turning theology into philosophy:

> I would argue that the divide between theory and practice, as it is usually presented in Practical Theology, fundamentally misunderstands how ideas about God function in the life of the Church. To be a Christian, I would want to say, is to indwell and to be indwelt by God. This presence of God is mediated in language and in practices.[112]

A theology of practice in the context of the church, including church plants, should integrate practice, belief, and the presence of God. This kind of practical theology can bring "empathetic and focused attention on the particular and the lived".[113] This means that lived theology is the complex and performed starting

---

[109] Smith (2009), p 17. Author's emphasis.

[110] Murphy (2001), p 323, she refers this expression to Palmer, *To Know as We Are Known: Education as Spiritual Journey* (San Francisco: Harper Collins, 1993).

[111] Murphy (2001), p 323.

[112] Pete Ward (2012a), "The Hermeneutical and Epistemological Significance of Our Students", *International Journal of Practical Theology*, 16 (1), 55–65, p 60. Cf. Ulla Schmidt (2021), "Practicing as Knowing", *Studia Theologica – Nordic Journal of Theology*, 75 (1), 30–51. Schmidt likewise points to the ability to perceive God's presence as a certain knowledge in theological practice: "The kind of knowledge associated with [ecclesial] practices is an ability to see, perceive and apprehend reality in certain ways. They might for example predispose practitioners towards perceiving a divine presence in immanent things through practices such as prayer, care for the ill, the eucharist, leadership etc"., p 35.

[113] Ward (2012a), p 60.

point of practical theology.[114] By studying *lived Christian identity*, I study how identity is being performed and changed through formative practice.[115]

Discerning Theology in Practice

According to James K.A. Smith, an overly intellectual understanding of Christian formation has consequences for discerning what forms the church. Christian congregations in the secular West are formed not only by practices of the Christian tradition but also by secular liturgies. Because of the flawed models of Christian formation, Smith argues, "we have failed to recognize the degree and extent to which secular liturgies do implicitly capitalize on our embodied penchant for storied formation".[116] Churches and individual Christians are formed by and according to the secular narratives that permeate Western culture. I agree with Smith that secular teloi form people into something other than Christians and that churches need to offer some kind of counter-formation. This means that there is a need for discernment in the formative practices.[117]

John Swinton and Harriet Mowat locate the task of practical theology within the Church community as a way of discerning and being faithful to the script of revelation and the task of the church to participate in God's salvation of the world. In doing so, they point towards practices' continuously contested and dialogical nature. Practical theology is the critical, theological reflection on the practices of the church "as they interact with the practices of the world, with a view to ensuring and enabling faithful participation in God's redemptive practices in, to and for the world".[118] The practical theological reflection has a vital role in "the guiding and transforming of future practices that will inform and shape the life of faith".[119] In

---

[114] Pete Ward (2017b), *Introducing Practical Theology: Mission, Ministry, and the Life of the Church*, Ada, Michigan: Baker Academic, p 62. Cf. Nancy Tatom Ammerman (2021), *Studying Lived Religion: Contexts and Practices*, New York: NYU Press. Nancy Ammerman and others use the term "Lived Religion". Bonnie Miller-McLemore, in my opinion, fails to clarify the difference. I use lived theology, as I find it to match the intent and field of study better. Bonnie J. Miller-McLemore (2022), "Understanding Lived Theology: Is Qualitative Research the Best or Only Way?", in Ward, Pete and Tveitereid, Knut (eds.), *The Wiley Blackwell Companion to Theology and Qualitative Research* (London: John Wiley & Sons), 461–70.

[115] This is how Etienne Wenger speaks about identity, see p 90.

[116] Smith (2013), p 39.

[117] Ward (2017b), p 66. Ward says: "Not all lived theology is good".

[118] John Swinton and Mowat, Harriet (2016), *Practical Theology and Qualitative Research – second edition*, London: SCM, p 7.

[119] Swinton and Mowat (2016), p 11.

addition to locating practical theology as an essential ecclesiological discipline, Swinton and Mowat also define it as missiological:

> Practical Theology is a fundamentally missiological discipline which receives its purpose, its motivation and its dynamic from acknowledging and working out what it means to participate faithfully in God's mission. While staying close to experience, Practical Theology understands particular situations within the wider, overarching context of God's ongoing mission of redemption to the world. This mission provides the critical hermeneutic which guides the practical theologian in each dimension of her task.[120]

Practical theology also involves what God is doing beyond the ecclesial community. The missional contextualisation which is present in church planting raises theological issues. I agree with missiologist Cornelius J.P. Niemandt when he writes: "Discernment is the core practice of a missional church seeking the presence or movement of the Triune God in relationship with all of creation".[121] How Christian formation is perceived and practised in ecclesial contexts has consequences for the authenticity of the church communities and the persons in them. The task of practical theology is not only to describe the state of things and discern theology in practice. As Miller-McLemore notes, it has an errand: "It makes demands on those who practice it to live by the sacred and transcendent convictions it professes".[122] When studying the formative practices in church plants, I discern theology in practice in missional situations in the secular context as a contribution to the discussion of the nature of this errand.

Researching Lived Theology

Knut Tveitereid points to several turns over the last decades that have brought a focus on lived aspects of religion:

> The spatial turn has brought attention to theological situatedness. The *spiritual* turn has signified unorganized and non-institutionalized religious practice. The *practice* turn has recontextualized theology as a performative act. The *subjective* turn has moved the self to the center of theological hermeneutics. The *pragmatic* turn has situated theology in experience. The linguistic turn has drawn attention to theolinguistic negotiations. The *esthetic* turn has brought materiality back to the theological repertoire. But most importantly, at least in this volume, the *empirical* turn in theology has reconstructed the

---

[120] Swinton and Mowat (2016), p 26.
[121] Niemandt (2012), p 6.
[122] Bonnie J. Miller-McLemore (2012), "Five Misunderstandings about Practical Theology", *International Journal of Practical Theology*, 16 (1), 5–26, p 25.

entire field of practical theology by locating the shaping of theology in *empirical* reality as much as in the world of ideas.[123]

He further notes that the lived theology of the churches has been studied through ethnographic perspectives and methods.[124] The interest in lived perspectives is not new but has been studied as part of anthropology and related fields. I use situated learning theory, which has a heritage from anthropology through one of its influential proponents, Jean Lave, who studies learning from the perspective of social anthropology. As a result of a greater emphasis on lived theology in practical theological research over the last decades, theological ethnography has emerged as a common method.[125]

A lived perspectives approach enhances the voices which are part of embodied and performed cultural environments in gathering and constructing the material.[126] In this study, I have positioned myself in the middle of things, taking part in most of what was going on in the church plants through field studies. I have taken part in different gatherings and also interviewed church planters, other leaders, participants, and newcomers to understand the meaning they attribute to the formative practices that their voices represent.

Using sociological methods in theological study raises the question of the relation between these two fields. As Andrew Root points out, neither sociological nor empirical methods are innocent when it comes to representing reality:

> Empirical methods may be naively presumed to be able to provide something purely objective, but this is to ignore what method is. For any method in the hard sciences, social sciences, or even theology, is, as said above, a reasoned reduction or framing of reality so that a particularity of reality might be explored.[127]

Root argues on the grounds of critical realism that the methods become problematic when they exclude the possibility of divine action at a fundamental level. The methods risk reproducing the reductionistic immanent frame, part of the secular

---

[123] Knut Tveitereid (2022), "Lived Theology and Theology in the Lived", in Ward, Pete and Tveitereid, Knut (eds.), *The Wiley Blackwell Companion to Theology and Qualitative Research* (London: John Wiley & Sons), 67–77. See also Meredith B. McGuire (2008), *Lived Religion: Faith and Practice in Everyday Life*, Oxford: Oxford University Press; Ammerman (2021).

[124] Especially the Ecclesiology & Ethnography network, with Pete Ward, Christian Scharen, Knut Tveitered and others conected to Durham University, should be mentioned.

[125] The ethnographic perspective in this thesis will be further described in the chapter on methodology.

[126] Ward (2017b), p 63.

[127] Andrew Root (2016), "Regulating the Empirical in Practical Theology", *Journal of Youth and Theology*, 15 (1), 44–64, p 52.

condition. For example, this could mean that people's descriptions of their experiences of divine action are unequivocally in psychological, social or cultural terms.[128] This approach would reduce the understanding of the world and, therefore, the theological value of a practical theological study like this one. Still, empirical methods and social theories are of great benefit since they allow the practical theologian to study human action deeply. I aim to use sociological theories and empirical methods mindfully in order to avoid reductionism. The theological analysis of the interviews and observations in this thesis does not exclude or attempt to reinterpret claims of divine action.

Pete Ward, likewise, refers to the merits of critical realism for practical theology. "For critical realism, ontology refers to the 'real', but the description of this 'real' is epistemological and therefore relative".[129] This, Ward argues, doesn't mean that the "real" isn't real. There are, in fact, two levels of what is real in ecclesiology that need to be critically distinguished: the lived and the theological. Descriptions of both are preliminary, contested, and liquid:

> The theologian builds a world, but the status of this world is not guaranteed, nor does it have any particular claim to apprehend the divine. At the same time, this does not mean that the divine is closed off from theological discourse. Theology is part of the expression of the Church and as such conditioned and contingent. Theology does not have any special claim to visibility, but neither is it occluded from the vision of God. The point is that what theologians say about God is a contested and contesting field, and to claim anything beyond that is problematic. Ecclesiology is liquid, in other words.[130]

In the thesis, I take critical realism, as described here, as the approach in constructing practical theology. The descriptions of the lived and the theology I interpret and discern are conditioned descriptions of the real that can be contested and engaged in discussion with other voices in the field.

Reflexivity: Personal Engagement in the Research Context

A reflexive approach to one's relation to the objects, processes and questions of research is part of theological ethnography. This is especially relevant when taking on an interpretative or evaluative role. Tone Stangeland Kaufman calls the researcher a "Gamemaker", a term that underlines the fact that the person doing research stages the situation and then describes how the characters within the play

---

[128] Root (2016), p 50.
[129] Pete Ward (2017a), *Liquid Ecclesiology*, Leiden: Brill, p 23.
[130] Ward (2017a), p 20.

go about practising theology.¹³¹ In other words, the researcher is not a neutral observer but is involved in many decisions that could affect the results and findings. A responsible Gamemaker is transparent about assumptions, location, and pre-understanding. As James J.S. Bielo puts it:

> The observations and arguments depicted in a piece of ethnographic writing are always partial in several senses. They are a particular selection of empirical evidence, born from a particular research design, translated by a particular individual, understood through a particular set of analytical frameworks, and presented via a particular style of writing.¹³²

Therefore, some sense of partiality is hard to avoid in ethnographic studies. The edges between emic and etic – the insiders' and outsiders' worlds – are often blurred. The researcher becomes part of the research and the main tool in the research practice. Therefore, it is important and fair to the reader that the researcher is clear about the reasons and backgrounds that are involved in the game-making.

Behind this study is my curiosity about church planting and learning. During the early 1990s, I was part of a group that grew into a new church connected to the Vineyard movement in Sweden. Vineyard emphasises church planting, and it is fair to say that church planting is at the centre of the movement's identity. This was especially the case in Sweden, where the Vineyard movement was just taking root and being part of a church meant being part of church planting and imagining ways to bring new communities of faith to life. In the late 1990s, my wife and I also volunteered in a church planting team in St. Petersburg, Russia. After undertaking theological studies from 2003 to 2007, I worked as a pastor in the Uniting Church in Sweden. When studying Adult Learning and Medical Education at Linköping University, I was exposed to different theories of learning that opened new horizons for understanding the ecclesial environments in which I worked.

I initially found that, within UCS, planting churches was considered rather obscure. There were still a few church-planting initiatives, which I frequented with different levels of engagement. Around 2010, UCS started to support-church planting initiatives in response to the increasing number of churches that were shuttering across Sweden. As someone who had been pastoring established churches in UCS, I never missed an opportunity to visit and support church plants and their leaders. When the University College Stockholm announced positions

---

¹³¹ Jonas Ideström and Stangeland Kaufman, Tone (2018), "The Researcher as Gamemaker – Response", in Ideström, Jonas and Stangeland Kaufman, Tone (eds.), *What Really Matters* (Eugene, OR: Pickwick Publications), 173–82.

¹³² James S. Bielo (2009), *Words upon the Word*, New York: New York University Press, p 23.

for doctoral studies in practical theology, including one that was focused on church planting, that opened the possibility to delve deeply into questions about Christian formation in these contexts.

I suspect that my knowledge about what church planting involves has made it easier for church planters to accept me as a researcher studying their practices. It has also affected how I read the practices and contexts. I am, at least partly, an insider. Observations and conclusions would be different should that not have been the case. I consider church planting to be a necessary strategy for the reinvigoration and long-term survival of the church in Sweden. But I also see a need for improved practice. My position is, therefore, that of a critical friend as well as an active participant.[133]

Disposition and reading guide

This thesis revolves around themes regarding Christian formation presented in this introductory chapter. This closing section of the introduction describes how the chapters relate to each other and address the different themes:

The first four chapters serve as background and description of the study. This chapter has introduced the problem to be addressed in the thesis: Christian formation practised in church planting in the secular urban context of Sweden. It has presented the research design and located the study in the field of practical theology. Chapter 2 presents the most relevant research regarding Christian formation in church plants, while Chapter 3 describes the methodological choices made in the research process, and Chapter 4 describes the theoretical perspectives of the study.

In the second part of the thesis (Chapters 5 through 8), the findings are presented with analyses of interviews and observations recorded during the field studies in the three church plants. Chapter 5 analyses those church plants as formative contexts. By listening to the church planters, I am able to formulate a calling describing their intentions and how the telos of Christian life is imagined in each church plant. In this way, I answer the first research question, namely: *How are the callings and intentions of the church plants articulated, and what do the callings and intentions mean for Christian formation?* It follows that after reading Chapter 5, the reader should be acquainted with the three church plants of the study.

Chapter 6 addresses the research question regarding *what practices of Christian formation are present*. For each of the three church plants, one main formative

---

[133] This will be further discussed in the chapter on Method and Methodology below.

practice is described and analysed in detail to articulate its particular telos. Each church plant's described practices are discussed in relation to the free church tradition. Practices are at the centre of the study. They hold together different aspects: community and individual persons, what is shared or negotiated, and the locations and doings in the church plants. The practices are interpreted theologically, and possibilities of participatory engagement are discerned. The practices should be understood with a view to the callings and intentions articulated in the previous chapter.

In Chapter 7, the perspective changes from analysing practices to zooming in on individual participants. Three persons are selected in each church plant to show *how people are formed towards a lived Christian identity.* I use the concept of formative trajectories, which helps not only to add to the descriptions of the formative practices and the intentions of the church-planting communities themselves but also to describe what factors support and prevent a formation towards a lived Christian identity.

Chapter 8 addresses the last research question – *What cultural tensions do the church plants negotiate, and what do the negotiations mean for Christian formation?* – by approaching Christian formation as a matter of negotiation of the various contemporary cultural issues that have emerged in the analysis of the field study material. The chapter emphasises the changing relationship between the communities of formative practice and secular society. This relationship is important because it shows that Christian formation is complex, especially in a secular context. The chapter can be understood as providing depth to the formative practices and the identity formation described in the preceding chapter.

Chapter 9 summarises the thesis's results in an attempt to integrate them as a practice perspective on Christian formation in church plants. These results are discussed within the context of recent research and present the thesis's main contributions to the field.

The final chapter, Chapter 10, addresses some theological themes that are related to the conclusions drawn in the preceding chapter. These themes are of particular interest for Christian formation practice in missional situations in the wasteland.

2. Research on Christian Formation

This chapter adds to the scholarly discourse presented in the introduction by looking at the most relevant contributions in recent research. I will begin by presenting research on Christian formation through practices and then turn to studies associated with the formation of Christian identity. The final part regards the negotiation of faith in church plant contexts.

For the sake of transparency, I should note that the research cited below was evaluated according to four criteria. The first criterion is *relevance* to the present study, as reflected in the research questions. The second criterion regards the research's *geographic domain*, that is to say, where the research is performed. Preferably the West, Northern Europe, and Sweden in particular. Thirdly, *theory and methods*: ethnographic, case studies and other qualitative studies have been prioritised. Studies employing theories of practice are of special interest. Finally, since culture can change significantly over just a decade, I have prioritised studies that were published in the *past ten years*.[1] The presentation follows the four research questions and tries to match their concepts with the themes in the body of research.

2.1 Callings and Intentions in Christian Formation

Church plants and their communities have callings that lead them to act with a pro-social intention.[2] How church planters articulate these callings and intentions

---

[1] I have searched for peer-reviewed articles, dissertations, monographs, and anthologies related to theology, religion and sociology. I have used the EBSCO database search engine through University College Stockholm. Google Scholar and search engines provided by University College Stockholm, Linköping University, and Mid Sweden University.

[2] Elangovan et al. (2010). The authors define calling as "a course of action in pursuit of pro-social intentions embodying the convergence of an individual's sense of what he or she would like to do, should do, and actually does". They describe the Christian roots of the term and suggest a typology of religious vs. secular, and occupation-related vs. non-occupation-related. In the case of church planters, the calling is clearly religious but could be described both as occupational and not strictly occupational. However, what is clear is that there is a sense of clarity of purpose and personal mission leading to action with a pro-social intention.

with regard to their church plants sheds light on their own theological and personal motivations. Richard R. Osmer sees a difference in how Christian leaders describe these callings. His empirical study in the Missional Leadership Project investigated missional leaders' views of formation and how those views related to their own sense of missional vocation. In contrast with other spiritual leaders who described different forms of prayer, teaching, and sharing of spiritual experiences, the missionally-minded leaders emphasised practices that are open to and involve new people in the church. Those activities include worship and preaching, discipling lay leaders, sharing the gospel with others, and small groups.[3] While these two groups of leaders are not entirely different, the need for a break with tradition and the openness to outsiders were significant among the missionally-minded leaders. Further, Osmer points to a congregational two-pole continuum. One pole represents identity, and the other relevance:

> The church lives in the tension between identity and relevance, between the pole of gathering and upbuilding, on the one hand, and the pole of sending and self-giving, on the other. [...] When the church lives as a community of centred openness, living in the tension between identity and relevance, it serves as an *analogia Trinitatis* (an analogy of the Trinity). [...] Therefore, missional formation is the process of the congregation "taking form" as it lives in the tension between *identity* and *relevance*.[4]

Osmer argues that the congregation and its participants are being formed in the tension between the poles of relevance and identity, and the Holy Spirit is the primary actor in this formation towards the likeness of Christ.[5] Therefore, the two callings to relevance and identity should not be considered discordant but, with the right tension, as complementary. This formative tension might be realised when gathering as a church for worship. This is the context in which James K.A. Smith connects the telos of being human with a calling:

> To be human is to be *called*. But called to what? Gathered for what? The congregation gathers in response to a call to *worship*, which is the fundamental vocation of being human. God is calling out and constituting a people who will look "peculiar" in this broken world because they have been called to be renewed image bearers of God (Gen 1:27–28) – to take up and reembrace our creational vocation, now empowered by the Spirit to do so. So this is not just a call to do something "religious," something to be merely added to our "normal" life. It is a call to be(come) human, to take up the vocation of

---

[3] Osmer (2012).

[4] Osmer (2012), pp 50–51. Author's emphasis. Here, Osmer finds inspiration in the theology of Jürgen Moltmann.

[5] Osmer (2012), p 52.

being fully and authentically *human*, and to be a community and people who image God to the world.[6]

This connection between calling, telos and worship indicates a formative understanding of the liturgy as fundamental to being human. The liturgy becomes the practice through which the Christian is formed to desire God.[7]

A less liturgical perspective on Christian formation is proposed by Andrew Root. He makes a strong theological case for Christian formation as a union with Christ that is a result of divine action in and through Christian ministry. In commenting on the findings of Smith and Lundquist Denton, Root – who studies faith formation and ministry among youth – finds Moralistic Therapeutic Deism (MTD) to be a problem afflicting the American culture: "If we are still brave enough to try to reimagine faith formation, then we must begin at the back end, with the D of MTD deism exploring and rethinking how it is we encounter divine action itself".[8] Root also refers to Charles Taylor's different takes on secular culture.[9] Root argues that the American church is often fighting the wrong kind of secular. Instead of opening up to the possibility of divine action, it tries to attract youth on other grounds. That is to say that the church, rather than finding legitimate practices of Christian formation, is trying to be youthful, according to Root. The calling of the church is to lead people to union with Christ through the church's ministry in the Holy Spirit.[10] What Andrew Root is not answering in his proposal is *how* this is done, that is, what concrete formative practices are undertaken to reach this goal?

Another way of discussing callings in Christian formation is by looking at different models. In a study of four church plants in Seattle, Christopher B. James presents four different practical ecclesiological models (Great Commission Team,

---

[6] Smith (2009), p 162.

[7] Smith (2009), p 18.

[8] Root (2017a), p 94.

[9] A short summary of Taylor: The first meaning of "secular" (secularised public spaces) refers to the medieval division between secular and sacred. Secular then means temporal or worldly activities and things. Vocations like butcher or farmer would then be secular, while priest or nun would be sacred vocations that aimed at dealing with the divine rather than with earthly things. The second way of approaching the secular is the modern distinction between religious and non-religious (the decline of religious belief and practice). An example of this type of secularisation is the widely held view that the political sphere and the religious sphere should kept apart. Taylor's third take on secularisation regards the way we see the world (loss of the transcendent). The religious option is but one of many and is no longer the default choice in the West. Taylor (2007), p 20.

[10] Root (2017a), p 130.

Household of the Spirit, New Community, and Neighbourhood Incarnation) that draw from different spiritualities and foster different kinds of missional and identity formation practices. Like the communities described in this thesis, James' models embody the callings and intentions of Christian formation: The Great Commission Team and Household of the Spirit models nurture a contrasting posture towards the surrounding culture. The Household of the Spirit communities fosters a temple ecclesiology where the miracle-working God is present inside the community. The Great Commission model emphasises evangelisation of the city in obedience to the Gospel. Important formative practices include bible study, relationship groups, community service, and Sunday worship with Christocentric preaching. In comparison, the New Community and Neighbourhood Incarnation models are more socially progressive and positively inclined towards the surrounding society. The New Community model strives to embody inclusive and participatory corporate life through liturgical practices and contemporary arts in continuously innovative ways. The Neighbourhood Incarnation plants, on the other hand, understand their local neighbourhoods as sites of beauty, need, and hope. Building relationships and practising hospitality are central to both mission and formation.[11]

James's models reflect different teloi of Christian formation. The question: "What does it mean to be Christian?" would have rendered quite different answers from the different models. This, in turn, means that the church planters have initiated different formative practices. In the different models, James' study also shows that the church plants' callings are connected to place. As a consequence of this, he develops a missio-ecclesial understanding of place that he calls neighbourhood incarnation. At the heart of this placemaking posture lies a turn to the local and a radical appreciation of geographical proximity. To start with, James suggests that the church understands itself as being neighbours:

> The church as neighbours attends to the presence of God in the neighbourhood (which will one day permeate it in a palpable way). They pattern their lives in the ways of the Reign of God, training themselves to live in its approaching reality. In so doing they make the future manifest. It is in this way that they join God in the renewal of the neighbourhood.[12]

The church is local, and the people who represent it know their neighbourhoods and what goes on there. They are parishioners, humbly carrying the neighbour-

---

[11] James (2018). The New Community and Neighbourhood Incarnation models seem to overlap in James's descriptions.

[12] James (2018), p 210.

hood in eschatological expectation. The second part of this vision is the church as a neighbourhood. Here, James portrays the church as a social and material reality in the known-but-strange environment of houses, roads, cafes and shops. He speaks of "recognitional solidarity", a "sense of unity one shares with acquaintances and familiar strangers".[13] In the third part of the vision, James points to the diversity of the different ecclesial models and the ecumenical traditions they represent. Just as each neighbourhood differs, each church is different but fits together. In James' view, this is the vision of the heavenly city of Jerusalem and an ecumenical reality that impacts the neighbourhood. In this way, James connects the telos of church planting with the eschatological vision that holds unity and ecclesial diversity together with an appreciation of place.

2.2 Practices of Christian Formation

This section will present studies of formative practices related to missional situations and contexts. I will start by noting the turn towards the practice-oriented understanding of Christian formation in practical theological research. I then present various studies that are related, in various degrees, to this theoretical development.

Back in 2007, Paul D.G. Bramer wrote an article in which he argued that there was a strong emphasis on cognitive orientation in Christian education research.[14] Christian formation was primarily discussed as formal catechetical activities, like baptismal schools, confirmation, or Alpha courses. Christian belief was often understood as intellectual comprehension of the contents of belief, generally from the individual's perspective. While an individual cognitive understanding of faith is an important aspect of Christian formation, Bramer argues for a broader understanding of Christian formation, one which includes the embodiment of faith, meaning-making, and authenticity.

Around this time, Paul Heelas and Linda Woodhead, like Bramer, argued that societal changes had made the traditional view on Christian formation inadequate. They distinguished religion and spirituality, defining religion as congregational

---

[13] James (2018), p 212.
[14] Paul D.G. Bramer (2007), "Christian Formation: Tweaking the Paradigm", *Christian Education Journal*, 4 (2), 352–363. This article represents an example of the discussion of the inadequacy of the teaching perspective, at the time. C.f. Dorothy C. Bass and Dykstra, Craig (2008), *For Life Abundant: Practical Theology, Theological Education, and Christian Ministry*, Grand Rapids, Michigan: Eerdmans. The anthology represented a practice-oriented perspective of different contexts in pastoral and ecclesial life and ministry.

and connecting the individual to an authoritative tradition. Spirituality was instead associated with the subjective turn that makes the "inner sources of significance" the primary authority.[15] Geir Afdal interprets Heelas and Woodhead's distinction as mirroring two different learning cultures. Religion is instruction-oriented and provides the learner with authoritative knowledge. Spirituality provides a culture of learning through dialogue and experience – discovering rather than receiving. Practice theory offers ways of analysing this broader view of learning.[16]

Formation Through Liturgical Practices

As mentioned above, practical theology has largely embraced a practice-oriented perspective.[17] For instance, take James K.A. Smith's description of the liturgy, referred to in the introductory chapter.[18] Smith provides philosophical and theological concepts that are helpful to a practice-oriented comprehension of Christian formation, but his discussion is mainly on liturgical practice.[19]

María Cornou takes this analysis one step further in her thesis on the worship of Methodists, Baptists, and Free (Christian) Brethren in 19th-century Argentina. She researches formative practices with a practice understanding that leans on Smith, Dorothy Bass, and Craig Dykstra. Cornou shows that in 19th-century Argentina, the worship practice was significant in forming believers' values and ethical views on the church's social engagement. From that insight, she argues that the worship of Christian communities not only forms individuals' faith but also has the power to "build the church's identity, shaping how it sees itself and the world and how it envisions its mission and involvement in society".[20] Cornou's study does not match the methods or geographical selection criteria of my study. Still, it is relevant since it uses a practice-oriented view of Christian formation. Formative practices, according to Cornou:

---

[15] Paul Heelas and Woodhead, Linda (2005), *The Spiritual Revolution*, Hoboken, New Jersey: Wiley-Blackwell.

[16] Geir Afdal (2013), *Religion som bevegelse*, Oslo: Universitetsforlaget; Kathleen A Cahalan (2005), "Three Approaches to Practical Theology, Theological Education, and the Church's Ministry", *International Journal of Practical Theology*, 9 (1), 63–94.

[17] See p 43.

[18] See p 28.

[19] The telos concept is especially useful in the analysis of Christian formation. In the chapter on situated learning theory, I explain how I operationalise this concept.

[20] María Eugenia Cornou (2016), *Worship as a Formative Practice: The Worship Practices of Methodists, Baptists, and Free Brethren in Emerging Protestantism in Argentina* (1867–1930), Amsterdam: Vrije Universitet, p 213.

bear meaning that is appropriated while doing, so that through active engagement in liturgy Christians are formed in a particular understanding of God, of others, and of themselves, and of what it means to live a Christian life in this world.[21]

This understanding of formative practices in Cornou's historical study is close to how Elisabeth Tveit Johnsen describes the formation of gathered communities of worship in the Church of Norway. With a particular focus on children, she analyses the worship service as a community of practice with a set of practices in which the gathered people participate. She finds that Etienne Wenger's analytical concept of learning trajectories helps to clarify the complexity of learning in social practices. The analysis shows the significance of facilitating central, peripheral and marginal participation in a worship setting. In other words, children need to be able to choose their degree of participation to grow in faith in the worship service.[22]

Thor Strandenæs argues that traditional Norwegian churches must also embrace a sense of being missional. In an article addressing the design of liturgical practices in a secular culture, he suggests that there needs to be an inclusive nature and contextual orientation. The liturgical practices must balance the collective and individual needs of Christians and non-Christians. In addition, the churches need to have an affirming view of society without leaving the normative foundations of the church.[23] In other words, while Strandenæs views the liturgy as the formative centre for Christian formation practice, he links it to a secular environment that needs a missional reflection, which should also include the everyday life of Christians.

Formation in Missional Situations

The aforementioned studies primarily focus on Christian formation in and through the liturgy. In missional contexts, Christian formation carries a different sense of situatedness than in the context of a traditional church. The ordinary

---

[21] Cornou (2016), p 19.

[22] Elisabeth Tveito Johnsen (2014), *Religiøs læring i sosiale praksiser. En etnografisk studie av mediering, identifisering og forhandlingsprosesser i Den norske kirkes trosopplæring*, Oslo: Universitetet i Oslo. Especially the article "Gudstjenestelæring gjennom deltakelse", in which Tveit Johnsen uses Wenger's trajectory analysis to study children's participation in liturgical practice. See also Elin Lockneus (2023), *Kyrkbänksteologi*, Skellefteå: Artos Norma Bokförlag. Lockneus studies liturgical practices of ordinary church goers in two churches in Sweden.

[23] Thor Strandenæs (2010), "Missionally Relevant Rituals for the Secular City: A Quest for Christian Rituals which Adequately Interact with Citizens' Lives and Needs", *Swedish Missiological Themes*, 98,3 341–360, p 357.

liturgical language might not be formative when practices are performed in a culturally alien environment.[24]

In a recent study of three Fresh Expression communities in the UK, Philip Wall investigates how three pedagogies are operant in new churches and shows how pedagogy is linked to missiology and soteriology.[25] Wall's underlying argument is that there is a need for stronger sensitivity to the questions posed in missional contexts in the West. The instructional pedagogy mainly uses a word-centred, monological mode of communication to convey a message of salvation by faith by the individual. This pedagogy reflects the modernist distinction between the cognitive, social, and material. Wall finds the instructional approach to be insufficient in communicating the gospel to the people in the church plant. In the critical praxis pedagogy, people of different faiths and views are involved. The focus is on humanising society through facilitated dialogue as an embodiment of the Kingdom of God. The enculturation pedagogy uses narrative and ritual in communal practices in order to constitute the church as the community of salvation. This pedagogy allows the rite of practising the liturgy to be viewed as a missional activity.

When analysing his case studies using these pedagogical models, Wall finds an inconsistency that somewhat undermines his hypothesis that pedagogy depends on missiology.[26] None of the three communities were committed to "the liturgically focused methods and objectives of Christian education as advocated by the chief proponents of the enculturation approach".[27] While Wall may be right in considering that this finding points to a limitation of the link between pedagogy, missiology, and soteriology, I would suggest that it also shows a limitation of the missional practice in the church plants. The pedagogical approaches of how the church plants reach and form new Christians are not consistent with the theology of the practitioners. In other words, while the link between pedagogy, missiology and soteriology is strong in theory, the practice tells a different story.

I draw several conclusions from Wall's study. The pedagogical views brought into missional practices – like starting a Fresh Expression community – impact

---

[24] In the introduction, I referred to the discussion of the attractional versus the missional perspective. See p 28-30.

[25] Wall (2014). Wall studies three new churches that are part of the Fresh Expressions movement in the Church of England. Wall establishes pedagogy as an integrative part of mission and even though soteriology is the determining factor, pedagogy is found to be a crucial part of these innovative initiatives.

[26] Wall (2014), p 229.

[27] Wall (2014), p 229.

how Christian formation is organised. Also, while different pedagogical views and practices can enact different ecclesial imaginations connected to missiology and soteriology, there are signs that a strictly instructional pedagogy is insufficient to meet the existential needs of contemporary culture. Theology and practice need to work together. For a church plant, this takes creativity and reflection.

The innovation of practice is significant to Christian formation in missional situations.[28] Church planters are active agents in this process. In a study of the formation of church planters in the UK, Christian Selvaratnam finds that creativity is an important feature of the church-planting practice and for revitalising the church. Using a mixed-methods approach, Selvaratnam shows that church planters perceive creativity as God-given, human tacit knowledge that is foundational for human identity. The manifestation of creativity in church planting is seen in the ability to take risks and be youthful and playful. Selvaratnam also finds that church planters are best trained through an apprenticing model in the context of a church plant.[29] Selvaratnam establishes the understanding of church plants as innovative church contexts in secular society, which is a premise for this thesis.

The astute reader will note that thus far, I have been referring to studies of missional situations that were conducted in the UK. In the only significant study directly addressing church plants in Sweden, Peter Svanberg described a highly secularised 1990s Sweden.[30] He looked for effective methods and principles to plant Methodist churches in a secular context and assessed them using church growth principles and reflecting the logic of a more churches paradigm.[31] Svanberg studied three of the 34 known church plants that were started between 1992–96. They were selected because they reported a relatively high number of new converts. The study does not focus on practices of Christian formation but looks at church planting as a missional strategy and the necessary factors for success. Svanberg finds that there has been a shift from traditional free-church organisations, similar to other member-based associations, towards strongly relational communities that not only envision Christian life as a journey towards God but also try to be culturally relevant.

---

[28] Paas (2016), p 181. Stefan Paas gives an excellent background to the new churches paradigm.
[29] Christian Nathan Selvaratnam (2020), *The Craft of Church Planting: Guild Training Models for Apprenticing Church Planters*, Wilmore, Kentucky: Asbury Theological Seminary, p 190.
[30] Svanberg (1999).
[31] Paas (2016), p 111.

2.3 Christian Formation as Identity Formation

Christian formation, to a large degree, concerns identity and identification. In a secular culture, church communities can be perceived as islands that, in different ways, offer alternative visions of life, including a life of shared and practised religious faith. The individual's formation and practice of Christian identity are supported and regulated by the faith community. Church plants are places where both individuals and the community are making voyages of emerging identities:

> Both individuals and the mission community make identity voyages, which involve a starting identity comprising ecclesial and personal identities; possible identities, which are imagined pictures of the self (or the community) helping to birth the proposed contextual church; a contextual church identity, which is the self (or the community) concretely helping to birth the church; it continues to evolve.[32]

Michael Moynagh describes the formation of churches as journeys that start in one of two ways: either by gathering a large crowd as a worshipping community that is inviting newcomers or by starting with a smaller group that builds relationships through serving the community.[33] The significant observation here is that individuals' identities change as the church plant grows. There is, in other words, a formative link between the community and the individual regarding identity.

The relationship between the individual and the church community is, however, not without its complications. In her study of young adults in the UK, Ruth Perrin describes three groups of young people in the churches of her study. The first group is the "leavers", who find it untenable when faith does not appear to help with life's difficulties. When exposed to "convincing alternative worldviews", they leave both church and faith behind. The second group, which can be named "leaving believers", are those who leave the church but still consider themselves believers. This group's reasons for leaving could include a "breakdown in relationships with leaders, feeling exploited or undervalued, and church conflict or resistance to change". Perrin also found that this group expressed discontentment with simple answers to complex issues and theological tensions. The third group, the "stayers", ranged from "disappointed but persevering" individuals, the "realistic pragmatists" who had managed their expectations, and the "confident and calmer" ones who had recognised God's faithfulness and received the support of

---

[32] Moynagh (2012), p 229.

[33] Moynagh (2012), p 197. The author describes the presentation of these models (among other things) as being part of "a series of hypotheses that combine theory and experience-based wisdom" that have "intuitive appeal" and should be systematically tested.

the church community in times of trouble. Finally, the third group included passionate late-coming "deeper enthusiasts" and the "radical risk-takers" who had engaged in ministry voluntarily and experienced God's provision and faithfulness through the challenges. Perrin's study forms a valuable background to the conditions for forming Christian identity between conflicting worldviews.[34] This study is valuable since it brings the complexity of the relationship between the individual and church communities to the front. This complexity is partly generated by the pluralisation and privatisation in secular societies.

It is also relevant to look at positive examples of this relationship. Anne Mie Arndt Skak Johanson describes how people find faith within the Danish folk church. The Danish society, like its Swedish neighbour, possesses an ambiguous view of religion. Few participate in the folk church, but a majority believe in God. She chooses to describe this situation as post-secular.[35] Skak Johanson, starting from a broad and dynamic understanding of salvation, investigates contemporary Danish faith stories – narratives of people coming to faith in the Danish folk church. She analyses the journeys to faith, partly by using Missiologist Paul G. Hiebert's social mindsets theory.

The mindset theory starts with the question: "What does it mean to be a Christian?" According to Hiebert, the answer to this question depends on how we view a Christian community.[36] He discusses different views: A *bounded* set means that being Christian is defined by essential characteristics that can be judged from correct belief (orthodoxy) and behaviour (orthopraxy). This means there is a clear distinction between being Christian and being non-Christian; consequently, all

---

[34] Ruth Perrin (2022), "Qualitative Research and Young Adult Faith", in Ward, Pete and Tveitereid, Knut (eds.), *The Wiley Blackwell Companion to Theology and Qualitative Research* (Wiley Online Library), 162–172.

[35] Anne Mie Arndt Skak Johanson (2020), *When What We Know Is Not Enough: Exploring Danish Contemporary Faith Development in the Local Congregation*, Pasadena, California: Fuller Theological Seminary, p 64.

[36] Paul G. Hiebert (1994), *Anthropological Reflections on Missiological Issues*, Ada, Michigan: Baker Academic. The mindsets were first described in 1978 but were later revised and developed. Bounded sets make clear distinctions between categories and set up opposites – there are apples and there are pears. Fuzzy sets avoid those clean distinctions and describe a scale – green fruits and greener fruits. We use fuzzy sets as qualifiers to categories – a green apple. Fuzzy sets are continuums that flow into each other. Thirdly, there are centred sets with a centre point of reference to which other things are related. The related objects can move closer or farther away from the centre until they disconnect entirely. Fuzzy sets are continuums that flow into each other. Hiebert argues that the West carries on a Greek worldview characterised by bounded sets, and Hebrew culture leans toward a centred set of thinking.

Christians are considered essentially the same. A *centred* set means identifying the direction of attention in a person's worship. A Christian is a person who has Christ as God and seeks to follow Christ. While there is a distinction between being a Christian and non-Christian, the difference means less than the direction. Some Christians are closer to Christ in their knowledge and maturity; others need to grow, and all are called to move closer to Christ. The centred set pattern emphasises growth and continuous change. Conversion is not the end but only the beginning.[37] *Fuzzy*-set Christianity means a high degree of fragmentations, where Christ and faith can mean very different things, which makes it hard to develop a deep sense of community around something shared.[38]

In the case of the Danish folk church, Anne Mie Arndt Skak Johanson finds that a "centred mindset" best describes the situation.

> The idea of defining church and faith in a centered set model has influenced the contemporary western church life. Such an understanding links well with postmodern thinking of individualism and inclusion. Especially in the context of the Folkekirke, this understanding of church and Christianity goes well with the broadness and spaciousness of the Folkekirke.[39]

Four factors stand out as important reasons as to how faith is found: Spiritual experience, attending Sunday service, gaining knowledge about the Christian faith, and Christian fellowship. Skak Johanson argues that to be helpful in supporting journeys of faith, churches need to offer practices and places where people can be "touched, taught, and transformed".[40] In other words, she argues for the significance of a personal experience of a living God in Christian formation. In addition, Skak Johanson finds that metaphors can be helpful in explicating the faith as they "do not give an unambiguous definition of salvation and faith, but a helpful opening into faith as connectedness and participation in the living God".[41]

The emphasis on experiential faith is one reason new Pentecostal churches have been relatively successful in attracting newcomers in the secular context. Karl

---

[37] Hiebert (1994); Paul G Hiebert (1978), "Conversion, Culture and Cognitive Categories", *Gospel in Context*, 1 (4), 24–29.

[38] Hiebert (1994). Michael Lee asses the value of Hiebert's theology when applying a centred set to what it means to be Christian. Michael H. Lee (2007), *Assessment Of Paul Hiebert's Centered-Set Approach To The Category "Christian"*, Dallas: Dallas Theological Seminary. He finds that this application "rightfully shifts the emphasis from intrinsic, humanly observable characteristics to relatedness or allegiance to the person of Christ" (p 62).

[39] Johanson (2020), p 83.

[40] Johanson (2020), p 150.

[41] Johanson (2020), p 85.

Inge Tangen finds that these churches offer individuals ways of finding meaning through dynamic events built around close-to-God experiences and produced at a very high aesthetic level. Other features, such as supporting the community and empowering leaders, are also crucial to the individuals' identification with these churches.[42] What Tangen calls "spiritual homes" facilitate processes of formation. People experience a kind of "self-transcendence" in that they can "serve a cause larger than themselves and live out their sense of being called by God to serve in the world".[43] Tangen finds that the two Pentecostal churches of his study are relevant "in relation to the experience of living in the late modern habitat".[44] New churches provide impulses that motivate urban, secular individuals to engage and identify with a late modern church as part of their Christian formation. Tangen's findings correspond to Andrew Root's argument "that Charismatic and Pentecostal expressions of Christianity have fared much better [than other Christian traditions] in the age of authenticity because, at a minimum, they are entertaining. Still, at their best, they create space for experience – most powerfully, experiences of transcendence".[45]

While not investigating it further, Tangen notes in passing that there are levels of the member's commitment to the identification processes.[46] The relationship between individuals and communities is, as seen in Perrin's study, for example, complex. Analysing the change of engagement in church plants is therefore important to understand Christian formation in secular culture. This thesis connects with Tangen's study and significantly adds to it by investigating the levels of engagement using the trajectories concept.

2.4 Christian Formation as Negotiation of Faith and Culture

In secular culture, faith needs to be negotiated when individuals move between different life rationalities. This negotiation involves reevaluating the doctrinal beliefs, moral values, and practices in the religious communities. In the introduction,

---

[42] Tangen (2012).
[43] Tangen (2012), p 312.
[44] Tangen (2012), p 312.
[45] Root (2017a), p 9. Cf. Harvey Cox (2010), *The Future of Faith*, New York: Harper Collins. Cox: "By far the fastest growth in Christianity, especially among the deprived and destitute, is occurring among people like Pentecostals, who stress a direct experience of the Spirit" (p 9).
[46] Tangen (2012), pp 42, 58, 62. Tangen points to "commitment scripts" and "levels of commitment".

I referred to these processes in church communities as detraditionalisation and internal secularisation.

In his study of the Quaker movement in England from the 17th to the 20th century, Ben Pink Dandelion describes the process of internal secularisation as a "cultivation of conformity" where church communities who are confronted with cultural changes re-negotiate language and adapt their theology in order to be accepted by the wider society. In the Quaker case, he identifies two parts of the internal secularisation process: individualism and subjectivisation on the one hand and change of language on the other. Religion, in other words, becomes a privatised matter of choosing from different options regarding morals and beliefs. For churches and organised religion, the common lived faith erodes when it conforms too much to cultural demands. The other element of internal secularisation entails language: "[F]or the religious mask to remain intact, linguistic culture, or how religious group identity is expressed in the public sphere, is key".[47] According to Dandelion, religious communities that suffer from internal secularisation no longer motivate moral choices or express a cosmology with religious language or theological arguments.[48] The negotiation of morals and theology is, therefore, part of Christian formation in secularised societies.

According to Stefan Paas and Philipp Bartholomä, it is not easy for secularised people who participate in new Christian churches to unpack the Christian message in a way that connects with their own "cultural sensibilities, feelings and questions of life of secular contemporaries".[49] The socio-cultural language of the church plants cannot carry the faith of new believers when the Christian faith, as presented, does not make sense in light of the beliefs and value systems of the surrounding society. This can be understood as an effect of secular pluralisation and privatisation.

Two studies investigate the importance of language, narrative, and negotiation of cultural issues in church plants. First, Jessica Moberg observes individual and communal features of cultural negotiation within an evangelical/charismatic church in Stockholm.[50] She describes the embodiment of spirituality in the lives of

---

[47] Dandelion (2019), p 144.

[48] Cf. Woodhead and Heelas (2000). "Detraditionalisation" is described by Heelas and Woodhead as a weakening of tradition, the sacralisation of the self, individualisation, the instrumentalisation of religion, and the universalisation of religions (p 344).

[49] Paas and Bartholomä (2020), p 171.

[50] Moberg (2013). New Life was started in 1993 and works actively to plant new church communities in Sweden. Moberg leans on theories on detraditionalization, religious consumption, mobilisation and intimacy.

late modern individuals and the ritualisation in the congregation. There is a cultural negotiation around issues such as how to relate to the opposite sex or the use of material objects in prayer. She identifies an "inward turn" and a therapeutic culture where individuals "open up" to God and others, where they "take off their masks" and are encouraged to "be themselves", as well as open their homes and use their God-given abilities as gifts for service. Moberg finds the emphasis on therapeutic authenticity, a characteristic ingredient in the late-modern secular culture, to be present in practices of prayer for healing, in singing intimate worship songs and in small groups gathering in homes to share lives.[51]

In the second study that investigates the negotiation between church and culture, Anna Strhan notes how the separation of secular institutions from religious practices in modern Britain discourages Christians from bringing faith into spheres of life that are not explicitly religious. She describes Evangelical Christians' attempts to speak openly about their faith at workplaces and public places in London. While they describe an adverse reaction to their evangelistic practices, they find this to be expected as they grow a self-understanding of being public and unpopular: "Jesus promises that Christians will be opposed, and Christians will be persecuted and will be hated", as one informant puts it.[52] Anna Strhan identifies how the Evangelical church community perceives borders to the majority culture in London. She points to the fragmentation of modern cities as a reason for this experience. The imaginative division between the earthly and the spiritual city, which, according to Strhan, characterises evangelical spirituality, draws them together as a church community in the big, fragmented, and hostile city.[53]

John Fitzmaurice discusses the negotiation between Christian and secular and is critical of the use of contemporary culture in Christian formation. His study on virtue formation concludes that the Christian church needs to stay faithful to its narratives and communal practices to form Christian virtues in a secular age.

> Thus for the church to become more fully the church it needs to consciously engage with those activities that make it the church, and not be too concerned with its external successes or failures as it perceives them. The building up of the inner nature is what will

---

[51] Moberg (2013).
[52] Strhan (2015), p 84.
[53] Strhan (2015), p 201.

ultimately enable the church to be effective in what God is calling it to – indeed the church will only discern what true mission is when it is true to itself.[54]

Fitzmaurice connects formation with mission and sees possibilities for incorporating into Christian formation those deeply Christian community-based practices like baptism and the Eucharist. In addition, he finds that an excessive focus on church growth generally undermines the character and mission of the church. Instead, the church should perform the Christian narrative through a repertoire of shared practices.[55]

As part of the process of secularisation, pluralism dictates that different religious providers compete in a market where individuals choose their preferred flavour of spirituality. In his study of church-planting networks and the rational choice theory, which describes the supply and demand relationship and its implications for social behaviour, John D. Boy finds that the market logic only partly impacts new urban church plants.[56] Church planters hesitated to engage fully in the "market", dominated as it is by secularity. Boy concludes:

> It could even be harmful, because it could further undermine the possibility of forming a community. Instead, these church plants view themselves as safe spaces, making community possible in the midst of a hostile environment. The environment is seen as hostile not because there are barriers in the religious economy preventing the church planters from competing. Rather, the problem is that one of the competitors, secularism, is dominating the market. The market itself is part of the problem.[57]

This means that ideological secular pluralism functions as a kind of majority religion or at least a standard option in the worldview market. Pluralism, whether good or bad, significantly impacts Christian formation in secular cultures.

Mattias Neve investigates the ecclesiology, mission, and worship of four emerging church communities in Sweden. Common to the four groups' reflection on missions was a personal approach that emphasised a "belong before you believe" mindset.[58] The groups showed little interest in the numerical growth of the communities. Following Jesus in everyday life, being a credible witness by serving the community, and responding to preconceptions and hostility towards Christians in a kind manner seemed more critical.

---

[54] John Fitzmaurice (2016), *Virtue Ecclesiology: An Exploration in the Good Church*, London: Routledge. Cf. Joel Appelfeldt (2023), *Dopet som hantverk*, Skellefteå: Artos & Norma bokförlag. Appelfeldt studies pastors and priests as liturgical actors in the baptismal practice.

[55] Fitzmaurice (2016), pp 227, 229.

[56] Boy (2015).

[57] Boy (2015), p 124.

[58] Neve (2021), p 188.

> In a pluralistic cultural context where exclusive or strong stances on truth and faith can be seen as suspect and an affront, a softer approach to mission that emphasise long-term witness and presence through service, dialogue and the possibility for people to experience God through a loving Christian community is favourable to emerging churches.[59]

Neve notes that Swedish groups cultivate identities of being alternative expressions of church. This can be seen in the places where the communities meet. They deliberately chose "neutral" places such as cafés, clubs, homes, or music festivals. In these groups, Neve finds an ecclesiological hermeneutics that is "highly relational" and fosters an open and inclusive culture, blurring the lines between church and world. The groups' emphasis on innovation and deconstruction of boundaries could be understood as consequences of the core values of this kind of Christianity, which Neve describes as "a protest against what is perceived as either unhelpful or downright destructive elements of evangelical Protestant doctrine, ecclesial forms and culture".[60]

The intense interaction with the cultural context present in the emerging churches leads Mattias Neve to suggest a kind of discernment tool. The trifocal lens enables "a critical exegesis of and dialogue between Christian tradition, Scripture, as well as culture and human experience".[61] These inputs are "sampled" and "remixed" in a process that ideally results in authentic local ecclesial expressions and a modified Christian tradition. The merit of Neve's approach is the trifocal lens, which allows for the acknowledgement of both cultural authenticity and Gospel faithfulness. Indeed, the trifocal lens is a useful tool for discerning faithful and authentic Christian formation in secular culture.

2.5 Conclusion

The review of previous research on Christian formation shows a need for practice-oriented studies on how people form or are formed towards a lived Christian identity in missional situations in secular Sweden. Below, I summarise the research around each theme in this chapter, pointing to the need for further investigation.

Regarding the callings and intentions, Richard R. Osmer identifies a missional identity in the vocation of spiritual leaders. Christian formation occurs in the constructive tension between being true to community identity and being relevant in the culture. Osmer emphasises the telos of being formed into Christ's likeness.

---

[59] Neve (2021), p 194.
[60] Neve (2021), p 177.
[61] Neve (2021), p 240.

Andrew Root makes a theological argument that the purpose of the church's ministry is to lead people into a union with Christ. Christopher B. James's models of missional communities suggest different community identities, intentions, and practices leading to different teloi. In dialogue with these scholars, I argue that studying notions of "calling" is an integral part of understanding Christian formation in missional situations. Indeed, the concept of calling can be used to hold together the seemingly disconnected pieces of theology and empirical findings in the extant literature.

Many studies of practices of Christian formation regard the formation as a result of liturgical participation, including formative trajectories in liturgical situations. However, as Thor Strandenœs points out, there must also be a missional reflection in the liturgical practice. The review of recent studies shows a lack of research on formative practices in missional situations; thick descriptions of missio-formational practices are sparse, to say the least. While Philip Wall does not use practice theory concepts, his study is interesting in that it shows a mismatch between the church planter's theology and practice and that it shows a link between missiology and pedagogy.

The question of identity formation of individuals in Christian communities has received some interest in recent research. Ruth Perin's study captures a crisis of identity and belonging that can be found in many free churches, including several in Sweden. While looking at the Danish folk church, Anne Mie Arndt Skak Johanson emphasises that a personal experience of God is important for people who join the community and grow in faith. The most interesting study is Karl Inge Tangen's on newcomers' identification with new church communities. The "identification themes" add to the knowledge of why people join Pentecostal churches. Like Skak Johanson's study, several of Tangen's themes point to the importance of what Andrew Root calls "divine action". They confirm his hypothesis that instead of directly fighting secularity, the churches need to be open to and act with the presence of God. In his study, Tangen points to levels of engagement but does not analyse the idea further. Practice theory and the concept of trajectories can help understand these dynamic identity formation processes and the complex relationship between secular culture and faith communities.

The attention to negotiating cultural issues in Christian formation can be seen in several contributions, including those from Anna Strhan and Jessica Moberg. But this negotiation could be expected to be even more pronounced in missional contexts like church plants. Mattias Neve points to a negotiation model that involves the Bible, the culture, and Christian tradition. However, his study of emerging Swedish faith communities does not provide descriptions of the negotiation of cultural issues within the communities. Christian formation in a secular context involves negotiating what it means to be Christian in faith and practice.

In sum, despite the growth of church planting in Sweden, contemporary research in these contexts is very limited, Christian formation being no exception. While few of the aforementioned studies examine Christian formation using a practice-oriented theoretical perspective, there is a lack of studies focused on practices within missional situations, including the calling to new places. The formative relationship between the individual and community, particularly noteworthy in secular societies, has, however, received some attention. Still, there is a need for a stronger understanding of the negotiation of faith and personal trajectories of lived Christian identity within church plants in secular contexts.

3. Methods and Methodology

Before moving to the analysis of the material, I will account for methodological issues and describe the basic design of the study and how the material was gathered. In the next chapter, I will present the theoretical framework I use to interpret the material.

3.1 An Ethnographic Study With an Abductive Approach

This study is designed as an ethnographic practical theological study with an abductive approach. When describing the study as abductive, I emphasise the conversation between theory and context. With the words of Stefan Timmermans and Iddo Tavory, I am "making a preliminary guess based on the interplay between existing theories and data anomalies or unexpected findings".[1] A strictly deductive approach would mean starting in theory, studying what is already known about my field of research, finding a spot that is insufficiently investigated, and addressing that gap using what is known from other studies. An inductive study, instead, starts from one particular context, gathers data which is then organised and interpreted, and uses that data to form theories that explain what is going on. An abductive approach is something of a synthesis between the deductive and inductive approaches: it attempts to foster conversation.

---

[1] Stefan Timmermans and Tavory, Iddo (2012), "Theory Construction in Qualitative Research: From Grounded Theory to Abductive Analysis", *Sociological Theory*, 30(3), 167–186, p 179.

The Abductive Conversation Between Theory and Contexts

Theory plays an important role in understanding, analysing and interpreting the material.[2] However, theories exist on different levels and play different roles in research (Figure 1). The macro level includes grand theories of how society works on a systemic level. Micro-level theories relate closely to the empirical material and deal mainly with the interaction between individuals and, in some theories, also non-human actors. In between, on the meso-level, the theories try to describe and explain group-level phenomena in a specific field.[3]

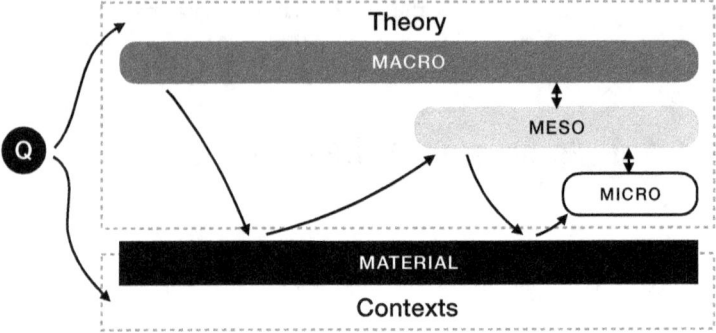

Figure 1: The abductive interplay of theoretical levels and material in qualitative research.

This study began with a general research question (Figure 1) motivated by my curiosity about how Christian formation occurs in church plants. The question was directed towards both the contexts of research and general theories that would help the process analysis. A practice-oriented concept of learning opens up the possibility to analyse Christian formation, both as individual-community relations (through the concept of trajectories) and on a social level (through negotiations of meaning). With that in mind, I decided to use theory related to sociocultural learning practices that provided me with conceptual tools for understanding Christian formation as a form of learning. I choose the situated learning theory by

---

[2] Berth Danermark, Ekström, Mats, and Karlsson, Jan Ch. (2019), *Explaining Society: Critical Realism in the Social Sciences*, Oxfordshire: Routledge. The authors describe theory as a language that includes an interpretation of social reality and provides interpretative frameworks. Theories are needed to conceptualise abstractions of properties, mechanisms and events.

[3] Trine Anker (2020), *Analyse i praksis: en håndbok for masterstudenter*, Oslo: Cappelen Damm Akademisk; Sandro Serpa and Ferreira, Carlos Miguel (2019), "Micro, Meso and Macro Levels of Social Analysis", *International Journal of Social Science Studies*, 7 (3), 120–124.

Jean Lave and Etienne Wenger as the theoretical point of departure since the theory relates learning to formation and provides conceptual tools to analyse the formation happening in and through the church plants.

Meso-level theories on Christian formation found in relevant research led me to formulate more detailed research questions regarding certain formational perspectives. One example of how I have used meso-level theory in the abductive process is when I turned to the contextual model theory by Stephen Bevans. This theory helped me to relate my findings with what had already been discovered about the missional interaction between Christian communities and their surrounding society. While this is a helpful theory in understanding Christian postures towards culture, it does not say much about how church planters engage the context in a new place, which was a significant finding at the micro-level in the interviews and observations. Again, this led to more reading and exploring new meso-theories and supplements to the situated theory, which resulted in new theoretical development. Ultimately, I found that Bevans' theory did not help me much, so I abandoned it in favour of ethnographic descriptions of what was going on in practice, which was supported by situated learning theory.

Focused Theological Ethnography

By labelling the study as "ethnographic", I refer to both methods and a tradition of research practice. To begin with, I use ethnographic methods, specifically field studies with participatory observations and interviews. Furthermore, the study is ethnographic in the sense that it aims to provide "thick descriptions" of contextual practices – describing with enough detail what is going on in the lives of local communities. The results of the study are these descriptions and their theological interpretations.[4]

Michael H. Agar describes the ethnographer's job as "to account for what goes on, on the ground, in living colour".[5] To be able to do this faithfully, the researcher needs to immerse herself in what goes on – studying heterogeneous communities, which might lead to a, at times, blurred line between emic and etic. Participatory observation is the common method used in ethnographic studies. Agar describes this method as delineating between, on the one hand, what he calls encyclopaedic ethnography to produce shared knowledge and, on the other, narrative ethno-

---

[4] Pete Ward (2012b), "Introduction", in Ward, Pete (ed.), *Perspectives on Ecclesiology and Ethnography* (Grand Rapids, Michigan: Eerdmans), 1–12, p 6.
[5] Michael H. Agar (1996), *The Professional Stranger*, Amsterdam: Academic Press Incorporated, p 10.

graphy, that is, giving insider stories, leading to deep contextual knowledge. In employing ethnography as the methodological perspective in this thesis, I am following closely what happens on the ground, so to speak, and study practices of the church interacting with the world.

What happens to ethnography when employed in the context of theological studies? Hubert Knoblauch argues that something happens to ethnography as it passes from anthropology to other fields.

> The purpose of stressing the category of focused ethnography lies in the fact that the image of ethnography until today is shaped by the image of long-term field studies common in anthropology. Only long-term field studies, it seems, epitomise what may rightly be called ethnography. With this ideal derived from anthropology, many of the ethnographies done in sociology and other fields frequently appear to fall short or to be "deficient".[6]

While short-term ethnographies may be considered deficient in anthropological studies, Knoblauch thinks they are valuable in other fields and ought not to be discounted. He proposes a way of framing this short-term ethnography, calling it "focused ethnography". Focused ethnography, Knoblauch argues, is oriented towards studying "alterity" – small elements of difference in one's own culture – rather than cultural "strangeness", and it demands intensive analysis of data, including transcriptions of interviews. Knoblauch finds that focused ethnography is well-suited for studying "the situated performance of social actions".[7] With that in mind, one might say that this study is engaged in focused ethnography.

The addition of "theological" to the description of the ethnographical approach acknowledges the fact that I am positioning the thesis in the field of practical theology. I agree with Peter Ward that in theological studies, ethnographical or sociological descriptions of what happens in practice are not enough: "Practical Theology also needs to find ways to be genuinely theological".[8] Natalie Wigg-Stevenson attempts to define ethnographic theology:

> Ethnographic theology is [...] an apprenticed spiritual discipline, through which the academic theologian integrates local theological knowledge, traditional theological

---

[6] Hubert Knoblauch (2005), "Focused Ethnography", Forum: *Qualitative Social Research* 6 (3), 1–14, p 4.
[7] Knoblauch (2005), p 11.
[8] Ward (2012a), p 60.

knowledge, and cultural critique of both to produce fresh theological insights and possibilities for Christian living.⁹

This definition – a baptising of ethnography, as it were – emphasises the research process and the nature of the results as being theological. Yet this definition is lacking in some regards. Directing the spotlight towards local and traditional theological knowledge is important, and using cultural critique constructively is a good start. However, the critique should also go in the other direction. Local and traditional – and I would add biblical, historical, and practical – theology bears phronetic knowledge that can provide useful and even necessary critique of contemporary culture. In sum, the telos of the practice also makes it theological. Knut Tveitereid mentions a theological "situatedness", which also qualifies the research domain for deeming ethnography theological. The research context of church plants raises theological questions about Christian formation.¹⁰

Theological ethnography needs to have space for ethnographic descriptions of transcendence. Andrew Root, starting from a critical realist view, holding that ontology precedes epistemology, rightly suggests that sociology cannot make truth claims that deny the possibility of transcendence. He argues that critical realism opens a space for transcendence in our conception. The ethnographic material contains testimony. The material of observations and interviews in this thesis contains things "which we have heard, which we have seen with our eyes, which we have looked at and our hands have touched" (1 Joh 1:1 NIV). It reports about experiences of God and doesn't try to interpret them as something else.

> Empirical methods of immanent social science are often not situated to see these higher layers of reality. So practical theology begins by inviting people to articulate their experiences of transcendence, seeking observations in ethnographic spaces, not simply of practices that give people meaning, but for how certain actions draw people into higher layers of reality. But these personal and communal experiences of testimony must always be heard as possibly true but nevertheless contested. Reality may very well have a higher layer(s) of transcendence, but people's experience of this is always from a lower layer, and therefore there is no way to conclusively claim such experiences as unquestionably true (this is why it is testimony).¹¹

---

⁹ Natalie Wigg-Stevenson (2018), "What's Really Going on: Ethnographic Theology and the Production of Theological Knowledge", *Cultural Studies – Critical Methodologies*, 18 (6), 423–429, p 426. For a longer argument and presentation of her approach to ethnographic theology, see N. Wigg-Stevenson (2014), *Ethnographic Theology: An Inquiry into the Production of Theological Knowledge*, New York: Palgrave Macmillan.

¹⁰ Tveitereid (2022), p 67.

¹¹ Root (2016), p 57.

Therefore, the testimonies are not taken as truth but as pointers towards significant matters that need theological discernment. To conclude, theological ethnography means starting in the mess on the ground – testimonies of theological value – and describing that mess of experience as significant for the ecclesial community. With that in mind, this thesis seeks to describe practical theology in fundamentally ecclesiological practices and contexts with a missional-theological purpose.

3.2 Ethical Considerations and the Question of Positionality

When studying contexts and practices where people are involved using ethnography, there needs to be a thorough reflection on how this is done in an ethical manner. In this section, I will address the most important issues. This research was given clearance from the Swedish Ethical Review Authority and has followed the guidelines presented in the process of this review.[12] Each church plant has received information about the project and the handling of research data in text, and the church planters signed a written consent giving me access to their respective church plants. Each individual in the descriptions of the observed gatherings and all interviewees have also received a document describing the research project and the handling of data, and they signed a written consent of participation in the study. Additionally, informants have had the explicit possibility to withdraw their consent at any time.[13] Even though the ethical approval included the possibility of naming the cities where the church plants are located, I have chosen not to do so to protect the study participants.

Having obtained written consent from participants and church plants, I was able to step into the role of a fieldworker. According to Jamal Brendan Thornton, "[F]ieldworkers are the primary instruments of ethnographic inquiry; they are the embodied scientific 'tools' of participant observation, and their personal experiences are a vital source of data".[14] Acknowledging that I am myself a tool in the research process is only appropriate. I entered the world of these church plants and

---

[12] This clearance [Dnr 2019-05848] was communicated on April 9th 2020, which was about two weeks after the announcement of the first pandemic restrictions in Sweden.

[13] Lauren Leve (2022), "Interlocutors", *Fieldwork in Religion*, 17 (1), 47–61, p 48. Lauren Leve suggests the term "interlocutors" as a replacement for "informant". I agree that there might be unfortunate references when referring to the persons I research and, in a sense, research with as "informants". They are, in fact, more than passive vessels of information. However, I chose to retain the term for the sake of simplicity.

[14] Brendan Jamal Thornton (2022), "Fieldwork", *Fieldwork in Religion*, 17 (1), 13–25, p 18.

3.2 Ethical Considerations and the Question of Positionality

stayed long enough to get to know persons and places, observe how persons are involved and formed towards a Christian identity, and see how the communities engage missionally in the cities. The observations were recorded through my own particular lens and judgement.

Throughout this project and thesis, I have intended to describe contexts and persons as clearly and objectively as possible. At the same time, I acknowledge my own bias. It is hard, after all, to claim a neutral position where distinctions and judgements can be made in qualitative research.[15] If that goes without saying today, it was not always the case – and a post-colonial perspective rightly questions the power of the stranger in naming the "exotic".[16] Likewise, personal engagement in the context is hard to avoid when engaging them over time, which blurs the edges between emic and etic. Having an insider's point of view means that you can see what the stranger misses, but at the same time, miss what only the stranger can see. When needed, I have pointed out my own position to be reflective about the process. In the process of interpretation, I have stated my own assessment at the same time as I have tried to be open to different possibilities.

It is also important to say that I had sporadic contact with the planters of one of the church plants before the study through my position as pastor, but I have not been personally engaged in any of the three church plants apart from the research. Since 2018, I have had a role as a member of a regional advisory board in the Uniting Church in Sweden (UCS). One of the church plants is associated with UCS and is monitored by this advisory board. This has meant that I have received information about the dealings of this church plant that I, in most cases, was already knowledgeable about through my own participation. The position did not have any impact on the church plants in this study.

It should be acknowledged that during the field studies, I was not only a researcher but also a participant in the contexts I investigated. In most cases, I was merely one in the crowd, but my participation became more significant in one church plant, Cathedral City. I studied the small group practice by participating in a bi-weekly online small group. The group was attended by three to five people, myself included. During our first meeting and in the group's Facebook Messenger chat, I volunteered and clarified my reasons for attending to the other participants:

> I informed you of the following in the meeting, but I also write it here in the chat. Until June, I am a hang-around in [the church plant]. It is one of three new churches that I

---

[15] For a further discussion see Ideström, Jonas and Stangeland Kaufman, Tone (eds.) (2018), *What Really Matters*, Eugene, Oregon: Pickwick Publications.

[16] Agar (1996).

study as a PhD student. I participate in different gatherings to try to understand what is going on and how people grow in faith. Since the group is a place for growth, I would like to be able to describe it in my research. For example, themes we talk about, briefly describe the participants, is there growth? I will not disclose any names or personal details! I will not write things you say without asking for your permission! I hope that is fine with you. Please ask me any questions if you have them.

Small group Messenger chat, Cathedral City, 17 Feb 2021

I received their oral and written permission to study the group, but it is difficult to know whether or how the group was affected by my dual role. The downside of being part of what is studied is that separating your assumptions, actions, and contributions from the group practice is nearly impossible. However, this problem is always present to some degree, especially in qualitative research.[17] As John Swinton reminds us, ethnographic observation "is not a neutral, value-free endeavour".[18] An entirely objective role is not possible:

> Ethnography involves an added dimension because fieldwork happens through interpersonal relationships that play out on complex and uneven social spaces. Our position in those spaces shapes our encounters with those we work with.[19]

If the value of being given access to the "inner room" of the small group is hard to overstate, it does bring issues of positionality: what is your relation to the people and contexts, and how do you judge your own impact on practices? My strategy as a participant observer has been to impact the practices as little as possible – which is to say, neither more nor less than what would be expected of any other participant. When asked about it, I have not tried to hide the fact that I am a researcher, minister, and Christian, though I have not felt the need to declare my status to all participants except for the small group and the leaders. As a participant myself, attending worship and small groups and engaging in other formation practices has come naturally. Still, I have tried to separate my roles of participant and researcher as much as possible. I have taken notes in the moment when necessary, but more often I reserved documentation and reflection till I had left the church plant space. The fact that I have visited most practices over an extended period has helped both me and others to "forget" about my research task as practices move along.

---

[17] E.g. Stephen Selka (2022), "Positionality", *Fieldwork in Religion*, 17 (1), 92–100.

[18] John Swinton (2012), "'Where Is Your Church?' Moving towards a Hospitable and Sanctified Ethnography", in Ward, Pete (ed.), *Perspectives on Ecclesiology and Ethnography* (Grand Rapids, Michigan: Eerdmans), 71–94.

[19] Selka (2022), p 93.

3.3 Selection and Material

A qualitatively and ethnographically oriented study strives towards a deep understanding rather than general theories. Since I do not intend to explicitly compare church plants as part of my analysis, one church plant could, in theory, offer enough material. At the same time, church plants are typically quite different from each other in their outset, motivation, and leadership, among other aspects. More than one church plant would offer variation within the material. Taking into account the need for balance between depth and width, as well as the time frame of the study, I decided to study three different church plants. These plants were selected using the following criteria:

- Stability and age of five years or less
- Urban location
- Different approaches to formation
- Access and availability

The pool of possible church plants was developed through contacts with denominational church-planting representatives in the *Vidare* network.[20] Since the year 2000, more than 450 churches have been planted.[21] Due to forces of urbanisation and relocation in Swedish society, the establishment of new churches is mostly focused on larger cities, and cities are environments where views, faiths, and lifestyles need to find ways to live side by side, resulting in intensified cultural negotiation and sharpening the culture's secular aspect.[22] I study relatively new church plants that are stable enough to provide valuable material over an extended research period, and as this thesis is concerned with the first formational years of the church plant, I ruled out any church plants older than five years. It is not an easy task to determine when a church-planting initiative is an established church. Still, the initial phase carries a special dynamic, and decisions made here could affect the survival of the church and its qualities. To observe the practices, there needs to be some stability and a sense of progress in the planting environment. While the study is not primarily concerned with "what works" in the process of church planting, I selected stable church plants to avoid finding myself studying the closing down of church plants.

---

[20] The main church-planting denominations are the Evangelical free church, Uniting Church of Sweden, EFS (evangelical/Lutheran), Vineyard, Swedish Mission Alliance and the Swedish Pentecostal movement.

[21] Tholvsen (2021).

[22] Berger (2014).

Furthermore, while the three church plants I selected all share a free church legacy, broadly speaking, they have a variety of expressions and approaches. Finally, the consent of the particular church plant and the availability in terms of distance and travelling possibilities were factors in the selection process, though I did not approach church plants other than the three selected since none declined participation.

It is worth pausing here to question the particular selection criteria. There is a potential methodological problem in discerning selection criteria and findings, especially in qualitative research.[23] A researcher is wise to ask herself if she selected particular contexts because of an initial perception or an established theoretical understanding. If so, the presentation of results offers little more than confirmation of preliminary views. In the case of this study and the selection of church plants with different approaches, how I judge their difference when selecting them is necessarily a part of the result in this thesis. However, the reason for the difference in the selection process was not to prove the difference as such but to be able to construct and describe a richer material in the field studies and analysis thereof.

After selecting three church plants to approach, I established contact with each church plant's leaders (called "planters" in this thesis). I met with other leaders (the planting team), described my intention, and received their written permission to enter the church plant. I have visited public gatherings, small group gatherings, and other activities. I intended to get to know the community, talk with people, get a sense of the atmosphere, and listen to the ongoing dialogue. What is talked about, and what is not talked about? Where do people come from? Why are they here? Where and how do they meet? What do they do? These were the types of questions that I was seeking to answer. While not specifically searching for contrasting views and disagreements, my intention has been to give a wide perspective representing the views I have encountered in the church plants. With few exceptions, the expressed views and perspectives have been notably harmonious. I have started interviewing the church planters and then approached persons I have met in various meetings, who either seem knowledgeable in the practices or new in the contexts. Two of the interviewees were suggested by the planters, which could be a double-edged sword since these persons might be amplifying the views of the planters. Still, they might also bring valuable perspectives otherwise not accessible to me as a researcher. In only one instance was I able to interview a person who left the church-planting community. It might be argued that the lack of material from

---

[23] Alan Bryman (2016), *Social Research Methods*, Oxford: Oxford University Press, p 393.

former members is a weakness of the study; however, as I aimed to investigate Christian formation in the church plants, involving the "leavers" to a higher degree would imply a different investigation even while providing results that were valuable and interesting in their own right.

After the initial phase, in which I gained an overall view of each church plant, I defined one main practice that I saw as significant for Christian formation in the church plant.[24] I have attempted to balance the different kinds of formative practices between the three research contexts in order to reflect the overall approach of each plant, take into account the culture of each plant's location, and add diversity and depth to the results of the thesis. The criteria for selecting a formative practice were:

- Availability for new-comers
- Intentional and re-occurring
- Possibilities for personal change and learning
- Ecclesiological significance
- Access to study

My intention in selecting interviewees has been to find persons participating in various degrees in the observed formative practices. This includes those in the periphery or who have left the community. In addition to the main leaders, I approached persons whom I suspected contributed to a wider understanding of the main practices. No one declined an inquiry to be interviewed. The field studies took part at a certain time in the histories of the communities, and the descriptions are snapshots of the time of my research.

The observations have been documented in field notes, and interviews have been fully transcribed. All documents have been gathered and analysed using *Atlas.ti* 9.1.3 software. When necessary, I translated quoted material into English.

---

[24] When I consulted the church plant leaders about my engagement in the groups, I was generally, welcomed to participate. Still, in one case, the leaders suggested that I shouldn't engage a certain kind of group, as my presence would interfere with the processes in the groups.

	Industrial City	Cathedral City	Harbour City
Public gatherings	9	10	1
Group meetings	4	10	6
Interviews	8 (9 ppl: 4 men, 4 women)	6 (7 ppl: 4 men, 3 women)	6 (9 ppl: 3 men, 6 women)

Table 1: Observed gatherings and interviews in the three research contexts.

As a fieldworker, I have noted and gathered observations along the way. Along with my reflections, they have guided my way forward, leading to curious interactions with experienced and new participants. In addition to my notes, I have gathered written material from the Internet and social media. Informal conversations with participants then served as a way of validating or correcting my preliminary understanding of contextual conditions.

As part of my observation and participation, I have used semi-structured interviews to deepen my understanding, especially about the motives and direct historical prerequisites behind the church plant.[25] I have interviewed both leaders and participators in the communities to understand the contexts and practices better. The interviews were conversations guided by the prepared interview guides, but at the same time, held broadly to provide rich material.[26] The main leaders were asked beforehand to participate in one or more interviews, and others were asked along the way as the shapes of the practices became clearer. One of the interviews in Harbour City was held as a group interview with the whole leader team participating. For practical reasons and to keep the duration around 90 minutes, I led the group session more through the different themes of interest.

3.4 Analysis and Presentation

The analytical process is, in one way, part of the whole research journey of selecting contexts and engaging with people on the ground to listen, transcribe interviews, name categories, and describe in text what that means. The analysis procedure, however, is the more structured process that results in the presentation of gathered material.

The words of Harriet Mowat capture the heart of the analytical process well: "The individual has a story to tell, even if they don't know they do, and the job of

---

[25] Bryman (2016), p 471.
[26] Interview guides are attached in the Appendixes.

the qualitative researcher is to hear, understand, locate, and analyze that story as faithfully as possible for the collective good".[27] I got to know the material well when listening, transcribing, and reading through the documents. In working with the material, I coded significant words, sentences, and passages. The aim and research questions guided me in seeing what was significant. The resulting list of codes exceeded 60, far too many to be useful, leading me to the next stage, which involved sorting and categorising the codes and going through each of the around 900 quotes. This process helped me eliminate unnecessary or redundant codes. The quotes were then categorised into nine preliminary groups: community, culture, leadership, meaning, mission, place, practice, theme, and trajectory. Again, going through the quotes of each group provided the bulk of material for each of the analytical chapters. However, the division of these chapters is influenced just as much by the research questions and an ongoing dialogue with theories. In each analysis chapter, I have presented the most significant quotes and complemented or nuanced them with summaries of other quotes.

Since the material is rich, working with theory on different levels has been helpful. Having a certain perspective and conceptual tools supports the analytical work. This does not mean that it is easy to connect the dots – far from it. I have described above how the research process has been an abductive interplay between theory and material. Using a practice perspective on Christian formation has kept the social practices – rather than individual persons, interactions, or communities – in focus from the beginning.

I intend to describe what I have heard and observed in a way that is not misrepresenting the voices. To that end, I have taken great care in listening and giving the voices their original context. There is obviously a balance between confidentiality and legitimate representation. If persons and situations are too specifically described, representation comes at the expense of confidentiality; if voices are depersonalised, confidentiality comes at the expense of representation. Qualitative research builds on trust between persons in the settings to be open about views and conditions, even when expressed views are uncomfortable. However, qualitative research must also, to be trustworthy and valid, present persons and contexts authentically and in detail. In this balancing act, the communities' and individuals' trust and confidentiality come first. Furthermore, since the church-planting movement in Sweden involves a limited number of people, the three cities in mid-

---

[27] Harriet Mowat (2022), "Interviews and Observation", in Ward, Pete and Tveitereid, Knut (eds.), *The Wiley Blackwell Companion to Theology and Qualitative Research* (Hoboken, New Jersey: John Wiley & Sons), 382–392, p 386.

southern Sweden will not be named to retain the confidentiality of the individuals. Faces and places are intentionally "blurred" in the descriptions.

I have presented the material itself in two different ways. The most common representation is the quote from a certain individual belonging to a certain church plant. Some quotes come from church planters and leaders, and these quotes often describe intentions and reasons for different choices. At other times, voices from ordinary members or relative newcomers are heard to give ordinary insights or contrasting views. Material is also presented in the following chapters through short scene descriptions that represent field notes.[28] The scenes – which are found between ❦ in the text – have been described from my perspective as a participating observer and are based on memories supported by my notes taken in the moment or shortly thereafter. Consequently, I have tried to concisely paint places, environments, and events as they have unfolded. There is always the risk that I might remember something incorrectly, or I could have misunderstood or misinterpreted situations. Such is the nature of fieldwork. Still, the scenes are authentic from my perspective, and they support the expositions of the analytical chapters.

3.5 Research in a Pandemic Situation

At some points in the presentation of results, it will be noted that the research project was carried out during a pandemic. This has affected both the study sites and the study itself to some extent. The faith communities included in the material have sometimes been unable to use their usual repertoire of involving new people or gathering for worship. Practices have sometimes migrated to the digital domain, creating thresholds for new people but also new possibilities for others.

Generally, I could adapt to Swedish COVID restrictions – which were admittedly looser than those of most European countries – and participate in the church plants. In 2020, during my time in Industrial City and Cathedral City, the restrictions allowed worship meetings with up to 50 participants assuming a 1.5-meter distance between individuals was mandated. Later, the limit changed to 8 individuals.[29] This was the case during my time with the church plant in Harbour City in the spring of 2021, and the restrictions made it difficult to hold public meetings

---

[28] Cf. Kristen Ghodsee (2016), *From Notes to Narrative: Writing Ethnographies That Everyone Can Read*, Chicago: University of Chicago Press. The author emphasises the importance of including descriptions of places, people, and events in the presentation of research.

[29] Action timeline from The Public Health Agency of Sweden: https://www.folkhalsomyndigheten.se/smittskydd-beredskap/utbrott/aktuella-utbrott/covid-19/folkhalsomyndighetens-roll-under-arbetet-med-covid-19/nar-hande-vad-under-pandemin/ [15 Aug 2023].

and other on-site gatherings. This negatively affected the gathering of material. While I attended online worship meetings and small group meetings, the possibility of participating in on-site meetings was strictly limited during this period. Since the participation in practices and direct communication with church participants was sparse, there may be some misunderstandings and misinterpretations on my part. Ideally, I would have more first-hand observations from an extended stay in Harbour City. However, the material has proven strong enough to include in the study, and it offers a valuable contribution to the overall perspective.

3.6 Introducing the Church Plants

The three communities I have studied follow a general pattern: the church communities are initiated and formed by church planters who experience a calling to a specific place. Others are involved, a team is assembled, and a plan evolves as the planters move into the area. They engage in relationship-building activities to encounter people in the neighbourhood. As people join the community, the planting team create practices of formation for individuals and the church community. The church plants, being innovative expressions of the church, have a mindset of being sent and sending others to plant in new places. I have chosen aliases to separate the cities in the presentation.[30]

- *Industrial City:* The church plant in Industrial City officially started in February 2018. The planters are a married couple in their thirties. At the beginning of 2020, when the field studies were performed, the church plant had worship services every other week, and those services were usually attended by between 70-80 people. Additionally, the church plant had six small groups, each with about eight participants and had eleven baptised converts since the start. The church is not focused on any particular area in the city but hopes to affect the secular wasteland culture. In the spring of 2022, they initiated a second church plant in a nearby city.
- *Cathedral City:* The church plant in Cathedral City was initiated in 2019 by a planting couple who had previously planted a church in a neighbouring area with some success. The neighbourhood where they decided to plant this church is divided into three sub-areas, each with a

---

[30] The aliases are arbitrary "city archetypes" and should not be taken as hints of the actual places.

distinct demographic. One part of the neighbourhood is populated by university students living in apartments; another by migrants, also living in apartments; and the final part by families living in villas. The planters state they want to be multicultural and present in the local community, and they run small groups and weekly gatherings in the local park.
- *Harbour City:* This church plant was started in 2016 when an old church was closing, and the planting couple was asked to start a new one. The old church was situated in a prominent part of the city centre; however, the planters wanted to reach the less-privileged, so the team of six people decided to sell the church's building and instead rent a store in a better-suited location in the city centre. The church plant encourages crossing cultural borders and likes to join things that go on in the city. The church plant consisted of about 60 people during my fieldwork, but there was no ambition to expand the community and build a larger church. Instead, the church plant stresses the sending of people on a mission to other places.

All the church plants in this study view themselves as being sent – having formative agency and intentionality – with a message to people in a strongly secular context. In other words, the three church plants show evidence of being place-oriented – they have a clear location in mind for their missional work. They also show an ambition to be innovative in being church, have an open mind towards practicalities, and possess a thought-through approach to being culturally relevant.

4. A Theoretical Understanding of Christian Formation

This chapter describes the theoretical perspectives underpinning this thesis. A reminder of the wider scope of the study is fitting at this point. As described in the previous chapter, methodically, the thesis is a focused theological ethnographic study. Academically, the study is situated within the field of practical theology and examines Christian formation. The study investigates the formation of lived Christian identity through formative practices. The analysis of practices here is not limited to what is being done. Still, it includes the nexus of the situation, involving social, individual, and contextual perspectives of what is going on.[1] This chapter details the motivation behind the choice of theoretical perspectives. It also gives a general overview of the main features of situated learning theory and those parts of the theory that are employed in the analysis of the gathered material.

4.1 Christian Formation, Learning and Practice

In the introduction, I defined Christian formation as those social practices intended to shape Christian faith and a lived Christian identity. I related my understanding of Christian formation to definitions proposed by Astley, Sargeant, and Smith. Like Sargeant, I see these formative practices as both individual and social,

---

[1] A practice perspective does not exclude cognitive perspectives but holds cognitive, social and material issues together in a complex relationship. Geir Afdal (2021), "Two Concepts of Practice and Theology", *Studia Theologica – Nordic Journal of Theology*, 75 (1), 6–29. Geir Afdal suggests an understanding of society as nexuses of practice. Studying religion is best done by studying practices. These practices, he goes on, are "unpure" because they are never separated from each other. Many things are going on, all of which are entwined with each other. In this messy situation, we need theoretical lenses and concepts to analyse what is happening. Afdal is sceptical about the language of "communities of practice", which suggests a more ordered reality. While his objection has some merit, the term is helpful as an analytical concept. As mentioned below, Wenger responds to critics on the community issue and later pushes the language towards the landscape metaphor, which suggests a less ordered and isolated context of practice.

and I, too, argue that they shape both identity and theology. Further, like Astley, I find tradition significant but locate it as an aspect of a formative practice. Along with Smith, I study Christian formation in the context of secular culture.

In studying the phenomenon of Christian formation in church plants, I acknowledge that the formation is aimed at the lived Christian identities of both persons and communities. Etienne Wenger points to a double perspective of "lived identity". Identity, according to Wenger, is:

> [...] the pivot between the social and the individual so that each can be talked about in terms of the other [...] The resulting perspective is neither individualistic nor abstractly institutional or societal. It does justice to the lived experience of identity while recognizing its social character.[2]

The emphasis on identity follows Wenger's understanding of membership in a community of practice and is helpful in describing Christian formation. Inspired by this understanding, I use lived identity neither as an abstract static essence nor as entirely fluid.[3] Identity, rather, is a person's practised, dynamic, and socially grounded experience. It is lived. An elaborate discussion of different views on identity is beyond the scope of this thesis, but what is important here is the attention to the change of identity towards a Christian self-understanding in terms of a lived experience. As a consequence, faith in Jesus Christ within the Christian community involves changed engagement as manifest in formative trajectories.

Learning and Practice

In the introduction, I noted that learning in the modern ecclesial context has often been understood as a mainly individual and cognitive process. This has affected how learning has been understood as knowledge transfer and acquisition. But learning is a broad concept that needs to regard change at an individual, collective, organisational, or societal level.[4] General theories of learning often divide theories

---

[2] Etienne Wenger (1999), *Communities of Practice*, Cambridge: Cambridge University Press, p 145.

[3] Afdal (2013) I agree with Afdal, who argues that Wenger's use of identity avoids a romantic, essentialist, and collective understanding while also avoiding an entirely utilitarian, procedural, or voluntarist understanding of the concept.

[4] Per-Erik Ellström (2010), "Organizational Learning", in Peterson, Penelope, Baker, Eva, and McGaw, Barry (eds.), *International Encyclopedia of Education*, Vol 1 (London: Elsevier Science), 47–52; Staffan Larsson (2006), *Didaktik för vuxna – tankelinjer i internationell litteratur*, Stockholm: Vetenskapsrådet; Knud Illeris (2016), *How We Learn*, Oxfordshire: Routledge, p 3. The Danish professor of lifelong learning Knud Illeris defines learning as "any process that in

into behaviouristic (changed behaviour), cognitive (changed thinking), and sociocultural (changed participation) theories. In the article "On Two Metaphors for Learning and the Dangers of Choosing Just One", Anna Sfard identifies two rivalling metaphors: learning as acquisition and learning as participation. In the first metaphor, knowledge is often thought of as objects accumulated in a metaphorical "container" at the learner's disposal – as something one has – and learning is the process by which the individual gathers it. This leads to an emphasis on teaching and education as the handing over of knowledge. The second metaphor, participation, suggests that "learning a subject is now conceived of as a process of becoming a member of a certain community".[5] The learner enters a new zone as a "newbie" before developing a growing capacity to operate in the zone over time, which results in a changed identity in the community.[6]

The turn to practices that have occurred in social sciences over the past decades involves fostering a certain perspective on human activity. Nicolini states it well: "The attraction of the practice idiom stems in particular from its capacity to resonate with the contemporary experience that our world is increasingly in flux and interconnected".[7] While this perspective accommodates several traditions, one common aspect is a general holistic view of social phenomena. By starting with "the doing" instead of "the thinking", a practice view acknowledges that human activity involves more than the individual and cognitive perspective.[8]

I study Christian formation as a form of learning and turn to a theory of learning practice to analyse identity in practice. When using the concept formation related to learning, it is relevant to ask what is actually being formed. Is it a particular understanding of life? Behaviour, rituals, and virtues? A common appreciation of self as an individual or community? A practice perspective can involve all these aspects. Hager, Lee, and Reich propose five lenses for theorising practices of learning:

---

living organisms leads to permanent capacity change and which is not solely due to biological maturation or ageing" and could refer to the outcomes of processes of learning, the psychological processes of change within the learner, the interplay between the individual and the socio-material context, or sometimes as synonymous to the activity of teaching.

[5] Anna Sfard (1998), "On Two Metaphors for Learning and the Dangers of Choosing Just One", *Educational Researcher* 27 (2), 4–13, p 6.

[6] Sfard (1998).

[7] Davide Nicolini (2012), *Practice Theory, Work, and Organization*, Oxford: Oxford University Press, p 2.

[8] Nicolini (2012).

1. Practice theory involves both doing and thinking, which cannot be easily separated.
2. Practices are socio-material phenomena involving human and non-human actors in space and time.
3. Practices are embodied and relational and thus involve dialogues of speech and activity.
4. Practices exist, evolve in historical and social contexts, and take shape at the intersection of complex social forces.
5. Practices are emergent complex ecologies rather than stable and foreseeable systems.[9]

I approach Christian formation as a form of learning, which means it can be investigated with learning theories such as the situated learning theory. This provides a way of analysing the lived aspects of Christian formation in local communities. One might add that studying practices in the local church community, especially using ethnographic methods, is a way to examine lived faith on "the ground".[10] An essential aspect of the practice turn is the inclusion of a plurality of voices in the same setting and acknowledging that what is said and what is done are not always in harmony.[11] The practising faith communities negotiate heard and not heard voices.

By studying Christian formation through the lens of practice theory, I can hold together the different aspects of what is "lived" in a certain situation – what is said and thought, what is done or performed, as well as the material, relational, and spatial aspects. Therefore, a practice perspective is suitable for my study's aim to understand the practices through which people are formed as Christians.

---

[9] Hager et al. (2012).

[10] Sune Fahlgren (2015), "Studying Fundamental Ecclesial Practices", in Fahlgren, Sune and Idestrom, Jonas (eds.), *Ecclesiology in the Trenches* (Eugene, Oregon: Wipf and Stock), 87–105. Fahlgren finds that studying practices is especially helpful in church contexts that are less credal and, therefore, are less keen to put words to their theology.

[11] Cameron et al. (2010). The ARCS team (Action Research Church and Society) introduced the "Four voices" terminology, acknowledging the *operant* voice (theology implicit in practices), the *espoused* voice (theology explicitly articulated by practitioners), the *normative* voice (normative theological traditions such as scripture or church dogmas), and finally the *formal* voice (academic theology and other disciplines).

4.2 Situated Learning Theory

The theoretical framework of situated learning theory by Jean Lave and Etienne Wenger attracted me because of the emphasis on a practice-oriented type of learning, which fits well with studies of Christian formation in church communities.[12] A second reason is the theory's tools for analysing trajectories and negotiations that bring light to how Christian formation practices are performed in a secular context. Lave and Wenger's theory is framed as a situated theory of learning because the interplay between persons in practising communities is in focus. As the name implies, the situation in which learning occurs is taken into consideration. The elegance of this theory is reflected in how the individual and social levels are held together in and through practice.[13] The community becomes a vehicle of formation and is simultaneously formed by individuals' participation in the common practice. Thus, the community and the practices are dynamic and changing, continually reformulating themselves as well as their centre, direction, and borders.

There are several alternatives to the situated learning theory that would have been possible to utilise in analysing practice.[14] One alternative that uses a mediative

---

[12] E.g. Elisabeth Tveito Johnsen and Afdal, Geir (2020), "Practice Theory in Empirical Practical Theological Research", *Nordic Journal of Practical Theology*, 37 (2), 58–76. In the Nordic context, the Norwegian LETRA project used practice theory perspectives in researching different aspects of Christian communities. Elisabeth Tveito Johnsen used sociocultural learning theory by Lave & Wenger in Johnsen (2014); Johan Lövgren (2017), *The Reflective Community: Learning Processes in Norwegian Folk High Schools*, Oslo: MF Norwegian School of Theology; Ingrid Christine Reite (2014), *Between Settling and Unsettling in a Changing Knowledge Society: The Professional Learning Trajectories of Pastors*, Oslo: MF Norwegian School of Theology. Ingrid Christine Reite uses the trajectories concept in her study of the professional learning trajectories of pastors in Norway. Following the LETRA project, Johan Löfgren used the community of practice framework to research Norwegian folk high schools. Fitzmaurice (2016) used a combination of the theory of practice by MacIntyre and Lave & Wenger to study virtue formation in churches under the influence of capitalism and utilitarianism. Westerlund (2021) has studied faith development in the youth work of the Church of Sweden. Zackariasson (2012) has used situated learning to study faith formation in free church youth work. Björn Asserhed (2013), *Discipleship in Community – Learning trajectories of church community leaders in the discipleship enterprise*, Linköping: Linköping University. As a matter of fact, my first encounter with Wenger's book (1998) made me curious about his religious background, of which I have found very little. Even though the case in the book is about insurance claim processors, it seemed to me that he was describing the socio-cultural ecology of a Swedish free church.

[13] Westerlund (2021), p 3.

[14] There are several other theories of practice than those mentioned here, such as Pierre Bourdieu's concept of habitus, and the Actor-network-theory by Bruno Latour. A good overview is found in Nicolini (2012).

4. A Theoretical Understanding of Christian Formation

approach to learning in organisations is the Cultural-Historical Activity Theory (CHAT), developed by Yrje Engeström.[15] An advantage of this theory is that it provides a rigorous systematic conceptual framework for analysing inequalities and conflicts in the community system. There are concepts for analysing the division of labour and the use of different tools in the knowledge-producing activity of the community. Another alternative can be found in Theodore Schatzki's socio-material theory.[16] Schatzki offers a natural inclusion of socio-spatial perspectives, which have some significance in this thesis. At the same time, compared to Lave and Wenger, Schatzki gives a diminished role to learning perspectives. Yet another alternative is Alasdair MacIntyre's practice-virtue perspective, which has had a strong position in developing practical theology, especially in North America.[17] A strong ethical perspective and formation of virtues in practices are central

---

[15] E.g. Yrjö Engeström (2001), "Expansive Learning at Work: Toward an Activity Theoretical Reconceptualization", *Journal of Education and Work*, 14 (1), 133–156; Nicolini (2012); Tara Fenwick (2012), "Matterings of Knowing and Doing: Sociomaterial Approaches to Understanding Practice", in Hager, Paul, Lee, Alison, and Reich, Ann (eds.), *Practice, Learning and Change* (Berlin: Springer), 67–84. CHAT has its roots in the Marxist tradition and draws from the theories of learning by Lev Vygotsky that suggest that learning is always mediated. Engeström developed a systematic model of mediated learning with activity as the unit of analysis and offered a map that can be used in analysing collaborative efforts with a common goal of identifying inequalities in the system.

[16] Theodore R. Schatzki (2001), "Practice Theory", in Schatzki, Theodore R., Knorr-Cetina, Karin, and Savigny, Eike von (eds.), *The Practice Turn in Contemporary Theory* (New York: Psychology Press), 1–14. Schatzki views practices as "embodied, materially mediated arrays of human activity centrally organized around shared practical understanding" (p 2). See also Nick Hopwood (2016), "Sociomaterialism, Practice Theory, and Workplace Learning", in Hopwood, Nick (ed.), *Professional Practice and Learning: Professional and Practice-based Learning* (Cham: Springer International), 53–115. He suggests that material entities of times, spaces, bodies, and things are intimately related in practice. How these entities are organised as "teleoaffective structures" in social practices is central to the socio-materially oriented analysis. Tara Fenwick finds Schatzki's theory imprecise on how "material phenomena become interlaced in practice, and how [...] they affect learning and action". Fenwick (2012), p 67.

[17] Hans Schaeffer (2022), "Concrete Church: Qualitative Research and Ecclesial Practices", in Ward, Pete and Tveitereid, Knut (eds.), *The Wiley Blackwell Companion to Theology and Qualitative Research* (London: John Wiley & Sons), 151–162; Alasdair C. MacIntyre (2013), *After Virtue*, London: A&C Black; Tone Stangeland Kaufman (2018), "Mapping the Landscape of Scandinavian Research in Ecclesiology and Ethnography – Contributions and Challenges", in Ideström, Jonas and Stangeland Kaufman, Tone (eds.), *What Really Matters* (Eugene, OR: Pickwick Publications), 15–37, n 88.

to the MacIntyrian tradition.[18] Situated learning does not exclude but is not limited to the formation of virtues. While I address virtue formation to some degree, I do so without explicitly employing MacIntyre at any length.

To summarise, the first reason for choosing situated learning as the main theory in the thesis is its focus on learning. A second reason is the analytical tools it provides for analysing trajectories and negotiation in communities of practice. The concept of trajectories gives us a way of analysing an individual's movements between margin and centre in a community of practice. The theory's focus on negotiation as an aspect of communal practices provides tools for analysing the meaning in and of practices. While some aspects are considered in the other theories, the situated learning theory holds them conveniently together.

Learning as Changed Participation

What does learning entail in situated learning theory? Jean Lave describes learning as changed participation in the community:

> [T]here is no such thing as "learning" *sui generis*, but only changing participation in the culturally designed settings of everyday life. Or, to put it the other way around, participation in everyday life may be thought of as a process of changing understanding in practice, that is, as learning.[19]

In their co-written book on communities of practice, Lave and Wenger describe learning from a master-apprentice tradition of situated learning rather than from the classroom teaching paradigm.[20] They study how people become midwives, tailors, quartermasters, meat cutters, and non-drinking alcoholics; in doing so, they show how the people involved in their study gradually learn how to do, how to be, and how to behave in fellowship with others of "their kind". The situated view of

---

[18] E.g. Michael D. Palmer (2016), "Ethical Formation: The Theological Virtues", in Chandler, Diane J. (ed.), *The Holy Spirit and Christian Formation: Multidisciplinary Perspectives* (London: Palgrave Macmillan), 107–127; Nancey C. Murphy, Kallenberg, Brad J., and Nation, Mark (2003), *Virtues & Practices in the Christian Tradition*, Notre Dame, Indiana: University of Notre Dame Press; MacIntyre (2013). MacIntyre's definition of practice, as part of his reformulation of Aristotelian ethics, bears a normative orientation. Virtues, as the defined purpose and telos of practice, are seen as relevant to Christian formation. Yet another feature of MacIntyre's practice theory is the appreciation of tradition as part of the practice. When it comes to learning, a MacIntyrian perspective points to a perception of knowledge mainly as phronesis (practical wisdom) manifested in practices forming virtues.

[19] Jean Lave (2018), "The Practice of Learning", in Illeris, Knud (ed.), *Contemporary theories of learning* (Oxfordshire, UK: Routledge), 200–208.

[20] Jean Lave and Wenger, Etienne (1991), *Situated Learning*, Cambridge: Cambridge University Press. The anthropological gaze is strongly present in this volume.

learning they propose introduces the analytical lens of legitimate peripheral participation, which points to this gradual process of becoming in a certain practising community:

> "Legitimate peripheral participation" provides a way to speak about the relations between newcomers and old-timers, and about activities, identities, artifacts, and communities of knowledge and practice. It concerns the process by which newcomers become part of a community of practice. A person's intentions to learn are engaged and the meaning of learning is configured through the process of becoming a full participant in a socio-cultural practice.[21]

A significant contribution of their study is the finding that apprentices learn not only from masters but also from other apprentices. The term legitimate peripheral participation points to the value and opportunity of being a newcomer and the fact that learning is never completed but instead aims at full participation. The concept of communities of practice, they say, "requires a more rigorous treatment", which is exactly what Wenger offers a few years later.[22]

Critique of Situated Learning Theory

In his book, Wenger introduces theoretical concepts for the analysis of learning in communities of practice. However, what he fails to address to any extent is the "unequal relations of power" that he and Lave had documented in the master-apprentice relationships.[23] Joanne Roberts finds situated learning theory lacking in addressing issues of power in communities.[24] This is one of the main critiques of the communities of practice concept, a critique that Tara Fenwick finds fair:

> The whole orientation of "practice-based learning", then, could be criticized for promoting what is essentially a highly conservative, a-critical direction where what is valued as the most important knowledge and skill is simply that which ensures the continued dominance of historical routines and hierarchies. A practice in itself does not necessarily embed the seeds for change, either through innovation or self-critique – or does it?[25]

To be fair, Wenger does warn about a romantic view of communities. I believe that the absence of power analysis in the situated learning theory should also be

---

[21] Lave and Wenger (1991), p 29.
[22] Wenger (1999).
[23] Lave and Wenger (1991), p 42.
[24] Joanne Roberts (2006), "Limits to Communities of Practice", *Journal of Management Studies*, 43 (3), 623–639. Roberts argues that communities of practice, among other things, lack in addressing issues of power in communities. See also Alistair Mutch (2003), "Communities of Practice and Habitus: A Critique", *Organization Studies*, 24 (3), 383–401.
[25] Fenwick (2012), p 68.

attributed to the theoretical tradition in which the theory emerges. Lave and Wenger stand in an anthropological tradition and aim to describe common features of groups, and emphasises social learning. Theories in the Marxist tradition, in contrast, emphasise differences and conflicts of interest more strongly.[26]

Participation in the Community of Practice

What, then, does the concept of practice bring to the theory of situated learning? According to Wenger:

> A concept of practice includes both the explicit and tacit. It includes what is said and what is left unsaid: what is represented and what is assumed. It includes the language, tools, documents, images, symbols, well-defined roles, specified criteria, codified procedures, regulations, and contracts that various practices make explicit for a variety of purposes. But it also includes all the implicit relations, tacit conventions, subtle cues, untold rules of thumb, recognisable institutions, specific perceptions, well-tuned sensitivities, embodied understandings, underlying assumptions, and shared worldviews. Most of these may never be articulated, yet they are unmistakable signs of membership in communities of practice and are crucial to the success of the enterprises.[27]

Understood from Wenger's perspective, the formation is not exclusively cognitive and individual but also involves a change in identity for both individual participants and the practising community. There are levels of participation and engagement that correspond to the formation of individuals and the community and to the relation between the individual and the practising community. In a particular community, this could be a formal or informal reification of membership, with conditions for belonging, initiation rituals, and expectations of certain engagements in the community. According to Wenger, however, the meaning of the practice is not fixed but continuously negotiated:

> Practice is a shared history of learning that requires some catching up for joining. It is not an object to be handed down from one generation to the next. Practice is an ongoing, social, interactional process, and the introduction of newcomers is merely a version of what practice is. That members interact, do things together, negotiate new meanings, and learn from each other is already inherent in practice – that is how practice evolve. In other words, communities of practice reproduce their membership in the same way they come about in the first place.[28]

Understanding community as something evolving and diverse acknowledges a negotiation of meaning of the practice and the community. I find this to be an

---

[26] Afdal (2013).
[27] Wenger (1999), p 47.
[28] Wenger (1999), p 102.

essential part of the learning that is going on in the kind of communities I study. There are few constants, and those that exist are interpreted differently and change slightly depending on who verbalises the meanings. According to Wenger, a give-and-take is involved:

> I intend the term negotiation to convey a flavour of continuous interaction, of gradual achievement, and of give-and-take. By living in the world we do not just make meanings up independently of the world, but neither does the world simply impose meanings on us.[29]

According to Wenger, participation and reification are interplaying parts of the negotiation of meaning and experiencing the world. Reification is "the process of giving form to our experience by producing objects that congeal this experience into 'thingness'".[30] By taking part and participating through living, acting, and interacting, we project, form, and produce meaning for things and actions.

According to Wenger, there are three dimensions to communities of practice: mutual engagement, joint enterprise, and shared repertoire. Mutual engagement means doing things together in complex social relationships; joint enterprise means that practice interpretations are negotiated into common rhythms. The shared repertoire consists of stories, artefacts, tools, styles, discourses, and actions that give and receive meaning in the social flow of practice.[31] The community is joined together by what is mutual and shared.

What does it mean to belong to a community of practice? Wenger mentions three modes or aspects of what this means: engagement, alignment, and imagination. Engagement means that you take part in the ongoing negotiation of meaning in the community, which results in trajectories, which are paths of unfolding histories of practice. This engagement is limited and strengthened by the limits of

---

[29] Wenger (1999), p 53.

[30] Wenger (1999), p 58. Reification is not used as a concept in the analysis but is presented here to give background to Wenger's theory. Participation, however, is a central concept in the analysis.

[31] Wenger (1999), p 73. Regarding tools, Wenger doesn't elaborate on the mediative aspect. That is, how different objects or programs are used to produce a certain type of community. The use of the concept of tools in practice leans on a long tradition of practice theory. Cf. Engeström (2001); Nicolini (2012), p 113. Davide Nicolini argues that there is a link between Marx's theories of how work is done in the production of material goods and the social learning theory by Lev Vygotsky, in which mediation plays a part in goal-directed action. Yrje Engeström develops the activity tradition of practice in Cultural Historical Activity Theory, in which a subject, a person or a collective produces objects and reaches outcomes, material or symbolic. This object/outcome in this theory has "a telic dimension" and is achieved by the use of tools in a community.

being in space and time.³² Alignment means the approach of the participants, which says that "we become part of something big because we do what it takes to play our part".³³ I understand this mode as adapting to what already is – whether for good or bad reasons. Wenger describes imagination with the delightful image of "looking at an apple seed and seeing a tree".³⁴ As we will see later, there is a lot of imagination going on among church planters.³⁵

Trajectories

In presenting how newcomers grow towards successful participation in certain practices, Lave and Wenger suggest that there is a trajectory – a change of identity from being an outsider to being knowledgeable within the social sphere of a specific practice. This movement occurs in relation to a community of practice – a movement from legitimate peripheral participation towards fuller participation.³⁶ Ole Dreier discusses psychological development in terms of "life-trajectory, structure of personality, and identity":

> [T]hrough the history of their participations persons unfold a particular subjective composition to the significance of their participations in particular contexts and with particular others. By relating their various participations, concerns, and stances persons gradually configure a particular subjective composition to the way they feel located in the world. It seems to me that this is what is meant by the term identity. The feeling of belonging to particular practices and with particular persons and places develops on the background of being part of them, reflecting on one's personal relationship to being part of them, configuring those reflections into personal stances and configuring those stances into mapping of what one stands for and where one belongs (which is what we mean by identity).³⁷

Dreier thus connects identity with the community using the trajectory concept – albeit from the perspective of psychology rather than learning, but nevertheless as a change of identity. Somewhere along and between the contexts, belongings and participations in the Christian communities, a person can foster or lose an identity as a Christian. Wenger describes different types of trajectories (Peripheral,

---

³² Wenger (1999), p 174.

³³ Wenger (1999), p 179.

³⁴ Wenger (1999), p 176.

³⁵ For example, the prayerful imagining of a church in Industrial City (p 113), how God's justice could be made in Harbour City (p 133), and the collective imagination of a virtuous community in Cathedral City (p 159).

³⁶ Lave and Wenger (1991).

³⁷ Ole Dreier (1999), "Personal Trajectories of Participation across Contexts of Social Practice", Outlines. *Critical Practice Studies*, 15–32, p 21.

Inbound, Insider, Boundary, and Outbound) in categorising the different movements a person is taking as a result of their participation in the community of practice.[38]

Negotiation of Meaning

Finally, I want to emphasise the concepts of identification and negotiability in the community of practice framework. Identification is "the process through which modes of belonging become constitutive of our identities by creating bonds or distinctions in which we become invested" made by ourselves or others, negatively or positively – what we are not and what we are.[39] In other words, through engagement and participating in common practices, imagining the possibilities of common endeavours, and aligning to traditions or understandings of the community, we identify ourselves with and connect to the community. Negotiability, Wenger writes,

> [...] refers to the ability, facility, and legitimacy to contribute to, take responsibility for, and shape the meanings that matter within a social configuration. Negotiability allows us to make meanings applicable to new circumstances, to enlist the collaboration of others, to make sense of events, or to assert our membership.[40]

Wenger points to the fact that among the possible "economies of meaning" in the community, there emerges ownership of meaning – "the degree to which we can make use of, affect, control, modify, or in general, assert as ours the meanings that we negotiate".[41] Not everyone has the same control over meanings produced within the community, and not all meanings have the same degree of currency. In the negotiation of meaning, there are bids for ownership where some meanings are given a higher value than others. This is where Wenger discusses power issues within the communities of practice in terms of social structure, social status, and identity formation:

> By incorporating both power and belonging into an ecology of identity, the duality of identification and negotiability provides a sophisticated way of talking about the social construction of the person. It does not simply create an opposition between individuality and collectivity, but neither does it simply assimilate them. Instead, it takes a different cut at the individuality–collectivity dichotomy by recasting it in terms of processes of identity formation. Neither identification nor negotiability is inherently collective or

---

[38] These different trajectory types are described on p 181.
[39] Wenger (1999), p 192.
[40] Wenger (1999), p 197.
[41] Wenger (1999), p 200.

individual. Yet their interplay in specific settings is what defines the meaning of the collective and the individual as an experience of identity.[42]

To echo critics of Wenger's theory, I must acknowledge that this does not make sense in all contexts. For example, when the focus is on the unequal distribution of power in a community, situated learning theory does not provide the tools for such analysis.

Another related issue that is seemingly absent is the appreciation of social heterogeneity.[43] In describing a community of practice in terms of what is mutual, joined, and shared, Wenger gives the impression that communities should be understood as homogeneous and harmonious. But according to Wenger himself, this is usually not the case:

> Because the term "community" is usually a very positive one, I cannot emphasize enough that these interrelations arise out of engagement in practice and not out of an idealized view of what a community should be like. In particular, connotations of peaceful coexistence, mutual support, or interpersonal allegiance are not assumed, though, of course, they may exist in specific cases. [...] In some communities of practice, conflict and misery can even constitute the core characteristic of a shared practice, as they do in dysfunctional families.[44]

Wenger argues that the tensions of unity and diversity are an important part of every community of practice, making engagement possible.[45] He further develops this as a matter of negotiation of meaning in practice in which the individual finds and refines their identity. The community, with its practice and the meanings attributed to it, is in flux. When considering communities of practice as a theory of learning, I take Wenger's seemingly double perspective on communities as both heterogeneous and homogenous to have enough balance to be helpful in the analysis of formative practices. As with any theory, there needs to be reinterpretations when meeting real-world contexts. No community of individuals is entirely homogenous, but there must be something shared in a social practice.

Conclusion

Above I have outlined why I use the situated learning theory in the analysis of Christian formation and described its main theoretical concepts. Situated learning theory offers an integrated perspective that involves individual and social learning

---

[42] Wenger (1999), p 212.
[43] Roberts (2006).
[44] Wenger (1999), p 76.
[45] Wenger (1999), p 75.

defined through participation in common practice. When analysing Christian formation, this reminds us that formative practices involve forming both individuals and church communities. Thus, lived identity is perceived reciprocally as "the pivot between the social and the individual so that each can be talked about in terms of the other".[46] This integrated view of situated learning offers analytical concepts that will be employed in my analysis of formative practices:

- *Trajectories*: The theory offers a dynamic view of formation through the concept of trajectories in the communities of practice. Using this concept, I can analyse the levels and directions of participative engagement.
- *Negotiation*: The theory offers the concept of negotiation, which points towards the social meaning-making processes of formation. I apply the negotiation concept to cultural issues raised in the material.
- *Imagination*: The situated learning theory involves a perspective on community-based creativity through the concept of imagination. This concept is helpful in analysing the orientation of the church plants and what they perceive themselves to be formed towards.

In addition to these central concepts, I want to add two other aspects to the practice analysis that are not explicitly part of the situated learning theory:

- *Telos*: I found strong intentionality and direction in the practices involved in the church plants. While Wenger discusses the meaning of practice negotiated in the communities, he does not suggest that practices have clearly defined purposes. In searching for a way of describing this intentionality, I found that several theories use the concept of telos to discuss how Christian formation has a direction.[47] In this thesis, I analyse the practices' teloi – what is suggested in the words of the

---

[46] Wenger (1999), p 145.

[47] Andrew P. Rogers (2016), *Congregational Hermeneutics: How Do We Read*, Oxfordshire: Routledge, p 215. In discussing the merits of Wenger's Community of Practice framework, Andrew Rogers finds that when studying congregations that are eschatological, a directional component needs to be added. For the same reason, I use telos to indicate the ultimate formational goal in the church plants.

planters and communities in addition to the choices they make and priorities they hold.⁴⁸
- *Tradition*: The gathered material also points to a strong use of free church tradition in developing formative practices. Even though Wenger doesn't operationalise the concept of tradition, the idea is partly present in how he uses meaning of practice, which is negotiated in the community.⁴⁹ The negotiation by practitioners means that the tradition is continuously changing.⁵⁰ While traditions are present in the formative practices, this is not much developed by Lave and Wenger, so I chose to include the concept of tradition to illuminate the historical rootedness of practices.

In addition to these practice-related concepts, I employ the concept of calling. The reason for including this concept is the planters' articulation of a strong sense of calling from God to plant a church in a particular place.

---

⁴⁸ Smith (2013). In studying cultural liturgies, James K.A. Smith shows how people are formed towards other, and sometimes conflicting, teloi. He describes humans as liturgical animals and grounds his theory of practice – or liturgical anthropology – in the phenomenology of Maurice Merleau-Ponty and theories of the social body by Pierre Bourdieu. The prominent place Smith gives to the body and "being-in-the-body" for Christian formation references Heideggerian philosophy and the view that doing comes before thinking, which is essential to developing theories of practice. Smith understands this as a feature of incarnate theology, that human beings meet God not as a merely cognitive experience but in and through the body. Bodily practice and habits are essential in forming a Christian life in connection to telos. This is how Christians are "re-storied" through the narrative practice of worship with Jesus Christ as an example. MacIntyre (2013) has had a strong impact on practical theology in the US. He elaborates on the development of ethics in the practising community, emphasising the telos of a practice. According to MacIntyre, practices, to begin with, are social and cooperative. Secondly, practices have internal goods. That is, the practice has value in itself. It is more than a means to an end. Thirdly, it is possible to grow in and through practice and, finally, develop the practice itself (p 218). Smith's take on the telos concept is more prominent in my analysis and discussion.

⁴⁹ Smith (2013). Smith uses the Bourdieauan concept of habitus, which he defines as "the orientation to the world that is carried in the way of life and oriented fundamentally toward action, toward tangible being-in-the-world" (p 84). To become a "native" (Christian) as part of a social body (the Body of Christ) is "a matter of having acquired a habitus that has become second nature […] having absorbed, and been absorbed into the plausibility structures of a people". (p 92).

⁵⁰ Nicolini (2012), p 81. Nicolini finds that in Lave and Wenger's early concept of Legitimate Peripheral Participation, there is an inherent generational "micro-conflict", meaning that the new participant needs to choose between adapting to the practice tradition or changing it through their increased engagement in the practice.

- *Calling*: I use the understanding of calling articulated by Elangovan et al.: a sense of clarity of purpose and personal mission leading to action with a pro-social intention.[51] Using this definition provides a way of discussing personally grounded intentions, including a perception of God's urge and the paths taken in the missional work in society. Bielo's concept of "dwelling" is also brought into my use of the concept of calling. Dwelling, in this context, involves cultivating a sense of place that directly reflects and recreates their social and religious lifeworlds, which closely relates to the calling described in the material.[52]

4.3 Analysing Christian Formation from a Practice Perspective

In Chapters 5 to 8, I will present the analysis of my material according to the aim and research questions.[53] The four chapters will analyse different aspects of Church planting as Christian formation (Table 2):

Analysis chapter	Theoretical concepts	Research question
5. The Calling to Christian Formation	Calling, intentions, telos, imagination	1. How are the callings and intentions of the church plants articulated, and what do the callings and intentions mean for Christian formation?
6. Formative Practices	Participation, tradition, tools, telos	2. What practices of Christian formation are present in the church plant communities?
7. Trajectories of Formation	Engagement, alignment, trajectories	3. How are people formed towards a lived Christian identity in the church plant communities?
8. Negotiating Secular Culture	Negotiability, culture	4. What cultural tensions do the church plants negotiate, and what do the negotiations mean for Christian formation?

Table 2: Theoretical concepts in relation to research questions and their location in the thesis.

---

[51] Elangovan et al. (2010), p 430. The authors define calling as "a course of action in pursuit of pro-social intentions embodying the convergence of an individual's sense of what he or she would like to do, should do, and actually does".

[52] James S. Bielo (2013), "Urban Christianities: Place-making in Late Modernity", *Religion*, 43 (3), 301–311.

[53] Aim and research questions are found on pp 23-24.

The Use of Theory in the Analysis Chapters

In Chapter 5, I will use the lens of calling and intentionality to present the church plants as contexts for Christian formation. The presentation mainly follows the understanding of calling by Elangovan, Pinder, and McLean, which points to the embodiment of identity and intentions and pro-social action.[54] In addition, I describe the strong connection to place in the realisation of the callings with the inspiration of Bielo's understanding of "dwelling". The analysis leads to articulations of a telos of Christian formation in each church plant.

In Chapter 6, I analyse significant formative practices in the three church plants. The practice descriptions show how Christian formation occurs on an individual and community level in church planting. The analysis relates the formative practices to the traditions, tools, and teloi and describes ways of engagement in the practices.

In Chapter 7, I analyse formative trajectories and formative practices in the church plants. Here, I employ one of the main concepts from the situated learning theory. By looking at how personal participation and engagement change over time, I discover how a lived Christian identity is formed in the practices.

In Chapter 8, I focus on each church plant's relationship with secular culture. Wenger's negotiation/negotiability concept is used to analyse the complex processes of contextualisation in the church plants. This cultural negotiation provides depth to the understanding of Christian formation in secular culture.

---

[54] Elangovan et al. (2010), p 430.

5. The Calling to Christian Formation

This chapter investigates the callings of the church planters and communities and thus addresses the first research question: *How are the callings and intentions of the church plants articulated, and what do the callings and intentions mean for Christian formation?* Here, we get a glimpse into the church planters' ecclesial imaginations and how they are realised in the lives of the communities. The chapter also serves as an introduction to the communities where the formative practices are carried out.[1]

The ecclesial imagination of the church planters begins to take shape through the planters' and communities' calling to a certain place and task. In this sense, the calling to plant a church represents a missional impulse to form a church community in a secular context, and this impulse is realised through formative practices in the communities.[2] The practices will be addressed in the next chapter, while in this chapter, I analyse the planters' place-related pro-social action and their embodiments of identities and intentions. What emerges from the analysis are three visions of lived Christian identity.

My understanding of calling leans on the definition by Elangovan, Pinder, and McLean: The sense of clarity of purpose and personal mission that leads to action with a pro-social intention.[3] The calling of church planters is rooted in their belief

---

[1] As mentioned earlier, the names of the cities and church plants, as well as all names of persons, have been changed for reasons of confidentiality.

[2] Hirsch (2006), p 127. Hirsch uses the term missional-incarnational impulse to describe an important aspect of missional theology. The church is sent into the world, not mainly to attract people to come to the church but to be embedded powerlessly present in the local community and proclaim the gospel. I use the term missional impulse to mean calling to mission more generally, without Hirsch's qualifications.

[3] Elangovan et al. (2010), p 430. The authors define calling as "a course of action in pursuit of pro-social intentions embodying the convergence of an individual's sense of what he or she would like to do, should do, and actually does". They describe the Christian roots of the term and suggest a typology of religious versus secular, occupation-related versus non-occupation-related. In the case of church planters, the calling is religiously oriented but could be described both

they were sent to the community by God. That the calling is pro-social means that the activity of the church plant is not limited to the private sphere but includes a sense of concern for the whole society. However, one of the main findings regarding the calling is that all planters strongly relate to a particular place.[4] The interviews also show that the church planters identify strongly with the vocation of being church planters.[5]

According to Etienne Wenger, taking part in the imagination of a community is a "mode of belonging" to a community. As mentioned previously, Wenger describes imagination as "looking at an apple seed and seeing a tree".[6] The church plants are embodiments of this kind of imagination. But the planters are not content with merely looking at the apple seed. They put it in the soil and water and care for it so it grows into a tree. In the material of interviews and observations, different aspects of calling become visible: How it shapes identity, the significance of place, and the nature of the pro-social action. The following presentation is structured around these aspects. Towards the end of the presentation, the descriptions of the callings are related to visions of lived Christian identity: the telos of Christian formation.

5.1 The Calling to Industrial City

The church plant in Industrial City is engaging secular culture at the centre of the city. They use social media to create interest and invite people to attend culturally sensitive worship services. The planters have a strong missional identity and experience a calling that extends beyond Industrial City to other cities of the same size and character. Ultimately, they want to create a movement of similar church plants in other Swedish cities.

---

as occupational and not strictly occupational. However, what is clear is that there is a sense of clarity of purpose and personal mission leading to action with a pro-social intention.

[4] Bielo (2013). As I noted in the previous chapter, James S. Bielo uses the concept of "dwelling" to indicate how Christian communities cultivate senses of place that directly reflect and recreate their social and religious lifeworlds. While I don't use the term "dwelling", my understanding of calling is enriched by the orientation towards place reflected by Bielo's concept.

[5] Osmer (2012), p 30, speaks of a missional vocation; Moynagh (2012), p 229, discuss church planter journeys.

[6] Wenger (1999), p 176. In this sense, the church planters are actually belonging to a community of church-planting practitioners, where church planting is the practice. I do not analyse church planting as a practice but, rather, as formative practices within the church-planting community.

Identity and Intention

In this section, we will see how a strong missional identity and cultural sensitivity characterise the identity of the church plant in Industrial City. The planters feel called by God to plant a church and want to be a voice that is heard in what they describe as a secular wasteland.[7]

Missionally oriented

Einar and Margareta are married and lead the church plant together. Before they planted this church in Industrial City, they had been part of missional projects and church plants in several places in Sweden. This has provided them with much experience and knowledge about church planting. Over the years, they had occasionally visited Industrial City for various reasons and had discussed with each other if this might be where God was leading them. But by the time they felt a sense of clarity and affirmation in this calling, they were engaged in another church plant. As such, they put their plans for a church in Industrial City on hold. But after a dream, which they interpret as encouragement from Jesus to walk in faith, they decide to move to Industrial City. They do so with a sense of joy tempered by some fear of failure.

> [Margareta]: I know that this is where we are going. We are kind of meant for this city. [...] So this dream about [Industrial City] started to come alive again. So we were very scared. Do we dare to take this step? What happens if we do? What if we think we should do something again, and it becomes a mess? All these fears came over us.

They arranged public church services in the city centre and got unexpected help from the local newspaper. The media took notice of the new church initiative since the church plant gathered in a well-known building that serves as a symbol for Industrial City. Einar and Margareta felt that the first meeting was a moment of truth for their church-planting dream, and around a hundred people attended it. They considered this as a success.

> [Einar]: At the inauguration, if you want to get the feeling, we read from Paul, the word that spoke so clearly into our situation. He writes: I came to you weak and afraid, but I had decided that I didn't want to hear about anything but crucified Christ.[8]

---

[7] Cf. James (2018) p 104; The model that is closest to Industrial City church plant is the Great Commission Team model, which sees itself as a response to a context that has forgotten about God. James describes churches in this model as "missional communities with rhythms of study, relationship, and service and worship services that prioritize Christocentric, exegetical preaching, and emotionally intense singing".

[8] Einar refers to 1 Cor 2:1-5.

The reference to the apostle Paul connects the church plant to Paul's legacy of evangelisation and church planting and affirms their own missional identity. But church planting, as they see it, involves more than moving to a new city and engaging in evangelistic activities. They want to build an ecclesial community and see a new church emerge. This intention is clearly expressed in the following statements:

> [Margareta]: We are planting a church here so that [...] people will get to know Jesus and be his disciples. [...] We want to help people, firstly, to hear who Jesus is, to discover him, to have a relationship and then comes the process of transformation that God is doing in the heart. That's how we think.

> [Margareta]: Being a Christian... I think it means you have decided to let Jesus be your Lord and saviour. It is the decision of the heart and the confession of the mouth. From this, you discover more about what the word of God says and who God is, and you start having a relationship with him. You are part of a church.

This understanding of what it means to become Christian echoes a text in the New Testament (Romans 10:9) that points to an inner decision and a public confession in the community. In other words, Margareta seems to argue that the process of becoming Christian starts with an individual, but it is also connected to the community. Similarly, God is understood to have an active part in the process, first by revealing himself to the individual and then by leading them to be part of the church. The church plant focuses on people new to the Christian faith, and it is built around leading people to Jesus and introducing them to the path of Christian discipleship.

Cultural Sensitivity

The church plant's Sunday gathering resembles a revival meeting, which will be addressed at length in the following chapter. In engaging the city's cultural centre, the church plant perceives a need to adopt practices that are not too foreign to the secularised visitor. This cultural sensitivity can be seen in the plant's contemporary style of music and approachable language. They want to present a culturally attuned worship meeting, and to that end, the church plant has different teams responsible for various tasks and functions in the meeting. It becomes a platform to which the members invite friends and people who have encountered the church on social media.

When secularised people come to the services, the church planters want them to meet a community that feels "real". To be this kind of community is part of their missionary identity:

[Margareta]: I think we as a church are Christ-like wherever we are, reflecting him. We don't meet only to experience God but to reflect him in the larger society. I take that as our beautiful goal. [...] and this sense of being a family that is not artificial or constrained is also important to the church.

[Einar]: Real, Relational, Relevant. I guess that would summarise us. That is what we want. It should be real, and you should be able to come and be at your worst but still feel welcome.

The image of a family is contrasted with a formal or shallow community, whereas their church community strives to reflect the values of being "real, relational, and relevant", particularly in their fundamental practices.[9] Sven and Birgitta, church plant leaders working with Einar and Margareta, state the importance of culturally sensitive language:

[Sven]: We call it "churchese" when we speak the language of the Christian culture where we grew up, a language that those who grew up outside the Christian culture do not understand. We don't want to speak "churchese"![10]

[Birgitta]: We try to use words that people who have never been in a church will understand at a service. I would say that this is significant [to us]. Because I have experienced elsewhere that when coming to churches and inviting friends who are not Christian, you feel very uncomfortable wondering if they actually understand one word.

The language, both in public meetings and smaller gatherings such as leadership meetings, is quite informal and youthful, or "fresh", as Birgitta says.[11] Sven underlines that the language is shaped in and through leaders: "As leaders, we urge other leaders to be mindful of the language". The focus on approachability extends beyond language, though. The planters consciously try to create a sense of community that allows newcomers to feel comfortable.

[Margareta]: We have noticed that some people are discovering the Christian faith and who God is, and we have communicated from day one: you are allowed to make your journey. You can belong without believing. I think that is key for people to feel that, okay, I don't need to buy in on everything at once. I own my process.

While the goal that people should come to faith is clear to the planters and leaders, this is not a prerequisite for participation in the life of the community. Rather,

---

[9] Neve (2021), p 236, finds in the Emerging churches a fundamentally positive understanding of culture and a missiology that is a pursuit of cultural proximity. While Neve accepts this as partly valid, he finds a critical reflection on culture to be lacking.

[10] "Churchese" is a translation of the word "kyrkiska", used by Sven.

[11] Root (2017a) p 17, criticises the churches' turn to youthfulness as a solution to secularisation. According to Root, youth culture is a feature of secularisation and is therefore not helpful when trying to be an alternative to it.

they want to create an environment where people can bring their understanding of themselves and faith into a discovery process in a not-too-foreign setting.

Relation to Culture

The Industrial City church plant seeks influence in the cultural centre but also, in certain ways, functions as a counter-culture. However, the planters' aim at the centre should not be understood in terms of seeking power and control. The planters reference John the Baptist in describing the role they seek:

> [Margareta]: We think Sweden, in a way, is a spiritual wasteland. We have material wealth and engage in all this self-fulfilment. Still, compared to other countries and contexts, Sweden is somewhat like a spiritual wasteland, and we hope to be a voice that preaches the gospel and God's truth in our region.

John was speaking from the periphery. He is described as strange, with "clothing made of camel's hair, with a leather belt around his waist, and he ate locusts and wild honey" (Mark 1:6 NIV). The church plant in Industrial City does not come across as odd or deviant to contemporary culture. In fact, in their attempts to be culturally sensitive and relevant, the planters could be seen as the opposite of John the Baptist. But John did not seek the role of a king at the top of the structures of power. He embraced the role of the prophet – a voice speaking from outside to the established order. His strategy was not to change the system from the top down through power and force. Instead, he names the wrongs at the system's core and calls people to repent before the Lord. This lack of power combined with preaching a counter-cultural message – about faith in a spiritual wasteland – are themes in the story of John the Baptist that resonate with the church planters in Industrial City. Margareta, for instance, describes Sweden as a desert wilderness, indicating that the context does not provide the soil needed for a good and godly spiritual life to grow.

In conclusion, the material from the church plant in Industrial City indicates a missional self-understanding. They aim for the cultural centre and foster sensitivity to contemporary cultural language.

The Significance of Place

Einar and Margareta, the couple who planted the church, have a strong sense of calling, one that is intimately tied to the particular location of Industrial City:

> [Margareta]: I really loved [Industrial City]. Just like that... I knew this was where we were going. We are kind of meant for this city.

It became clear during our interviews that while the planters expressed warm feelings for Industrial City, my questions were not evoking a discussion of the particularities of the place. To try to move beneath the surface of the matter, I designed a workshop where the planters painted a map describing the city as they saw it.[12] Einar and Margareta were given the following task:

> **Task: Draw the city** (15-20 minutes): A city is comprised of people and meetings. Infrastructure, politics, culture, sports, religion, and many other things exist in one geographical space. Draw your map over the city/place where you are present as a church plant. The map doesn't need to be realistic. Include places and areas important to you, personally and as a church. While you are drawing, explain why those places are important, what they represent, and their role concerning your goals.
>
> [Björn]: What would you say? We plant a church here because…
>
> [Einar]: Yeah, I would say… so that people will get to know Jesus and become his disciples.

They write this goal at the base of the map, then draw the culture hall where they gather. They place this at the centre of the map. The hall has a big door and a flag with the church plant logo (which has been removed in the version in Figure 2).

> [Einar]: I think [the culture hall] should be in the centre because what is important to us isn't the different local areas, but the people spread out over the city. [drawing a building typical for the city centre]
>
> [Margareta]: I think we should draw homes. The homes are where we meet people. Then we have coffee tables representing homes, with coffee cups. …wow, this is a real challenge for me…
>
> [Einar]: Then maybe arrows inwards and outwards.
>
> [Margareta]: Then, in addition to the important stuff…
>
> [Einar]: The arrows are about our Sunday gathering but sent out back into everyday life.
>
> [Margareta]: We should draw restaurants and cafes to represent the lives where the people are, living out their Christian lives where they are. A restaurant with many tables. Here is a sofa. It becomes…. can't you see it is a sofa?! [laughter] It symbolises cafes, restaurants, workplaces and all that.
>
> [Einar]: To see people becoming baptised.
>
> [Margareta]: Yes, we need water. That is water, right?
>
> [Einar]: You don't paint water like that.
>
> [Margareta]: How do you paint water? [laughter]

---

[12] This strategy was inspired by Boy (2015).

5. The Calling to Christian Formation

Figure 2: Map made by the planters in Industrial City, showing the city as they see it. Text in Swedish: "So that people will get to know Jesus and become his disciples".

The planters' conversation illustrates how this simple workshop opens doors to seemingly closed rooms of reflection. The intention of the church plant, that people will get to know Jesus and become his disciples, is connected to the planters' choice to gather in the city's centre, in a well-known building with a big door open for the masses. They are not called to specific areas but to reach the people of all parts of the city with the gospel. They have put their flag in the city centre, claiming the entire city. On the right side of the flag, they write "www", representing their strong focus on social media. This correlates with their bird's eye perspective on the city, where direct involvement with particular areas is lacking.

After putting the map to the side, the planters go on discussing Sweden as a secular country that needs the gospel. In their view, secularisation means that God has no meaning in the lives of the average Swede. Church planting is, therefore, a way to counteract secularisation. In describing their push against secularisation, the planters stress the value of the act of public preaching. By meeting in the well-known secular culture hall, the church plant engages in a contest regarding the cultural narrative. In this way, their choice of gathering place takes on a symbolic meaning. If the gospel is preached and heard regularly in this place, it becomes part of contemporary culture. The church plant rents the building and spends most of its financial resources to that end. Thus, financial resources become essential in claiming a place in the centre, but the planters consider the building to be a worthy investment.

The significance of the big, public meeting place is evident in the discussion above, and it is also – as we shall see – significantly different to the other church plants. The place of meeting illustrates something particular about this church plant:

> [Margareta]: At first, we gathered in [Historical building] because it is [Industrial City's] icon, the heart of [Industrial City]. Then we wanted to gather in [Cultural hall] because it is pretty visible in the city. It is convenient and a good place for us as a church. It expresses what we want to be…
>
> [Einar]: It is the same location as the first church in [Industrial City], so it is also a bit prophetic.
>
> [Birgitta]: [cultural hall] is where you have been with your job before or at a concert. Then it might be easier to go to a worship service again and tell someone that you have been in [cultural hall], and it's not weird. It might be more odd to say you have been to the Salvation Army. So I think it is less of an obstacle.

Still, the meeting in the culture hall is not the only place of significance to the church plant. Above their drawing of that building, Margareta and Einar have sketched small tables that represent homes. Cafes and restaurants, symbolised by a sofa and a table (lower left), represent the everyday lives of the people of the church plant. Small groups meet in homes, where faith is shared in conversation and other ways not possible in a large venue.

In conclusion, to engage the city centre and get the people's attention in the "secular wasteland", they chose meeting places familiar to people and representing the city's cultural centre. In addition to being a practical choice in regard to location and space, it challenges the image of the city as completely secular.

Pro-Social Action

The character of their calling to Industrial City is not only reflected in their choice of location and descriptions of their church, but also in the practices of their mission. The planters see themselves as called to preach the gospel in a culturally relevant manner. Here, in their ambition to influence the culture at large, lies the pro-social intention of their action. They engage the cultural centre, and their message is heard in the secular wasteland.

This evangelistic approach was on display at a baptism in a traditional church building rented for the occasion:

At the beginning of the service, where a young man and a middle-aged woman are being baptised, Margareta and Einar walk up to the podium. Margareta welcomes the twenty people in attendance and then opens with a prayer: "I put my trust in you, who are the Love and the Truth, the hope that remains through it all". A few worship songs are sung before Einar returns to the podium. He tells the story of his way to Christian faith and his awe as he started understanding what faith was all about. "What kind of God is this who can love me and forgive me? God is not interested in my good deeds – He wants me!" He then retells Jesus' parable of the father's warm welcome of the prodigal son.[13] Then Einar says calmly: "This is exactly what it is about for you as well. He has called you home! If you sit here and have not made that decision, God longs for you and wants to receive you". After the two baptisms and a prayer for the newly inaugurated, the service draws to a close. Afterwards, Einar approaches four friends of the newly baptised man who were sitting close to me. Einar

---

[13] This story is found in Luke 15:11-32.

seemed to have had these men as his target during the sermon. He asks them if they believe in God. One of them calls himself an atheist. Einar asks him why, and he has difficulty answering the question. One of the young men says he was baptised as an infant in the Church of Sweden. The discussion is friendly and frank, and they decide to meet again to discuss further about baptism and faith.

Scene: Industrial City, Oct. 26, 2020.

Inviting to the Meeting
The church plant in Industrial City wants to reach people with its message by inviting them to the worship service. To the planters, starting a church means launching a regular public meeting of sorts. They aim for what I call the "town square" – the city centre, the focus point of the culture – where they are most likely to grab the attention of unchurched people in Industrial City. While the worship meeting is not, as we will see, the only formative practice in their repertoire, the significance they put on the meeting shows that this practice is central to their identity. The ideal Christian of this church plant is the fisherman found in the Gospel of Luke, when Jesus calls his first disciples, who were actual fishermen, to catch people for God's kingdom instead: "'From now on you will fish for people'. So they pulled their boats up on shore, left everything and followed him". (Luke 5:10-11 NIV). The planters' own net is carefully prepared in the revival meeting, and the regulars are encouraged to invite their friends.

The Industrial City church plant has adopted what Michael Moynagh calls a "worship-first journey" strategy, which, in short, means that the planters start with an invitation to a public meeting. A handful of members come from closed-down churches; some have moved there from other cities, and others have left their former church and found a new home in the church plant. However, according to what the planters tell me, the church plant has also reached people outside the already "churched". That the planters, Einar and Margareta, would emphasise this is unsurprising; the ability to reach the "unchurched" is important to a church plant that wishes to be evangelistic. Still, in my own conversations with members and attendees, I found that the pastor was not exaggerating. Quite a few members and attendees come from a non-Christian background.

The focus on the public meeting is also connected to the planter's personal stories. Einar, who grew up in another religious tradition, later tells me how he visited a Pentecostal church and was moved by the preacher's message. At the end of the service, he responded to the altar call:

> [Einar]: Then [the pastor] asked: Can I lay my hands on you? I say yes. And when he prays, my whole body begins to shake, and my tears start falling. It felt like a heavy stone had been lifted off of me. I know today that this is Jesus removing my sins, all that burdens me. From that moment, I was entirely sure that what the Christians said was true, but I didn't know what they believed. I had never read the Bible, the Bible is taboo, and you can't have or even touch a Bible. This led me to search, and I read [other religious scriptures] for the first time, trying to understand it. I read the Bible and studied science, which eventually showed me how waterproof Christianity was.

The ambition of the church plant is to provide space for individuals to make formative journeys towards the Christian faith. This is done by addressing concrete problems and existential questions that people struggle with in their everyday lives and then presenting Christianity as a way to tackle those issues. The church plant also introduces practices where individuals can respond and engage with the Christian faith. The connection between these patterns and the planter Einar's story is interesting. The meeting was the site for an important experience in his own faith journey, and now he organises a church plant where the meeting is the main practice. An introductory course and small groups supplement the formation in the meeting, but the main formative practice of the church plant is the meeting itself.

Creating Interest in Social Media
The use of social media is significant in the approach of the Industrial City church plant. During the initial phase, the planters started a podcast discussing the Christian faith and the Bible. The ambition is to record episodes in a language easily accessible to the average spiritually inclined Swede. While there is no distinct membership in the church community, a Facebook group for internal information and discussion becomes a community hub. Sven, one of the leading team members, notes the strategic naming of the Facebook group:

> [Sven]: We have a Facebook group for those who see [Industrial City] as their church. There was some thought to the group's name, "We who consider [Industrial City] as our church", not to scare anyone away. "We who belong to [Industrial City]" sounds a little sect-like.

You need to apply to become a member of this private group, and this gives the leaders and other members a signal that you intend to be part of this community. By Oct. 26, 2020, this group had 59 members: 23 men and 36 women, their ages ranging from 20 to 55. Around the same time, the average meeting was attended by about twice as many people. Still, social media is a central strategy for reaching new people, as Birgitta, one of the leaders, notes: "Many of those who come have been saved in [our church] and have no church background whatsoever", she tells me. When I ask where people come from, she points to three categories of new contacts:

> [Margareta]: Some have listened to our pod at a distance for some time and then have dared to come. Some bring their friends, and others find us on social media and are curious.

The relationship between the meeting and social media could be likened to fishing. Social media draws people towards the meeting net. In this way, the podcast, the practice of inviting friends to the meeting, and social media work together:

> [Einar]: ...one notices a rumour in the city that you hear when you go to the hairdresser. They know someone who knows someone.
>
> [Margareta]: People follow us at a distance and check us out...
>
> [Einar]: We have gone through ordinary people, not from above.
>
> [Margareta]: I think that is the difference. Ordinary people recommend us and spread the word.

When Margareta speaks of a "difference", she refers to the relative success of gathering a significant number of people. In contrast to their church plant, many other church plants – and established churches, too – find it difficult to gather a crowd.

The use of social media is a deliberate strategy based on the know-how of Einar and Margareta, who have been working with social media on a professional level. They know social media is a big part of people's everyday lives.[14] Initially, they used their private savings to invest in ads on Facebook and Instagram. Birgitta sees digital media as "a tool that we believe God has given to our church specifically".

Forging a Church Plant Model

In my conversations with Einar and Margareta, it becomes clear that while they are fully dedicated to this church plant, they also nurture plans and visions beyond Industrial City. I get the sense of being in a laboratory where they test and develop

---

[14] E.g. Mia Lövheim and Campbell, Heidi A (2017), "Considering Critical Methods and Theoretical Lenses in Digital Religion Studies", *New Media & Society*, 19 (1), 5–14; Ruth N. Bolton et al. (2013), "Understanding Generation Y and Their Use of Social Media: A Review and Research Agenda", *Journal of Service Management*, 24 (3), 245–267. According to Internetstiftelsen (2021), *Svenskarna och internet 2021*, Stockholm: Internetstiftelsen, 95% of Swedes are active on social media, the majority of them daily. People of the ages represented in the Industrial City church plant are the most active users.

ideas that will eventually be part of a more general model that can be taken to other cities. At the same time, Margareta and Einar want to bring the church community into this process. The goal is to plant a church that plants other churches.

> [Einar]: It should become a movement that somehow provides a framework to enter a new place and immediately focus on people.
>
> [Margareta]: When we start in a new place, it's not something that only Einar and I are doing, but the whole church in [Industrial City]. It's not like we take our backpacks and go around alone. That's why it takes longer than when we started here. We start in new places because we want the whole church to feel that this is our identity.

Einar reflects further on the kind of places where they might plant new churches and the differences he sees between larger and smaller cities and those in between, like Industrial City, which seems to be the target size:

> [Einar]: We have sometimes seen how the church is imported from larger to mid-sized cities. [...] I think cities of the same size share similarities in mentality and how you think. [...] They differ in the number of Christians and history and such. Overall, I think that if you crack the code in one of the cities, it might work. It will be easier to cooperate as well. Then, you don't have to cover all different areas and all scenarios.

From their previous experience, Einar and Margareta know the difficulties of using a large-city church concept in a mid-sized or small city. There is no one-size-fits-all model. The model will always need to be tailored and adjusted to fit the contextual conditions of a community, though the hope is that those adjustments will be minimal in other mid-sized cities. In addition, Einar sees possible gains in having some standards and networks for mid-sized city church plants to help the plants focus on the main task – people – instead of getting distracted by organisational issues. While they are committed to maintaining a presence in the middle of Industrial City and becoming a prominent voice in the city's culture, they feel sent to the wider region and similar cities in Sweden. This becomes clear during the map-drawing exercise:

> [Einar]: Perhaps you could put Sweden there.
>
> [Margareta]: But, please, I can't reach that far...
>
> [Björn]: Not everyone has my arms... But if you put some dots, where are you heading?
>
> [Margareta]: We will reach this region first.
>
> [Einar]: There are many. [names 6 Swedish cities with around 150 000 – 200 000 citizens]

For Einar, Sweden is part of their city map. While the goal is to plant a local church in Industrial City, the focus lies beyond this one church. They aim to plant similar churches that make up a network. Rather than using the map to zoom in on the particularities of the local place, Einar uses the map as a way of zooming out, thus putting the local in the context of a larger geographical vision.

In conclusion, the pro-social action of the church plant in Industrial City is visible through their attention to drawing visitors to the Sunday meetings and creating interest in social media. Further, their calling goes beyond Industrial City, as seen in their attempt to create a model for church plants in similar cities.

Calling: Forming Fishermen

The calling of the church planters in Industrial City has been analysed through their identity and intentions, their relationship to place, and how their pro-social action is envisioned and organised. The assumption has been that the purpose and mission embedded in the planter's sense of calling are reflected in the church plant community. The church planters of Industrial City feel called to provide space for individuals to make a formative journey towards a personal Christian faith. A strong missional identity and an emphasis on cultural sensitivity characterise the community. As we shall see in the following chapters, their purpose and mission are also essential to how they approach Christian formation.

The planters describe themselves as called to Industrial City, but at the same time, they want to forge a model for church plants in mid-sized Swedish cities. The church plant is particularly aimed at people new to the Christian faith. The church plant wants to be a community that reflects the message and person of Jesus Christ in a culturally sensitive manner. In the words of the planters, to be "real, relational, and relevant" are essential for the community.

The telos of the church plant is to form fishermen. The relationship between the culturally sensitive revival meeting, their strategic use of social media, and their personal invitations to the meeting shows a strong intentionality to form Christians who adhere to the call of Jesus to leave their old lives behind and engage in mission: "From now on, you will fish for people". The church plant has prepared a culturally sensitive net, and the regulars only need to invite new people to it.

5.2 The Calling to Cathedral City

In Cathedral City, the church plant approaches the local area differently than in Industrial City. While there are similarities in the planters' identity and intentions, these are articulated in a different manner. The neighbourhood, outside the city centre, plays a much more significant role in how this church plant understands its calling. Here, the planters want to gather a community and create a spiritual home for people in the area. They have a positive stance towards the neighbourhood but foster a faith-based culture. Their calling is even more place-oriented than Industrial City, and they want to be a mission station that equips people and sends them to new neighbourhoods. Being faithful neighbours is a formative ideal for the church plant.

Identity and Intention

The church plant in Cathedral City was initiated in 2019. The planting couple, Peter and Sofia, had previously planted a church in a neighbouring area in the same city. Quite early on in the process of planting this first church, Peter sensed they would not stay there forever. They remained, however, for seven years, at which point they had done their part and moved to another neighbourhood in the same city:

> [Peter]: Knowing so far in advance prepared us in our minds and pushed us to train new leaders for the day we would hand over to them.

This indicates that for these planters, the calling is not to the city in general but to a particular neighbourhood. The decision to move resulted from the sense of a divine calling to this new area in Cathedral City:

> [Sofia]: To us, there was actually no alternative to planting again. We had built trust [among people] in Cathedral City, and with all those contacts, it felt logical and convenient to use what we had already built. [...] And then you [Peter], especially, had already had a calling and longing to [this area]. And it fitted well with our family situation as well.

After moving, Peter and Sofia tried to gather a team, but they were unable to find people who wanted to join them in planting a new church. In fact, for the first six months, the church-planting team was only comprised of Peter, Sofia, and one other couple. As months passed, they were discouraged by the slow pace and lack of interest:

> [Peter]: We kind of knew there were not many who wanted to join us. But discovering that no one wanted to do it came as a shock. We thought we had built a pretty good trust and reputation. [...] It also becomes a bit personal when you are a church planter. In a way, you say: "Follow me!" And to follow me, you need to like me as a person. Implied, the lack of response means… nope, no one wants to join me…

Peter's story illustrates that the call to church planting is deeply personal. The degree of success or failure of the venture feels, to some extent, like an evaluation of the planter's status, character, and faith. Eventually, they were joined by a two-person team that had been assigned to their church plant by a bible school with a church-planting orientation. Two years later, there were five people leading the church plant, twelve dedicated members, and another twenty coming to Sunday meetings. The church plant is organised into six small groups of three to five persons.

Mission Station
In the church plant's introductory course, which all people interested in joining the church plant are expected to attend, it is explicitly stated that the church plant has a missional self-understanding. This means that they want to form a community culture that gazes to the horizon, beyond the church plant itself. The calling is to be a church plant that fosters members who want to plant other churches. In the course of informal conversations with some leaders in the church plant, I had heard about plans to reach out to another area of Cathedral City. These plans were confirmed in the membership introduction meeting that I attended when leaders explained the goal of forming a network of small church plants in Cathedral City. Even though the church plant is only two years old, its participants and leadership feel that the church has reached a point of sufficient stability to go to another area.

The church plant is in an ethnically diverse area, and the leadership wants to plant the next church in another diverse area:

> [Peter]: We sometimes say that we plant a church, but we also want to, or what we are actually doing is starting a mission station. We want to train people. We want to see people come to us, meet Jesus, train them, and send them on.

During spring of 2021, a small team was formed to support one of the former bible school team members, and this team was sent to plant a church in another neighbourhood – all while under Peter's mentorship.

In line with the discussion in the membership class I attended, Peter emphasises that membership is more than having the right to vote in the church assembly meeting. To be a member is to share and carry out the church's vision. Sure, assembly meetings make decisions, but to Peter, they are first and foremost services where the church seeks the mind of Christ – not gatherings where individuals express their opinions, debate, and vote. Prayerful conversations that lead to consensus decisions are ideal. The community discerns God's will together and then moves forward as one.[15]

---

[15] Cf. Neve (2021), p 178, sees a less formal decision-making process, with an emphasis on prayer and finding the will of God, in the Swedish Emerging Churches that he studies.

This means that mission is not something reserved for a charismatic leader. Rather, the leader's task is to form a community focused on mission. Accordingly, Peter's main responsibility is not preparing and preaching sermons but including new people in this work. To that end, he considers himself a project leader rather than a pastor.

> [Peter]: I don't want my identity limited by being only a pastor, and it is always important for me to have other jobs [outside the church]. Because I don't want to define myself as such, I don't want to be a professional Christian. I want to meet people. [...] I have another role here, standing in the background, giving direction, and coordinating things.

This statement reflects a non-hierarchic and non-professional understanding of ecclesial leadership – the community's interpretation of the priesthood of all believers. It is clear that Peter and Sofia have a pastoral function, and they lead the church plant by giving direction, recruiting leaders, and handling practical matters. At the same time, they do not want to be in the spotlight. Instead, they emphasise the collective identity of the community and its focus on mission.

Close Communities of Shared Faith

The small-group practice, which is significant to the Cathedral City church plant, will be introduced here but explored extensively later in the thesis. The small groups are close prayerful communities where faith is discovered through Bible study and the invitation to certain shared habits in the church plant. Peter's telling of his own path to Christian faith includes several characteristics that can be recognised in the life of the church he has planted:

> [Peter]: It was really a matter of maturity to grow into it and make the faith your own. For me, it happened when I was around the age of fourteen. I can't say exactly, but something like a strong hunger for Jesus was kindled. This led me to a lot of Bible reading. I devoured it, many chapters a day during those years. Faith became a part of me, and I am so grateful for this.

Growing faith is linked to a strong inner longing for Jesus, and reading the Bible represents a communication with God that nurtures this hunger. Christian formation is described in didactical terms rather than connected with rituals or strong experiences. At the same time, reading the Bible is more than a quest for information or a study of old texts. It is a response to a felt call to a relationship with God. Over time, Peter's prayerful reading results in the formation of his Christian identity. As will be evident in the next chapter, these characteristics are also seen in the formative practice of the church he plants.

In conclusion, the church plant has a strong intention towards being a missional community where all members are carriers of this calling. The identity also involves being a community of close relationships and embracing a Bible-reading spirituality that affects all areas of life.

The Significance of Place

Being visible and close to people in the local area is important to the Cathedral City church plant. Observations from three situations in the field show how the planters relate to their neighbourhood.

Neighbourhood Proximity
The neighbourhood where the church is planted is divided into three areas housing university students, migrants, and families living in residential buildings. The church plant gathers people by meeting publicly in the area's activity park during summertime and gathering in one or two homes during the cold season from late September to early May.

The summer is fading into autumn. Though the sun is shining, it is chilly and windy, so much so that I regret not bringing a warmer jacket as I rush towards the crowd gathered in the park. They have set up a table with books and bibles in different languages, and they are serving coffee. A group of people are socialising, involved in discussions and friendly chats. I recognise Swedish and English, but not the other languages being spoken around the table. The other centre of activity is the inflatable bouncy castle, where many children are waiting in line for their turn. Families and individuals pass by walking or biking, seemingly curious about the commotion. Next to the bicycle path, several small groups are gathering on the grass. Peter finds me and pulls me into a group just about to start reading a chapter from the Gospel of Luke about Jesus' crucifixion. They discuss the Bible text with the help of questions on a sheet of paper. After the group session, I continue chatting with a former journalist and sociology student from Turkey. He calls himself an agnostic but likes to discuss spiritual matters and has made a few friends in the community. The church plant considers this lively weekly gathering in the park to be their worship service.

Scene: Cathedral City, Aug. 31, 2019.

The home-based meetings each gather around 20 people. During my time in the church plant, these meetings had to be suspended due to pandemic restrictions and were replaced by prayer walks on Sunday afternoons. During these walks, the participants pray for the schools, the inhabitants of the neighbourhood, and the employees at the local health care centre.

> [Björn]: So the park thing is quite important?
>
> [Sofia]: Yes, because otherwise, we would not reach these people
>
> [Peter]: It is possibly the most central part of our work. [...] We can make new contacts there and develop them during the rest of the year. We have little to build on and fewer contacts unless we do our job. At least if we want to reach…
>
> [Sofia]: …the multicultural part of [the area].

Reaching the neighbourhood and being part of the local life is important for this church plant.[16] Compared to the Industrial City church plant, the Cathedral City plant has relatively little emphasis on social media and instead aims to be physically present in the neighbourhood by organising its community into small, diverse groups. The members also try to attend neighbourhood network meetings to be active in dealing with local issues. Meeting outside in small groups was still possible if the participants kept a distance of at least 1.5 meters from one another. I attended one such gathering in April 2021:

Spring arrives slowly in Cathedral City, and the ice-cold wind whips our faces as we gather on Maundy Thursday for evening mass in the park. A group of eight people stand in a circle wide enough to meet pandemic restrictions. The leaders alternate between speaking Swedish and English so that everyone can follow. Anders, one of the leaders, begins a prayer and leads us in a few simple worship songs. The texts, he informs us, can be found online if we use our phones to follow a link embedded in a QR code. Frozen fingers start to fumble to find the texts. We sing "How great is our God, sing with me how great is our God!" and a song based on John 3:16: "For God so

---

[16] James (2018), p 136: "The Neighborhood Incarnation model is anchored in a fundamental identification with the local neighborhood as a God-given parish. [...] Neighborhood Incarnation churches are incarnations of Christian community in, of and for their neighborhoods. They manifest as social bodies (Christian community) and material presences (spaces for hospitality)". This model reflects the orientation to place that is present in the church plant in Cathedral City.

loved the world that he gave his one and only Son, that whoever believes in him shall not perish but have eternal life". The park is sparsely populated, but the group sings loudly enough that passers-by seem curious about what is going on at the park's hill. As the singing ends, we take turns reading the texts from the Gospel of Mark about the gathering in the upper room and the betrayal of the Master. A celebration of the Last Supper follows this. The simple liturgy includes the words of inauguration and a prayer, but no breaking of the bread or raising the cup. After we exchange the greetings of peace, the apple juice and salty crackers are prepared at the table for everyone to fetch, in turn, while maintaining their distance. Personal prayer in pairs and worship songs in Swedish and Arabic end the liturgy. As the sun sets, the community disbands and returns home from the cold park, hopefully with warm hearts.

Scene: Cathedral City, April 1, 2021.

This Maundy Thursday mass is particularly important for the community since it is a gathering in person – not online, as was the usual practice at the time. But it is also important because it is a public service and a window for the people in the area. It gives them a chance to see something of the inner life of the church community. Being present in the public space is an essential part of the missional strategy of the church plant:

> [Sofia]: As [Peter] said, we have the services in the park during summer to create a low threshold and raise curiosity. "OK, what is going on over there?" Perhaps they might overhear what we pray, which is a testimony. We can do this openly; we don't have to be ashamed of it, and anyone is welcome to sit along if they want to. And people we have met before or talked to, it is easy to invite [them] to celebrate worship or sit along and pray.

In reflecting on public services, Sofia refers to Isaiah 58 about the true meaning of fasting and emphasises that it means caring for the weak and poor:

> [Sofia]: Caring for people is a big part of what constitutes a service as we do it. We don't want to get stuck in a certain view of service, reduced to only standing in aisles and lifting our hands to sing or listen to a sermon. Of course, that can be a service, but it doesn't really constitute it. Rather, the service is something much deeper and much more than that.

What Sofia and Peter find difficult when celebrating the worship service in public is integrating worship songs and charismatic practices like prophecy and healing naturally in the ways they do it when gathering in homes. Prayer and Bible readings are easier and the primary liturgical elements in their current services; caring for people is mainly witnessed in personal prayer for each participant in small groups.

On Easter Sunday, the community returns to the park for a short service with songs and readings, but interestingly, there is no Easter sermon. The gathering is short because the main event is an activity a few blocks away close to the local shopping mall. Tables are assembled with coffee and pastries, while another table has a spread of drawing books and crayons. These are ancillary, though. The church members are gathering here to hand out daffodils to everyone passing by, wishing them a happy Easter. People seem to enjoy the commotion around the tables, and conversations break out as new and well-known faces approach those serving coffee.

Scene: Cathedral City, April 4, 2021.

Both the Maundy Thursday and Easter Sunday services present a "missional window" into the life of the church plant and their approach to creating and maintaining relationships with the neighbourhood. Meeting outside in the neighbourhood is a conscious move. This approach is more relational than instrumental. The planters do not articulate very specific outcomes when they describe the expected result from these new contacts. Instead, the church community seems to enjoy the moment and simply appreciate meeting their neighbours.

The prayer walk mentioned above is also an example of place-bound practice with the neighbourhood in focus. Being present in and for the local area is part of the vision of the church plant, and therefore the idea of regular prayer walks had been suggested as a way for the church to remain visible and present during the pandemic. The church organized prayer walks in the past, but they were not part of the regular schedule. But during the pandemic, prayer walks partially replaced the Sunday service gathering and supplemented the Monday online service. The following episode describes one of these prayer-walk events:

5.2 The Calling to Cathedral City

The congregants gather at the empty schoolyard this sunny winter afternoon, and Sofia divides them into groups of three or four. I was assigned to a group with a visiting Bible school team member, a woman named Ingrid, and an Iranian migrant Mirjam, both of whom live in the neighbourhood. We are equipped with a map that marks the start of the route and the five prayer stations, each of which had a different focus: (1) Pray for families and immigrants; (2) Pray for the people we have met in the area during the last two years; (3) Pray that people in the area should be safe and feel at home; (4) Pray that more people would meet Jesus and join the church; (5) Pray for students so that they might experience Jesus as their friend and saviour. We alternate between prayers and conversations as we follow the trail to our next prayer stop.

Scene: Cathedral City, Jan. 10, 2020.

Neighbour is a word with more than one meaning. It can mean those living close to you, and it can mean people outside your immediate sphere of close relationships. Yet Jesus challenges divisions between close relatives, those who are and think like you, and other people: "You have heard that it was said, 'Love your neighbour and hate your enemy'. But I tell you, love your enemies and pray for those who persecute you". And "You shall love your neighbour as yourself" (Matt 5:44, 19:19 NIV).

Something of this is present in Cathedral City church plant. Neighbourhood proximity is central here, which means that the local area and the people living there are as essential to them as the church community itself. It recognises the area as a place where God is at work. To present a public window to their inner church life by celebrating worship services in the park is part of their missional strategy. Further, they get to know people in the area, thus being faithful neighbours. They want to connect with the people living around them and seek opportunities to be part of the local community's common life. The church members do this by lifting their community before God through embodied prayer practices.

Pro-Social Action

The engagement in the neighbourhood through the place-bound practices described above demonstrates the pro-social character of the church plant's calling. Beyond this, the church planters feel called to foster a spiritual home that gathers a diverse community. They want to create communities that are small, close, and relational. They eschew hierarchies and institutions. Their vision is to grow by creating a community network rather than one big church.

A Spiritual Home

The practices of the church plant in Cathedral City show a strongly relational ecclesiology. Being a home for people in the neighbourhood brings a missional focus with intentions of reaching out to new people through personal relations, inviting them to meetings and small groups as their spiritual home.[17] This is seen in the following quotes:

> [Sofia]: The goal is actually that people should… get to know Jesus.
>
> [Peter]: It is clearly about people coming to faith.
>
> [Sofia]: [The church plant] has as its vision that it should be a close community that is like a home to people.
>
> [Ingrid]: [The church plant] focuses on building relations with people and neighbours. That is the actual culture in the church, to meet in the park where people are. We talk to them and just engage with them as we are. We are part of the everyday realities here, in our community.

In the activities I attend, it is evident that the church plant wants to be a home for people and create an interest in a personal faith in Jesus. One of the participants, Ingrid, describes the missional culture formed in the church plant: to be where people are, engage with them and become part of their lives. Activities are organised to be accessible for newcomers. Not only are they open to people who already believe, but they are also open to anyone who might be interested in asking these kinds of questions:

> [Peter]: Partly, it is clearly [the goal of the church plant] that people would come to faith. But that one is hard to measure since it is so much of a process. So, I would rather consider it a success that people take distinct steps closer to Jesus. In this, you see if people grow in their discipleship and whether they have chosen to follow Jesus.

---

[17] Cf. Neve (2021), p 171, identifies a relational ecclesiology in the Emerging Church.

Peter's words point to formation beyond the binary conception of saved/not saved. Instead, he emphasises the process and direction in life, where the goal is to move "closer to Jesus".

Gathering a Diverse Community

As we have seen, the church plant in Cathedral City tries to reach the ethnic diversity represented in the area by being present in public spaces and building relations in various ways. Doing this well would mean that they themselves become a multicultural community, reflecting the diversity around them. because they want to be open to everyone, gatherings of the church plant are usually bilingual, with both Swedish and English being spoken.

Another way the Cathedral City church gathers people from diverse backgrounds is by using different kinds of introductory courses to the Christian faith, like Alpha, MyLife workshop, and Al Massira, which is especially suited for those with a Muslim background.[18] Al Massira gathers almost 30 people this time, while the online Alpha course draws 17 people. Anders, one of the leaders of the online Alpha course that the church plant organises with the Christian student organisation at the university, had this to say:

> [Anders]: The Alpha course has been very meaningful, and it is also an obvious place to grow by discussing faith with people who are not believers but interested in twisting and turning on issues, giving their perspectives and listening to mine.

In addition to the courses, two women who are trainees from a bible school meet and talk to people outside the local neighbourhood grocery store. Some of the people they meet are interested in the opportunity to speak Swedish and to have contact with other people, a scarcity during the COVID lockdown.

Calling: Forming Faithful Neighbours

The analysis of the church plant in Cathedral City reveals an emphasis on simple structures, close relationships, and a missional focus in close proximity – that is, in the immediate neighbourhood of the church plant. The church members describe a calling to meet new people, see them come to faith, and give them a spiritual home. They want to create a network of mission stations with close communities of shared faith that gather people of diverse backgrounds into close communities with small groups as one of the main practices. The Bible has a vital role in forming

---

[18] Al Massira: https://almassira.org [4 Sept 2023]. Alpha: https://alpha.org [4 Sept 2023]. MyLife: https://www.mylifeworkshop.net [4 Sept 2023].

the community. They intend to build a network of faith communities as they grow rather than becoming one big church. The vision is to plant small churches that plant other small churches. The formative telos of the church plant can be described as shaping faithful neighbours. The fact that the church plant encourages virtues such as hospitality and kindness through their formative practices attests to this analysis.

5.3 The Calling to Harbour City

Like the community in Cathedral City, the Harbour City church plant has a positive view of engagement in society and the place where the church is being planted. As an example of this, the planters are actively partnering with non-religious organisations in their social work.

Identity and Intention

The church plant sees itself as a community on a mission with the peace and justice of the kingdom of God and endeavours to set up an "equalising table" in an unjust city. A typical ideal for this church plant is a person who leaves a comfortable place and position to cross cultural and social barriers to meeting a stranger. The Harbour City plant values diversity and has a strong sense of being sent on a mission.

Life-affirming Mission

As in the other cases we have studied, these planters' own journey significantly informs the approach adopted by the new community. The church plant in Harbour City started when an old church closed a few years earlier. The main planters, Karl and Sara, moved to Harbor City after a proposal from their denomination. Previously, they had been leading a church plant in the United Kingdom and brought their ideals and experiences with them. One lesson they learned there concerned priorities and the relation between life in general and the work of planting a church. Karl describes this hard-won experience from their time in the UK:

> [Karl]: I decided to go full steam ahead without building a life. So, the church was first in our visions. You know, just let's get this job done. And [we] didn't create sustainable friendships in the community. [...] I didn't enjoy this as much as I thought I would. So it was during that time that I would begin learning, reading, just putting myself in different spaces, different communities outside the [denomination].

"Building a life" seems to mean balancing church work and social life and forming a church community around close and real relations. He found no joy in his initial task-oriented way of planting a church, and the crisis led him to develop another approach to it and use a different language for what he was doing.

As the couple finished their work in the UK and moved to Sweden, they wanted to continue walking on this new path. Their denomination suggested Harbour City, and as they went there, they sensed that God confirmed this decision:

> [Karl]: We could have gone to several places in Sweden, but it didn't feel quite right, and then [Harbour City] was offered to us by the [Denomination]. So I had actually been here once, for about an hour for lunch, so we had seen Harbour City before. And for some reason, we went just: yeah, that's him, that's God.

At first, they decided to move to the centre of the city. Karl took daily walks on the nearby streets and visited the shops and hairdressers to make contact with the owners and workers. Sara started to build a network with different partners in the city, including hotels, local social services, and the police. Her focus was to help victims of trafficking, a known problem in the city. Today, Sara, together with Kristina, one of the other leaders in the church plant, visits massage salons and tries to connect with Harbour City's sex workers. Part of the vision is to build relations and partnerships with other organisations to make a greater impact in the city.

> [Karl]: We're here to join things, get to know our community and work out where God's will is being done.

Equality

Karl uses the table as a metaphor to describe the intention of bringing God's kingdom of peace and justice through the church plant. The shared table is where stories of life are told and interpreted in the light of the Gospel stories, which brings people from different backgrounds together:

> [Karl]: We want to create networks and friendships and invite people into their homes. Share the table. Where else does this happen? I think the church is called to share the table, which is an amazing equaliser. I think that is inherent in our Christian heritage – The table. [...] I think we often underestimate the power of sharing a story and experience. But we cannot do good theology detached from people's lives. So we really raise people telling their stories. And we don't edit out the pain.

According to Karl, being missional means making missions a part of your personal life. Rather than building a traditional church structure, he describes it as being on a journey of discovery, where they try to find out where God is at work and establish spaces – or tables – of kingdom expressions:

> [Karl]: What does the good news look like? For our city. Where is it broken? Where is it lovable? Where is it beautiful? Where is it not beautiful? Where is God's will being done? And the Lord's prayer, may your will be done, here in [Harbour City] as it is in heaven

> – I think it is both the unspoken longing and drive for all of us. [...] We are often quite surprised that even in the darkest places, He shows up. That has been part of our story, that we have found God in some unlikely people, unlikely places, and unlikely situations. That is the purpose of the church.

Shaping welcoming milieus for people with different backgrounds is a complex task. Having good intentions does not necessarily mean that people feel welcome. But Marianne, one of the members, is positive when she describes how the church plant approaches new people:

> [Marianne]: It is so good to know that you don't have to hide anything because [the church] accepts you anyway. No prejudice, nothing! They are actually amazing. Do you get it?
>
> [Björn]: What is that all about? Community or what?
>
> [Marianne]: It is the Christian community. I don't want to say just community. That would be unfair. It is the Christian [emphasis] community.

Karl tells the story of a member of the church plant who felt very uncomfortable when he tried to communicate with another man who spoke neither Swedish nor English. But the church member discovered they had one thing in common: they played chess. So they started to meet to play chess without being able to speak with each other. Karl says of the member: "But he did the hard thing. He got out of his comfort zone. And it is the mutual getting out of your comfort zone, which we place as a real high thing in church".

Stories like this, about crossing cultural barriers, are important in forming the community since they serve as heroic examples of making the mission personal. This ideal reflects what is communicated in Jesus' story about the good Samaritan. When the religious leaders pass by the wounded and robbed man on the way to Jericho, "a Samaritan, as he travelled, came where the man was; and when he saw him, he took pity on him. He went to him and bandaged his wounds" (Luk 10:33–34 NIV). The church plant in Harbour City places great emphasis on this ideal of crossing ethnic, religious, and political borders to care for fellow humans. They want to shape Good Samaritans.

Unity in Diversity

The church plant in Harbour City emphasises that God has called each person in a specific way and has given them a unique mix of gifts to serve the church and the world. This belief takes shape in the way different groups are formed as places to discover and develop gifts in people's lives. These groups are usually very small, and the leaders' main role is to provide a kind of apprenticeship for the participants.[19] Finding a common language has been important for the team and is a significant part of forming their church community. They use the language of the "APEST", a model developed by Alan Hirsch and Michael Frost. APEST is an acronym for Apostle, Pastor, Evangelist, Shepherd, and Teacher.[20]

In Karl's journey as a church planter, he describes a crisis that leads him to the writings of Hirsch and Frost and the discovery of APEST missional language and approach. This part of the missional movement critiques the established church for being too focused on shepherd-teacher leaders, normally called "pastors". This figurative church body has, they argue, a disproportionately large head sitting atop short arms and legs. It prioritises teaching as a cognitive exercise in preaching and caring for the already-gathered community. This means that the evangelistic, apostolic, and prophetic aspects are neglected in the larger mission. The APEST understanding lifts these aspects of the church life and helps the leaders see both how they can complement each member of the team and how each person can contribute to the whole. Someone can, for instance, have a strong apostolic gift with a prophetic orientation. This can be combined with a dedication to justice issues in an entrepreneurial church plant. Another person can be more of a shepherd, caring for the people in the community. This can be paired with a church that has an evangelistic sensibility, reaching outside of the community fence to meet new people.

A River, Not a Lake

The church plant in Harbour City has no intention of becoming a big church. Still, it wishes to multiply in the city and beyond and birth several smaller communities of faith and social engagement – a goal reminiscent of the church plant in Cathedral City. In discussing that long-term goal, Karl describes the church as a river rather than a lake:

> [Karl]: We try to learn a different way and not to fill [seats in a building] to get church done, but it's really about these people. So, the sending element is crucial. We want to be a river rather than a lake, which just holds water. We want to send people.

The point here is that there needs to be a flow of people sent into the world, otherwise, the church has failed its mission. To be able to plant more churches or

---

[19] The inner workings of these groups will be further discussed in the next chapter.

[20] This is taken from the book of Ephesians [Eph 4:11-13]. The APEST model is part of the missional movement discourse, of which Alan Hirsch and Michael Frost are proponents. This will be further described in the following chapter.

spark new initiatives, the leaders of the church plant in Harbour City have started an international network for missional leaders, and they also produce a podcast for "missionally minded" people.

It is the beginning of June, and I sit under the apple tree, trying to connect on Zoom again. This time, I am invited to be a guest at a missional network meeting, gathering people from all over the world, though mainly Europeans. Sara from Harbour City welcomes everyone as the intro presentation and music stop, and the meeting is about to formally begin. She extends a special welcome to me as a guest from Sweden. The fourteen people are all in some way involved in church planting or different missional projects. A woman from Brazil leads a short devotion with texts from the book of Psalms. She gives us three questions: who is God, what do I receive from God, and what is my response? These questions are discussed in breakout rooms, which I am not invited to attend. As the group is regathering, we watch a short video of Alan Hirsch discussing the theme of being gospel-centred versus Jesus-centred. Being something of a guru of the missional movement, his message is that we should not downgrade something living (i.e. Jesus) to mere words. We discuss this in groups for a while – this time, I am invited to be part of one – and summarise the wisdom we have received before we return. The gathering ends with prayer.

Scene: Harbour City, June 8, 2021.

In conclusion, the Harbour City church plant offers a stark contrast to the free church tradition of inviting people to big gatherings, as is done in the Industrial City church plant. The metaphor of being a river, not a lake, represents this well and characterises the church's calling in Harbour City. They want to be a community of equality in the city and gather people from diverse backgrounds in Christian unity for mission, all in a life-affirming way.

The Significance of Place

The church plant inherited a building from another church that was closing. This building was in a prominent part of the city, but as they were hoping to minister to a broad group of people, especially the less privileged, the team decided to sell it. In its stead, they rented a storefront in a better-suited location in the city centre.

❦

One of the church planters extends a warm invitation to the facilities of the church plant for our first in-person meeting. After sitting down for some coffee with the church-planting team, Elisabet, the current leader of the church plant, suggests a walk in the surrounding area. Due to the pandemic restrictions, the winding streets of the old city centre are empty on this cold spring morning. We head towards the location of the old church building that was left as the new church was planted. They tell me that the decision to sell the building was motivated, in part, by their sense that it represented a tradition that demanded adherence and respect that was suffocating. It did not seem like an inviting place to form a new church. But even more important, Elisabet says, is the location of the building. She points to the shops, hairdressers, and art galleries adjacent to the old church building. For Elisabet, it is obvious that the clientele that populates this area represents a privileged group in the city.

We turn southward, and Elisabet, who used to work at the municipal social services, points out how the buildings and the people we observe change shape and character. We reach a town square where people usually sell vegetables, fruits, and a variety of other things. There is also another church there, whose presence is manifested with diaconal workers. Police officers are often stationed here, and Elisabet tells me they are there to counter the drug trafficking that is going on beyond the gaze of a casual visitor like me.

Scene: Harbour City, March 25, 2021.

❦

Engaging the Margins of Society
This episode from the field studies in Harbour City has stayed with me for several reasons. To begin with, it shows how the church plant is sensitive to the social and material realities of the city they serve – and how the planters are more interested in attending to them by joining others than building their own organisation.

Further, I witnessed the leap of faith they took in selling their old church building, abandoning the traditional ways of being a church, and moving into a more contested and marginal space, where they are guests rather than hosts, representing a listening posture towards the surrounding context. This approach is not without risks, including the risk that the church plant will become activistic, performance-oriented, and overwhelmed since the needs of society will always exceed the capacity of the church body. Will the less wealthy residents only look at them as providers, no matter how hard they try to meet them at an equal level? According to the church planter Karl, leaving privilege and comfort comes with a price:

> [Karl]: For [Sara], this is a real struggle. You know, but for me, it is really life-giving, and I love it. It's second nature. I love to get to know my neighbours. And so just being a neighbour, not isolating myself, and I also don't like hanging out with Christians. I love Christians, and it's life-giving. But I can't… that has been the greatest drain of my life, to be in a Christian bubble. So, it doesn't come naturally to me. I like to be in the world. I would much rather be in the pub than in the church. That's just the environment where I tend to have more spiritual life-giving conversations for some reason.

Karl's comparison of the church and the pub and what they represent is noteworthy. The traditional church, for Karl, is a place and culture that is safe and pleasant but fails to be relevant for most people. Staying in the traditional church means being a guardian of the past, and Karl feels called to leave "the bubble" and do something that he finds meaningful – not only for himself but also for those who do not usually fit in the church. But if ministering at the margins of society is natural and life-giving for Karl, others may find it taxing and stressful. While this is a tension that the church plant is aware of, being among the marginalized is essential to the planters' understanding of being a church.

In fact, during my time in the church plant, the leadership was discussing finding a new locale far outside the city centre in a socially exposed neighbourhood. The particular area they had in mind was more ethnically diverse and had higher crime rates than their present location in the city centre. I interpret these discussions as expressions of a longing to deeply know and serve the less privileged, a kind of intimate, personal ministry that is difficult to foster in the commotion and anonymity of the city centre.

> [Elisabet]: This new place should be, perhaps even more than here, a meeting place where not only we have access but where we can bless the area in many different ways. We don't need to put our name on all the walls. We want the place to serve the area as much as possible, together with others as well.

Sara adds to Elisabet's comment by articulating a two-part vision. The place should serve as a house of healing, like a health care centre for the soul, while also equipping people for mission. She acknowledges that these two things could be difficult to combine. People who need healing might find themselves treated like objects of missional training. As pointed out earlier, these two conflicting visions are foundational for the church plant in Harbour City. Interestingly, in discussing a new location, the planters envision a potential move as part of their placemaking. In the upper room of the storefront they rent, the walls are covered with words of vision and prayers regarding this moving process. Clearly, this is very much a community-involving process. They left the well-known, old church building in the privileged part of the city and moved to the current place with dreams of an unknown future in the margins:

> [Elisabet]: We move farther and farther out in the margins, possibly both from the traditional view of the church – we try to get moving into the adventure as far as we can to be able to observe what God is actually up to – and also a movement closer to people that live outside the fringes of society. That is the journey we're on.

In the reflection about a place, Elisabeth connects their calling to a theology of restoration of beauty:

> [Elisabet]: We really believe that Christians can be part of bringing life to those places. A building can receive new life, and people will be able to see the good that comes out of it. Resurrection needs a physical dimension, getting a taste of... wow, this is the God they worship. I see the flowers, smell the freshly baked bread, and feel how people receive joy and community in this place that was so ugly. This manifestation of God's restoration power can also be involved in buildings and places.

In conclusion, I find that the church plant in Harbour City is intentional in its move towards the margin, both in the sense of leaving a privileged position and moving to geographical areas outside the centre of economic and political power. This move is theologically motivated since they believe that God works among people in society's margins, and therefore, it is the task of the church to do the same – to embody the journey of the good Samaritan. This approach to church planting is significantly different from the approach of the church plant in Industrial City, with its focus on being part of the centre of both the city and the cultural conversation.

Pro-Social Action

The Harbour City church plant aims to reach people by being guests rather than hosts and by doing rather than speaking the good news. They build relationships through the church plant's social work and have consciously decided to prioritise serving people over building the church.[21] This is slow work and depends to a high degree on the church-planting team.

---

[21] Moynagh (2012), p 205. Moynagh refers to this approach as the "serving-first journey".

Being Guests

The planters approached the city with a vision to embody the kingdom of God among the poor, weak and outcast. It's obvious that this is far more than a private project to the planters. However, the church planters find their lives meaningful when they mean something to others. They speak about coming as guests, not hosts, representing a listening posture towards the surrounding context.[22]

> [Karl]: The idea of being host is maybe something that we [as the church in the West] had some time ago when we had a position of authority. Maybe the Swedish church has got something of that. We had a position of authority. People respect who we are. People listened to our teaching. From what I see in the secularised Swedish context, no one really cares. So the idea of being a host and putting all your energy into inviting people to things really is the most ineffective model of a church you could ever come up with. [...] So our mindset was not... could we start something, open an event, or start a gathering for worship? We were much more having the sense that we were guests rather than hosts. We're here to join things.

When asking the leadership team what this approach means and when they have seen this vision manifested during the five years of church planting in Harbour City, I get a few different examples. Karl mentions the so-called "migrant crisis" that immediately offered opportunities to meet people as migrants arrived in the city and needed food, shelter, and contacts. They set up a project with another church that connected families, most of them Syrian, with people in the churches. Sara tells me about a woman who had been a sex worker and recently had an experience with God. Elisabeth gives an example of a woman in the church whose son they supported during his time in prison. Now, his mother never misses an opportunity to share her joy and appreciation with her friends and in the church. These stories exemplify the planting team's "guest approach" ideal and its goal of building relations with people – a clear departure from a "host approach", where they would instead build a church organisation and host activities to attract people.

Social Work

Social work is a central practice in this church plant, first and foremost, because the planters see it as enacting the kingdom of God. The social work flows from

---

[22] Neve (2021), pp 198, 203, argues that the church in the West is more inclined to come with ready solutions and answers than having a listening mind-set in mission and that the Emerging Churches, which he is studying, "remind us that the practice of listening is not only an important but essential missional practice in today's culture". James (2018), p 228, argues that "the overlapping and interwoven postures of guest and host to the world and to God express the true nature of the church".

their desire to live out justice and peace as a community on a mission in the middle of the city. As a result of this, people join the community, but that is a secondary effect, not a driving motivation:

> [Karl]: I think peace, shalom, is the ultimate expression of the gospel – peace with God but also peace with one another. You take Love of the enemy out of Christianity, and it is no longer Christianity [...]. The church has a great role in rehumanising the story of people's lives because hell, whatever that is, is what many people already live in. If the church was really serious about hell, then [the church] would recognise that they've got good news.

As Karl sees it, the church is practising the good news of the gospel. It is not enough to talk about the gospel in church gatherings. It needs to be acted out.[23] As Karl describes it, social work is good in and of itself, and as such, it does not need to lead to church growth. Karl emphasises this repeatedly during our interviews and informal talks. He distances himself from what he considers to be the conventional approach among church planters, an approach that prioritizes growing a church community by moving into the city, presenting a vision, and gathering a crowd.

> [Karl]: Our question is not how we can grow our church but how to grow the kingdom of God. [...] We don't want to be a church that just gathers just on Sunday. We want to see our city transformed and the kingdom of God take root in all of it, really.

Karl's focus is not at church meetings but elsewhere. Services are not their main method of reaching people. The church plant has not gathered for larger on-site meetings during the pandemic, but even before the pandemic, Sara explains, the Sunday services were not an altogether positive experience. The meetings were messy and lacked a natural flow. Instead, they get new contacts by being present in people's lives in other ways:

> [Kristina]: The new people who have joined during this time have largely come through our wider work, just because we are there or through relations.

Kristina and the other leaders rarely hold gatherings in the storefront. They meet people in other places, mainly through social work and build relationships with them. The pro-social action of the church plant in Harbour City is its theologically grounded social work. This is seen both in action and the reflection of the planters.

---

[23] James (2018), p 125, The church plant in Harbour City resembles the New Community model in that it embodies "a practical ecclesiology that is at once eschatological in its underlying vision"; however, the New Community's institutional, liturgical, and progressive identity are not as prominent in Harbour City church plant.

Calling: Forming Good Samaritans

The calling of the church plant in Harbour City is to engage the margins of society through social work and to present an open and equal community in the city where Jesus builds unity amid diversity. Karl's table metaphor describes the church's pro-social vision of bringing God's kingdom of peace and justice to fruition; as noted above, the shared table is where stories of life are told and interpreted in the larger story of the gospel. The planters intend to foster a life-affirming way of being a church community and are involving new people in faith and mission. The church plant aims to reach people not only by being guests rather than hosts but also by enacting and embodying the good news rather than just proclaiming and speaking it. The hero in the church plant is a person who, like the good Samaritan in Jesus' parable, leaves a comfortable place and position to cross-cultural and social barriers in order to care for the stranger. This is the formative telos of the church plant.

5.4 Conclusion

The callings of the church plants have been analysed through their identities and intentions, the significance of place and pro-social actions. The Industrial City church planters feel called to provide a space for individuals to journey towards a personal Christian faith, and to that end are creating interest through social media, inviting people to the professionally produced church services, and then introducing them to Jesus. This church plant's identity is bound to its calling of being a culturally sensitive voice in the centre of the city and the centre of the cultural discussion. This calling stretches beyond its Industrial City church plant in that the planters want to develop a missional model for planting churches in similar mid-sized Swedish cities. In their view, the vision of lived Christian identity is that of a person who follows Jesus to become a fisherman. This ideal is a culturally aware person who participates in church activities on social media and in worship meetings, and witness to people with the goal of bringing them to the church activities.

In Cathedral City, the planters feel called to reach and lead people to faith and create a spiritual home for them by establishing missional proximity in the neighbourhood. They embody a vision of creating close-knit, diverse Bible-reading and virtue-forming communities of shared faith and building a network of missional communities instead of one big church. Their vision of lived Christian identity is the faithful neighbour who reads the Bible and approaches it as God's voice in everyday life, shares life with others, forms the common virtues of the church community, and engages in the church's mission towards the neighbourhood.

The planters in Harbour City feel called to the margins of society, where they reach people by being guests rather than hosts and by doing and being the good news. They want to be an equalising table in the city, a place where Jesus builds peace, justice, and unity amid diversity. This calling is realised through their emphasis on social work. The planters feel called to build authentic life as a community, involving and supporting new people in the mission. Their ideal of lived Christian identity is a person who embodies the good news of Jesus by crossing cultural and social borders to engage with people as equals. This person, like a good Samaritan, is part of the common mission and uses her gifts in its service while supporting others in seeking God's kingdom in the city.

	Industrial City	Cathedral City	Harbour City
Identity and intention	Missional orientation, Cultural sensitivity	Missions station, close communities of shared faith	Life-affirming mission, equality, unity in diversity, a river, not a lake
Significance of place	Engaging secular culture at the centre	Neighbourhood proximity	Engaging the margins of society
Pro-social action	Inviting to the meeting, creating interest in social media, forging a church plant model	A spiritual home, gathering a diverse community	Being guests, social work
Formative telos	Fishermen	Faithful neighbours	Good Samaritans

Table 3: Callings of the church plants.

Calling is closely related to Christian formation as a sense of clarity of purpose and personal mission leading to action with a pro-social intention. The church plants understand a calling as God's urging of individuals or groups to take personal responsibility for a particular task directed towards people in a particular place. For the church planters, their calling becomes part of their identity. But the calling is also coming from, or related to, a sense of dissatisfaction with contemporary culture, which they think excludes God and faith from people's lives. The planters all feel a tension between what is and what should be, and they take on the task of being agents of change. This change is accomplished by ecclesial re-innovation and missional action, with the hope of leading people to become Christians.

6. Formative Practices

In the introduction, I stated that practices are at the centre of this thesis. The previous chapter laid out the ideals that each church plant aspires to, which included the kind of church the planters are trying to develop as well as the kind of Christian identity each church wants to form. In this chapter, I will look deeper at the formation of Christians. How are these churches actively working towards their ideals? I will study one formative practice that plays a significant role in each church plant and, in doing so, answer the research question: *What practices of Christian formation are present in the communities?*

6.1 Analysing Practices of Christian Formation

I have tentatively defined Christian formation as social practices intended to shape Christian faith and lived Christian identity. When a church is planted, different activities are initiated to reach people and gather them into a church community. Some activities have clear missional intentions, which means that they are initiated to get in contact with and gather new people. Other activities are intended to form a stronger sense of community or common ecclesial identity. In the church plants I have studied, formation involves developing a community with a common self-understanding, a purpose of being, organisational structures, a culture, and other issues that are essential to the church plants.

According to Lave and Wenger's theory, practices are always communal and dynamic. A community of practice has a centre and a periphery, and learning consists of a movement from the periphery towards fuller participation in the practice.[1] In this sense, the formation involves not only individual or cognitive matters but also changes in identity and practice for both individual participants and the practising community.

In analysing each of the three church's main formative practices – revival meetings, small groups, and apprenticeships – I will demonstrate how they are

---

[1] However, the movement can also be in a direction from the centre of the community of practice, resulting in another kind of change in identity and practice.

performed through a flow of sub-practices. The parts that build up the actual practice.[2] Further, I note that these particular formative practices are performed in a landscape of other community practices. I will identify important aspects of each practice for forming the church community and the persons in it. These include the telos, the ways to engage in the practice, and the traditions present in the formation practices. Finally, I will point to the use of tools in the respective practices. While the concept of tools is more significant in other practice theories, Wenger emphasises the significance of tools in providing imagination and a common language.[3]

Landscape of Practices

A particular practice does not exist in isolation but relates to other practices in a landscape. Wenger initially used the term "constellations of practices" to describe this phenomenon, though he later adopted the metaphor "landscape of practices".[4] When analysing a practice, we should understand it as related to other practices and not as an isolated phenomenon.

As part of planting each of the three churches, the church planters have initiated different practices within each church's unique context. Table 4 shows the main practices found in each church plant.[5] The three formative practices presented in this chapter have been selected based on their significance to Christian formation in the church plants, and they align well with the respective church plant's teloi.

In Industrial City, the public meeting is central to the self-understanding and missional strategy of the church plant as a public voice in the middle of the city. In Cathedral City, the small group is critical for the formation of common habits that support the telos of the church plant. However, the landscape of practices in the

---

[2] Fahlgren (2015), p 100. I follow Sune Fahlgren, who uses the language of practice – subpractice, where significant ecclesial practices are built up by their sub-practices.

[3] Wenger (1999), p 186.

[4] Wenger (1999); Etienne Wenger-Trayner et al. (2014), *Learning in Landscapes of Practice: Boundaries, Identity, and Knowledgeability in Practice-based Learning*, Oxfordshire: Routledge; Nicolini (2012); S. Kemmis et al. (2012), "Ecologies of Practices", in Hager, Paul, Lee, Alison, and Reich, Ann (eds.), *Practice, Learning and Change* (Berlin: Springer), 33–50. Davide Nicolini talks about the concept of "bundles of practices", while Stephen Kemmis instead refers to "practice ecologies".

[5] The term practice, in this study, is used as an analytical vehicle as part of practice theory. It is a way of describing what is going on holistically in a certain context that entails social as well as individual, material as well as cognitive and matters of identity as well as power structures, tradition and understandings of place.

Cathedral City church plant is not centred on one practice as is the case in the Industrial City church plant, where the meetings are central. At the Harbour City church plant, the landscape is even more flat, and it is an open question about which practice is the most significant to Christian formation. That being said, the practice of developing apprenticing relationships draws together many of the main features of the church's approach to forming Christians, and to that end, I consider it the church's main formative practice.

Industrial City	Cathedral City	Harbour City
Social media	Home/park meeting	Social ministry
Public meeting	Book table at the mall	Apprenticeship relationships
Intro course	Small group	Small group
Small group	Prayer walk	Public meeting

Table 4: The landscape of practices of the church plants.

Traditions of Formation

History is an integral part of the formative practices in these church plants. I will, therefore, analyse how these church plants draw from free church tradition in developing their formative practices. Three formative practice traditions are particularly relevant in the case of the three church plants in this study: the revival meeting, the conventicle, and social ministry; historically, these practice traditions have each played a significant role in forming Christian identities within the Swedish free churches.

The revival meeting tradition is recognisable in its aim at individual conversion and salvation through an experience and decision to become a Christian.[6] It has an informal liturgy consisting mainly of singing, preaching, witnessing, and common prayer.[7] Traditionally, the sermon represents the main part of the revival meeting, is delivered in a personal tone, is only loosely structured, and speaks to the heart to

---

[6] Gunnar Hallingberg (2010), *Läsarna: 1800-talet folkväckelse och det moderna genombrottet*, Stockholm: Atlantis, p 238.

[7] Joel Halldorf (2015), "'En församling i varje stad' – Ideal för lokal församlingsverksamhet i 1900-talets svenska pingströrelse", in Josefsson, Ulrik and Wahlström, Magnus (eds.), *Församlingsplantering i Pingst – Rapport från ett forskningsprojekt på IPS 2015* (Forskningsrapporter från Institutet för Pentekostala Studier, Nr 6; Institutet för Pentekostala Studier), 39–62. Halldorf refers to Lewi Pethrus, the founder and leader of the Swedish Pentecostal movement, who found the big meetings to be of great inspirational significance since the curious visitor can remain anonymous in the crowd (p 56).

lead the person towards conversion. The sermon can be accompanied by individuals offering testimonies of their personal experiences with God, while heartfelt worship songs give the participants a way to respond to the message.[8]

The conventicle is a small gathering for ordinary Christians. While there might be a designated leader, this is usually a layperson. The small, intimate community enhances relationships and the ministry of all believers by delegating leadership to laypeople.[9] This practice consists of simple worship songs; Bible reading, and personal, heart-led prayer – all in a home setting.

Urban social ministry can take many forms and complement the sermon as a way of expressing the gospel through action rather than just words. It explains what Christianity means in a way that is easy to comprehend.[10] The urban context, of course, makes the social misery more evident to the churches. In addition to helping people, the practice gives the Christian community a good reputation within the larger society. The emphasis on social ministry in the free church tradition has varied over time, and it has sometimes been secondary to the meeting and conventicle.

As I will show below, these practice traditions are present to different degrees in the three church plants. This is expected since they are part of denominations that carry the free church legacy.[11] In the previous chapter, I showed that the church plants share the evangelical conviction that individuals need to respond to the gospel, that is, the offer from God to receive eternal life in Jesus Christ.[12] While the

---

[8] Joel Halldorf (2018), "Mötet i frikyrklighet och väckelse", in Sundmark, Stina Fallberg (ed.), *Kristen gudstjänst: en introduktion* (Skellefteå: Artos), 137–168.

[9] Halldorf (2018).

[10] Christian T. Collins Winn et al. (2011), *The Pietist Impulse in Christianity*, Eugene, Oregon: Wipf and Stock; David J. Bosch (2011), *Transforming Mission*, New York: Orbis Books, p 259. Ulrik Josefsson (2005), *Liv och över nog: den tidiga pingströrelsens spiritualitet*, Skellefteå: Artos p 274.

[11] The choice to not disclose the denominational associations for confidentiality reasons, to a degree blurs the connections with these practice traditions.

[12] Cf. David W. Bebbington (1989), *Evangelicalism in Modern Britain*, London: Psychology Press. The "Quadrilateral" that Bebbington proposes to describe British evangelical Protestantism emphasises conversionism, activism, biblicism, and crucicentrism. While there are differences in nuance, I take these four marks of British Evangelicalism to be roughly accurate in describing the Swedish free church tradition as well. In the emerging Swedish free church movement, the emphasis on conversion was significant.

planters use various languages to describe this motif, it is present in each church and connected to their respective callings to plant new churches. This conviction is most clearly seen in the meeting practice in the Industrial City church plant. The conventicle practice tradition is helpful for relationship-building. While it can be found to some degree in all three church plants, it has a particularly prominent place in the Cathedral City church plant.[13] The emphasis on social ministry is much stronger in the church plant in Harbour City and Cathedral City than in Industrial City. While this can partly be accounted for by denominational legacy, I would argue that it, even more, is a result of a personal calling in the lives of the church planters.

6.2 The Revival Meeting Practice in Industrial City

The public meeting is the main formative practice in the Industrial City church plant. It is this bi-weekly public meeting to which the church invites visitors, and it is there the whole church gathers to hear the preaching of the gospel. Before the COVID-19 pandemic, a meeting's attendance averaged between 50–80 people, and it was obvious how much time, energy, financial resources, and focus are invested in the meeting. The first leadership team meeting I attended is largely devoted to evaluating the previous Sunday's worship meeting and planning the next meeting.[14] While small groups are important for building relations and growing deeper in faith, the meeting is also the gateway to the small groups. By attending the larger meetings, you can be invited to a small group or an introductory course to the Christian faith. The activities in social media are also aimed at reaching people and inviting them to the meeting. In this way, social media could be likened to a fishing net, while the meeting is the harbour where fishing boats deliver the catch.

> [Birgitta]: It often starts at the service. That is where people come in, and most go on to the introductory course. That is where we lay the foundation, but most work is probably done in small groups. There, you build relations, and you have a designated leader to follow.

At the church plant team leaders' meeting, they discuss ways to hold the bi-weekly meeting every week. Margareta shares a plan she and her husband have about a different kind of meeting. The ordinary Sunday service is aimed at newcomers, but now they have identified a need to offer practices that help the average Christian to grow in faith. The answer to this need is "My Church Meeting", a gathering

---

[13] E.g. Neve (2021); Moberg (2013).
[14] Jan. 7, 2020.

where they work with "why-issues and values, with the Bible and Q & A", she explains. Therefore, the monthly "My church meeting" would have a different telos than the ordinary meeting. It would be about strengthening the community's core group rather than reaching new converts.[15]

The need to develop a new kind of meeting that fosters a deeper faith indicates the mission-oriented character of the regular meeting. Indeed, most of the regular attendees have a task or responsibility during the Sunday meeting. For example, the welcoming team is tasked with ensuring that everyone who comes to church feels welcomed. Meanwhile, others are preparing coffee or gathering the children for a children's meeting. The collaborative structure holds the meeting practice together, which is evident from the moment visitors are welcomed at the door, throughout the worship service, and even after the service is over when they are socialising and drinking coffee in the mingling area. (When gathering without COVID restrictions).

Flow of Sub-Practices

The end of summer is approaching, which means that students are coming back to town from holiday adventures and returning to university.[16] This Sunday, the revival meetings are resuming after the pandemic restrictions of the spring and summer, including a semi-lockdown, made public meetings impossible. Using a commercial event service, I booked a ticket to the first of two meetings on this day. Each of them allows a maximum of 50 people, which is in line with the government restrictions at the time. During the service, I observed how a flow of sub-practices constitutes the practice of revival meetings:[17]

a) Entering

A beach flag with the church's name is flying outside the city's culture hall, and several persons are about to enter the meeting. The two greeters recognised me,

---

[15] Halldorf (2012) interestingly makes a distinction between two meeting practices in the evangelical revival in Sweden: "meetings to gather", which had an evangelistic telos, versus "meetings to be gathered" with a community building telos.

[16] The following is mainly from a meeting Aug. 23, 2020, but the intention is to describe the meeting practice in general, which is why episodes and conditions from other occasions are included.

[17] I will call the gatherings Revival meetings. The church plant uses the Swedish term *gudstjänst*, which is an ordinary term for the Sunday service that is used by many established free churches.

checked my name on the list, and welcomed me with big smiles. Sven describes the thought behind the welcoming team:

> [Sven]: When arriving at church, we want people to meet them at the door because many come alone, and you know how it is to come to a new place. Many don't go to a church or a place where they don't know anyone, so we want to remove those obstacles for people to come. Hopefully, they have been invited by someone who is meeting up. I can ask someone on that team to meet you early if possible. We put a lot of thought into this to make it all work.

But keeping a distance means that no one gets the usual hug, as I head towards the meeting hall, I notice there is no coffee being served. In the meeting hall itself, every other seat is cordoned off to ensure that the participants maintain social distancing. The cultural venue could hold 350 people, but today it is anything but crowded. Upbeat worship music plays in the background, building excitement as people enter. The big stage is empty save for a single guitar, music stands, two mics, and a huge backdrop emblazoned with the phrase "Welcome to church". This is yet another effort to make newcomers feel welcome:

> [Erik]: When we design the services and all that, we adapt to [the newcomers]. It is designed for them.

Erik, who was himself a newcomer to the church less than two years ago, reflects on the strategic environment of the revival meetings. The meeting place is in a modern, nice, and comfortable venue, easily accessible in the city centre and curated to make newcomers feel welcome.

b) Welcoming

Wearing black t-shirt and trousers, Einar takes the stage and greets us as the meeting starts: "If you are new here, you should know that you are allowed to make this journey at your own pace. We can let go of our masks and be who we are". Then he prays, "Thank you, God, for loving us unconditionally!"

> [Margareta]: I think a key has been saying almost the same phrase every Sunday, almost like a mantra: Now you are here... I don't know the Swedish word... "acknowledge", that there are new people. That makes the newcomer feel welcome and signals to all others that there are supposed to be new people there. If you bring someone, we work hard to make them comfortable.

Margareta, one of the planting pastors, emphasises the importance of making people feel they are entering the meeting on their own conditions. In hindsight, however, Dani, who was part of the church plant for several months before she left it, finds these opening phrases shallow and fake:

> [Dani]: I think they said you can come as you are... there shouldn't be any masks. You can be who you are and things like that. And later on, I thought that it didn't reflect reality. Sometimes, at the beginning of the service, the pastors could express the anticipation that everyone should feel great. Like... how are you? Are you fine? You know, something energetic where you were supposed to answer positively.

By creating an energetic and upbeat atmosphere, he feels that the church plant fails to acknowledge the actual mood of some of the people who come, thus denying them to be what they are. If Dani's observation is correct, this indicates an inconsistency between the authentic ideal – you do not have to wear a mask – and the actual practice.[18] This rhetoric aims to make new people feel comfortable being themselves, but how this message is presented undermines this possibility if one is not actually feeling positive or upbeat.

c) Singing

After the introduction, we are invited to stand up together. The worship is led by a small team of a guitarist and two singers. As the guitarist starts to play, one of the singers briefly describes what worship means, and again, the instructions are directed towards newcomers: "Worship is singing songs to God".

> [Sven]: We always mention from the stage before we start that worship is prayers set to music. It is a help for people to pray their first prayer. You read a prayer and sing along even if you don't believe it.

As I look around the hall, I see some people eager to sing worship in church again: "Jesus, you have set me free". Others look hesitant and seem to listen and observe rather than engage in the singing. The songs are repeated several times, and eventually, most people join in. One phrase is sung over and over again: "When I open up my mouth, miracles start breaking out. I have the authority, Jesus, you've given me". This seems to be almost an incantation to drive out or, at least, reject the voices that make me less than God has created me to be.

The songs usually follow without interruption, but sometimes, there is a planned break for a reading from the Bible:

> [Birgitta]: Many people who come have been saved in [our church] and have possibly no church background. So, the change has been quite noticeable in how the congregation responds more in worship. From the start, it was mostly us on stage who were singing and worshipping, and I think many wondered what we were doing and thought it

---

[18] Cf. Moberg (2013), p 178, where she discusses authenticity in religious meetings. She objects to the idea of the shallowness of this ideal.

was a bit strange. But now people engage in another way. You can see people being moved. It is awesome!

Worship is a sharp formative tool in the meeting practice. The contemporary sound is inviting, and the messages are convincing. The sub-practice of singing worship in the revival meeting is meant to draw the newcomer into a personal encounter with the gospel discourse.

d) Giving

Einar reads a passage about giving from Matthew 6. He says we should not give our money in order to receive praise from others. We give before God. He is aware of the presence of newcomers and the sensitivity of discussing money and religion in the same breath, so he adds that "football clubs need financial help as well". In other words, it is no different to give to your church than it is to pay the membership fee in a sports club. The church, he goes on to say, offers two ways of giving: on the church's website, there is information about becoming a monthly supporter. The other way to give is to "SWISH" money to the number projected on the screen along with the SWISH service's logo.[19] Einar concludes with a prayer for the money: "Thank you, Lord, that you have given us so much. Now, we give back to you so that more people in the city can hear about you. Amen". Newcomers might hesitate to give money, but by challenging them to do so, they are invited to invest personally in the church. Thus, Einar prompts them to ask themselves: "Is this worth investing in? For me?"

e) Preaching

The most significant revival meeting sub-practice is preaching. The sermons are 40 to 45 minutes long. Einar and Margareta take turns leading the meeting or preaching. Margareta underlines the central importance of preaching in a broad sense.

> [Margareta]: Simply put, we imagine ourselves being this voice that preaches God's grace as it is. If we do, people will be drawn to it. When they hear the true liberating message, they will respond positively to it. So that is what we thought, that wherever we [preach this message], people will come, and it will spread like ripples on the water because people thirst for the truth in the desert wasteland to learn the truth.

Margareta, the preacher of the day, places a big box on the stage. Gesturing to the box, she says, "I don't know if you are like me, but I sure don't like to be put in a box". She refers to statistical categories like risk groups identified in media during

---

[19] SWISH is a common app-based payment method in Sweden.

the pandemic and different age groups where you always end up on the wrong side of the age limit. "And they tried to put Jesus in a certain category, to box him in, along with other people. But he was the friend of sinners. He didn't fit the religious box". She continues by describing how Jesus broke the limits of his culture by speaking with women, healing the sick on the sabbath, and touching those considered unclean. Then she reads the text from Ephesians 3:16-21, where the verses 18-19 talk about the dimensions of God's love:

> I pray that you may have the power to comprehend, with all the saints, what is the breadth and length and height and depth, and to know the love of Christ that surpasses knowledge so that you may be filled with all the fullness of God. [Eph 3:18–19 NRSV]

Now, she turns to us. "And we do the same thing. We give God a zone where he is allowed to do his thing, but Jesus wants to touch your whole life!" This is where she enters the box on the stage and disappears completely, drawing giggles from the crowd. "Sometimes we put God in our box of beliefs, and we only take him out when we are in trouble", she says from inside the box, her voice carrying over the PA system. "Faith is really boring with a boxed God. He is bigger, and God can do more!" She describes a God that wants to impact our whole lives: "Sometimes we put ourselves in the box and listen too much to what others say we can't do. God asked us to step out of our box and start a church". Margareta, still in the box, goes on to talk about self-image and having the confidence to step out of the box. She offers an example from the book of Judges – the character of Gideon, whom she calls "a kind of Scandinavian" in his lack of confidence. "God doesn't see who you think you are but who you really are".

Forty minutes into her sermon, the worship team enters the stage as she turns to the audience and says: "Some of you have put God in the box, and you need to let him out. Others here have put yourselves in the box, and God calls you to live a full life". We are about to enter the next stage of the meeting. The calm and engaging music and Margareta's emotional closure help drive her personal message home for the listeners.

> [Björn]: I have heard several sermons, and I think you often come back to this… "You don't have to be ashamed". Especially you [nodding towards Margareta], you often return to this subject. Why is that?
>
> [Margareta]: I think it is partly personal, something you carry, having a sense of revelation on this particular subject. But also, I hear people talk about this a lot, at least the people I meet, that they have this shame. I am not worthy before God, or I don't fit in. You exclude yourself because you think that it is not for me. Both as a non-believer and when you have got hold of God, I can feel people struggling with this. Jesus came to set people free from this. You need to remind people 'cause now you have heard it, but in

three weeks, you fight it again and feel shame that affects your relation to God and how you make decisions.

Einar also points out the recurring themes of removing masks and being oneself.

> [Einar]: If we say that everyone is a sinner, there is no longer any point in keeping the mask on. I think this message is attractive to Swedes because [...] everything in the world is built on performance. Everything is about what you achieve, what you get out of it, and what you earn.

These themes of shame, being yourself, and basing your life on God's love instead of achievement are important for the planters and are clearly recognisable in the meetings. In the sub-practice of preaching, the listening participants are challenged to re-evaluate who they are and who God is.

f) Responding

After each sermon, there is a time of prayer, with the opportunity to publicly respond to the sermon's message. Usually, this entails approaching the stage and receiving personal prayer from one or more designated prayer ministrants. On some occasions, the preacher extends a direct invitation to the listeners by giving them a chance to respond by raising a hand or giving a sign while everyone is closing their eyes. In the sermon above, the invitation to people who recognise that they have limited God to a certain religious area of their lives or have seen faith as a religious system that is irrelevant and boring. Another group that is pointed out are those that, for different reasons, have limited themselves by listening to the wrong voices. While some of the participants in the hall are visibly affected by the message, just a few find their way down to Margareta and another prayer minister. Perhaps the regular admonitions to socially distance ring louder than Margareta's invitation to change ways of thinking and being.

The service is approaching its end as the worship team sings about God as the "Way Maker, Miracle Worker, Promise Keeper, Light in the Darkness" and then proclaims "How great is our God" as they sing the famous worship song by Chris Tomlin. Einar concludes the meeting by summarising the sermon and inviting the participants to an introductory course on Christian faith.

> [Sven]: We see worship as very important because it is a response to the service, to engage fully in what you have heard. I know personally that almost every time God has acted the most clearly [it is] during the worship. You hear the message, but it is in the worship you can process it. It is a mix, of course, but it is also where… "I agree to this. I understand it more when I can sing it out".

Sven points to the importance of singing as part of the "message processing". Worship opens a space for change in the meeting. Some criticize the use of music for evoking certain feelings in an almost manipulative way, and without discounting those concerns, it must be said that music can be a cultural resource that helps people understand and identify beyond the cognitive.[20] Singing worship is a significant formative sub-practice of the meeting, and in combination with preaching, the worship enforces the message of the service.

The Revival Meeting as Formation

How is the meeting organised as a practice of Christian formation, and what kind of Christian is formed through this practice? As outlined in the previous chapter, the telos of the Industrial City church plant includes the shaping of a certain culture, or as Einar puts it, "being relevant, the language, social media, the place and contemporary music".

In analysing the meeting as a formative practice, we should start by asking what is actually going on. People enter the situation, some as newcomers and others as regulars. Apart from the warm greeting at the door, they might be entering any of the other events held at this venue. But once the participants are inside the venue, being guided through the different parts of the well-planned program, there is no mistaking what kind of event they are attending. Activities like praying, singing songs to God, and giving money to the church might feel unusual to the newcomer, who might question whether to personally engage. The use of humour and the acknowledgement of the role of the spectator in the room (by talking about "your journey" and "being who you are") help create a comfortable environment. There is room for engagement as well as non-engagement in this church plant's meeting practice.

The meeting follows the traditional pattern of revival meetings.[21] This includes a build-up towards responding to the sermon's gospel message, which is typical for

---

[20] Strhan (2015), p 122, observes and discusses the distinction between word-oriented and ritual/emotionally oriented Christianity, with the word-orientated approach generally regarded as more authentic: "Yet despite the anti-ritualist discourse at St John's, church members are nevertheless conscious that their formation as listeners depends on the training of the body through specific techniques to develop a particular habitus that will enable them to hear God speak. One such technique is their engagement with music".

[21] Wall (2014), p 190, introduces a pedagogy with an instructional approach, which is somewhat similar to the meeting practice. However, while the meeting practice depends on preaching as somewhat "correct, didactic scriptural teaching", it is not instructional in the sense of "given by the ordained leaders", as Wall's model suggests.

the revival meeting but not for the majority of Swedish free church Sunday services. The telos of the meeting is to reach the invited non-believers with the gospel, lead them to a change of "the heart", and guide them into a new identity as Christians. Interestingly, the telos of reaching people with the Christian message is present throughout the entire meeting, even in the giving sub-practice.

The meeting is not held in a church building. No clerical clothing or other symbols identify the place as liturgical. Instead, this is a secular place in the centre of the city. Since there are no material signs of God or religion, the use of worship becomes even more important to Christian formation in this liturgically strange place. In addition to this, there is still no church in a formal sense. The church-planting team has the intention to gather people into an ecclesial community that will eventually become a church. This is the aim of the practice, but not a prerequisite for it.

From my observations, I note three levels of practice engagement for the meeting's new participants: These levels of practice can be interpreted theologically in the following way:

1. *Participation*: Forming an identity of non-membership in the community of practice.
2. *Active participation*: Accepting the identity of a legitimate peripheral participant in the community of practice.
3. *Active body engagement*: Forming an identity toward full participation in the community of practice through singing, giving, and responding to a call by raising a hand or stepping forward for personal prayer.

There is an assumption in the revival meeting practice that becoming a Christian presupposes some cognitive comprehension of the gospel, who Jesus Christ is, and what this means on a personal level. This is why the sub-practice of preaching, where the gospel is explained, is so significant. The meeting practice provides ways of responding bodily and socially from this inner re-negotiation of one's identity and response towards Jesus. In the meeting, the church planters challenge newcomers and others to become "who they really are" by letting go of any masks or shame before God. This challenge is evident in sermons but also in songs and prayers.

Being Christian is described as becoming "who you really are in Jesus" or "whom God created you to be": not perfect, but on a journey towards integrity and confidence in being loved by God, not defined by your sins or mistakes, but by whom God says you are, the "beloved child of God". This formative challenge is central to the church plant, and nowhere else is it as palpable as in the formative meeting practice.

6.3 The Small Group Practice in Cathedral City

Now, let's turn to the small group practice in Cathedral City. The church plant holds its meetings in the park during summer and in homes the rest of the year. Gathering in homes does limits the attendance to between 20 and 30 people, which is why the church plant now has more than one big home gathering during the week. Before the pandemic, there was a meeting in one home on Sundays and another in a second home on Mondays. During my field studies, COVID restrictions forced this practice to migrate to the digital meeting platform Zoom, where video meetings were held on Monday evenings. It's within the context of these bigger meetings that the small group practice, which is also held online, becomes an important building brick in the church plant.

> [Anders] You feel safer than in a [big] meeting. I am not involved in the other groups, so I don't know how they are doing, but I think there are many good talks. People can talk about things that are hard to discuss in the [big] meeting.

The small groups are made up of 3–5 persons of the same sex who gather for up to six months to read the Bible together and encourage each other to develop certain habits. The Cathedral City church plant makes a point of including both believers and interested non-believers in the groups. As Peter, one of the planters, puts it, it is a matter of taking steps closer to Jesus to form a personal faith:

> [Anders]: So I think that is the purpose, that the personal faith will grow and deepen in a safe environment. And another focus is seeing non-believers become believers in the groups. The idea is to include people curious [about the Christian faith] in a group with stable Christians.

The group I attended met every other week, with three or four men in attendance each time. Anders was appointed leader. The group has an agreement to not share with others what is said during the gatherings. Not everyone in the group engaged to the same degree, and this caused occasional frustration, for example, when one or two persons suddenly cancelled. But on the whole, the group was stable enough to become meaningful for the participants. This was not the case for every group within the church plant:

[Anders]: This was my second small group and the first one that actually worked. The other one didn't work because it was so insanely unstable. People didn't show up, so it fell apart. [...] It was too burdensome and demanding. People didn't show up.

When he reflects on the necessary conditions for a functioning small group, Anders mentions setting realistic goals for Bible reading. Otherwise, the burden might become too heavy resulting in persons leaving the group. The digital format makes the group, in a sense, even more fragile since the relations are at a distance. At the same time, it made the group possible since in-person meetings were not an option during the height of the COVID-19 pandemic.

Intentional Habits

An important part of the small group practice is performing habits that are linked to the church plant vision:

- *Prayer list*: Prayerfully make a list of five non-Christian friends and pray for them regularly.
- *Eat together*: Make it a weekly practice to eat together with someone in the church to share everyday life.
- *Bless someone*: Practice generosity towards someone.
- *Personal Bible reading*: Read the Bible regularly to get to know God and to hear his voice.
- *Personal prayer*: Pray regularly by thanking God and asking for help for ourselves and the world.
- *Gather*: Participate in church gatherings.[22]

Using intentional habits to inculcate the telos expressed in the church plant's vision statement is a recognition that formation is more than a cognitive matter.[23] In

---

[22] There has been an upsurge of the language of habits in the missional movement lately. E.g., Michael Frost (2015), *Surprise the World: The Five Habits of Highly Missional People*, Carol Stream, Illinois: Tyndale House uses the acronym BELLS that stands for *Bless* (acts of generosity), *Eat* (intimate community), *Listen* (hearing God), *Learn* (following master Jesus), *Sent* (evangelism). Frances Fulling Blomberg (2014), *Forming and Sustaining Christian Community in a Consumer Culture: An Analysis of and Search for Appropriate Models*, Cardiff, UK: University of Wales finds that "Contentment, stability, hospitality, commitment, communal discernment, and their subsidiaries are offered as 'powerful practices,' not because they are imposed on either believers or culture, but because they are transformative", p 347.

[23] The vision statement reads: "We want to be a generous and multicultural everyday community that helps each other to follow Jesus, and is sent with hope so that more people may find their home in God".

this way, the church plant also models a way of living the Christian life in community.

> [Sofia]: That is something we emphasise in the [the church plant], the habits of the small groups. How can you live close to people in formation and evangelisation as part of your discipleship?

The small groups are directly connected to the formation through intentional habits. It is also worth noting the inherent "missionality" of the habits. The Christian life is understood as having a clear centre – the life with Jesus Christ – but when it is lived out, the ambition is to move beyond the borders of the church. The habits are meant to form a life of being sent into the world. In reflecting on the use of common habits, Peter underlines the collective aspect, that it is something shared in the community.

> [Peter]: If you do this, you will grow your spiritual life. It will build the common vision that we are dedicated to. A vision can sound very good, but how can it be tangible and concrete? We are habitual beings, all of us. You recognise how habits can both help you and lead you astray. It is so helpful having someone ask you every two weeks, "how is it going with this?" in love. It is such a help. It makes us pray more, read the Bible more, and keep focus. So... a help to live the lives we actually want to live but cannot always do.

Peter also stresses the mutual accountability around the habits in small groups, which supports individual behavioural formation. Peter will not go so far as to say that living the habits equates to being Christian, but he maintains that by practising the habits, people grow spiritually. The next section will show how the small group practice forms these habits across the entire church plant.

Flow of Sub-Practices

I was invited to the small group via a message on Facebook Messenger:

> Hi, how are you? I wonder if you would be interested in joining a small group in the church? These groups meet every other week to pray together, discuss the Bible and support each other in our Christian lives. Between the meetings, we read the Bible, about one chapter each day. To be part of a group, you are expected to participate in the meetings, prepare, and be willing to learn. Would you like to join? /Anders

In discussions with the leaders in the plant, I have declared my interest in becoming part of a small group as part of my field studies. As people enter the community and become part of it, they are approached by one of the leaders who asks them if they want to join a small group. This time, the invitation came on Messenger, but at other times, it might be in person.

The first time we meet, Anders, who is the leader of the small group, describes what the group is for, what the gatherings will look like and how often we will meet. Anders describes the habits and explains that we will practice them throughout the coming months in the group. Later, in an interview, he reflects on his role as a small group leader:

> [Anders:] [My role] has been to put the group together and establish the meeting procedure, but I don't have an overwhelmingly strong kind of leadership. I consider myself one of the members, we are doing this together and making it work, so to speak. But I often find myself in the role of a conversation leader, both in the small group and the service.

In our introductory meeting, we introduce ourselves to each other and decide on a good time for our meeting. At this point, I explain my reasons for attending the group and ask for their permission to use the group for my research.[24] Before we leave, we also decide on reading the first half of the Gospel of Matthew before we reconvene, which means reading one chapter a day. Then, we end the first meeting with a short prayer. In the following section, I describe the pattern of the bi-weekly small group meetings.

a) Signing in

I enter the meeting by accepting the video call from Anders on my phone's Messenger application. In a few seconds, the faces of the other participants are more or less visible, depending on the quality of the connection. We speak English as one person is more comfortable in this language, and after exchanging initial greetings, Anders asks us how we are and what is going on in our lives. This might sound like a rather general question to get us going, but it also represents the act of signing in to a safe place where we share our lives.

b) Establishing habits

During the second meeting, Anders suggests that we make a list of people for whom we will pray. The idea, he explains, is to pray for up to five people that we are close to, people need to get to know Jesus. When we meet the third time, we talk about the fact that we do not meet many people during the pandemic lockdown. For this reason, it is hard to know what is going on in the lives of people around us and what to pray for when you are not meeting them in person.

---

[24] I described this earlier in the chapter on Methods and Methodology. During our meetings, I was one participant in the group. It is difficult to know whether the discussions were affected by my double role, but it is fair to remind the reader that I am a part of the material.

The same thing becomes clear as we try to implement the habit of eating with someone every week. We live rather different lives; while I am surrounded by my family, two group members live alone, and one is married without children. We talk about what these habits mean in our different situations, particularly in the midst of the COVID restrictions. We discuss how it could mean opening the family's dinner table to include others. Other times, it might mean breaking out of your isolation to share what is going on in your life with someone else. For one young member who lives alone and works from home at the time, eating with a colleague once a week becomes a "necessary lifeline for his soul".

In the fourth meeting, we decide to try to bless others by doing good in some way or by speaking encouragement to others. For me, this meant calling an old friend who recently lost his wife to COVID-19. In the following meeting, I share how this act encouraged both my friend and myself. Two of the others shared how they met beggars outside their local stores. One of them also helped an old lady to take down goods from a shelf in the store. We discuss the dilemma of giving money to beggars who might not keep the money because they have been trafficked and need to hand the money over to someone else. We acknowledge Jesus' exhortation to see and care for the least well-off in society. We conclude that our small group gatherings help us remember and actually do things like these. Anders reminds us what we have read in the book of Galatians this week: "Bear one another's burdens and whenever we have an opportunity, let us work for the good of all" [Gal 6:2, 10 NRSV]

We work through the list of habits as the meetings continue. We try the habit of arranging a certain time of prayer every day using reminders on the mobile phone, and we also attend the church plant's big gatherings in the bi-weekly Zoom meetings.

c) Bible reading

During the spring, we read a few books in the New Testament: Matthew, Mark, John, Romans, Galatians, Ephesians, and First Corinthians.

"What has been especially significant in your Bible reading these weeks?" Anders always asks. This time, our task was to read half of the Gospel of Matthew, and we had done our homework enthusiastically. Charlie, one of the group members, relates how he is challenged by "the Sermon of the Mount: "What does it mean to judge?" he asks. Having an opinion is not the same as judging, we conclude. If someone does what is wrong, it is important to be able to point that out. A good starting point might be to be aware of your own shortcomings, the speck in your eye, I suggest. Someone says that being aware of your own sin makes you look differently at others. We also discuss the passage in Matthew about tearing out the eye and cutting off the hand. Andreas later refers to this in a Messenger post:

> Hi! For those who weren't able to join this Wednesday, here's a recap. We first talked about the chapters that we had read in Mathew. Especially, we talked about how Jesus can be very hard against injustice and sin and that he is forgiving and merciful. We also talked about how our lives should become more like Jesus' life as we grow in our relationship with him.

When reading the Galatians, the group discussed what "the law", "the flesh", and the fight between "the spirit and the flesh" might mean. We could recognise this fight in ourselves, and we all agreed that sometimes you do what you know is wrong. Olof mentions the bad habit of looking at the phone all the time, something that results in a fragmented mind. "But how can we grow the fruits of the Spirit?" Anders asks. This leads back to the good habits, starting with God, praying, reading the Bible, blessing and being mindful of other persons. These habits should help us to bear "good fruit".

Later, after reading the Gospel of John, it becomes evident that one chapter a day is too much for Olof. He is rather new to faith and Bible reading, and most of the stories and issues in the texts are not familiar to him, which leads to a lot of questions and insights. We talk about the balance between the joy of spiritual engagement on one hand and the risk of losing joy and becoming proud from performing religious commitments. Finding that balance becomes important for the group, and our reading moves forward at a slower, healthier pace.

When discussing our reading of the first half of First Corinthians, Olof says that Paul is sometimes impossible to understand. He finds that there are too many prohibitions on life. "Today, among students, you are expected to have many sexual relations". This expectation does not fit with Paul's instructions and strict sexual morals, and Olof's comment leads to a discussion about relationships. Anders, who is married, distinguishes between being attracted to a woman and acting on that attraction. Someone says that it seems easier to be married and exclaims: "I should get married!" It is increasingly clear that reading the texts together is leading us to conversations about how life should be lived as a Christian as we build trust and share our thoughts. The group increasingly becomes a place where we can process these questions and challenges together.

d) Praying together

At the end of each meeting, we have a time of prayer. It usually starts with Anders asking for any prayer requests. The members of the group are open and share what is going on in their lives. Recurring themes are the future and work. Anders soon finishes his studies and is searching for a job, preferably one in the Cathedral City area. Olof is thinking of moving back to his home region and is trying to get a job there. Charlie is studying Swedish and is also looking for a job. We are all feeling the psychological toll of the pandemic isolation, with each of us feeling down or sad from time to time. In the midst of this isolation, sharing and praying become important to the group.

At one time, Olof connects his reading of Matthew's Gospel with a situation in his life. He tells us of a friend whose child has cancer. Olof, clearly affected and distraught, asks: "Why does a child get cancer?" He read in the scripture how Jesus predicted his own death even though he has cured so many people of their suffering and diseases. How can this be? The point of the conversation is not to find an answer but to share the pain. We pray together for the situation. In this way, the group becomes a vehicle to bring both joy and pain to God. We experience that God is there, together with us, and we share God's presence in the virtual space.

e) Signing out

Each of our small group meetings is about one hour long. Anders finds that one hour every second week is sustainable.

> [Anders]: Often, one hour is enough to have conversations and pray together, you don't feel that it takes too much energy, which is important if it is going to be sustainable in the long run.

After checking the date for the next meeting, we say our goodbyes, close Messenger, and go back to our lives. As spring turns to summer, the time for us to dissolve the group has come. By the time we have our final meeting, it is clear that we have come to know each other quite well even though we have never met in person.

The Small Group as Formation

The telos of the small group is to form Christians according to the vision of the church plant: "We want to be a generous and multicultural everyday community that helps each other to follow Jesus and is sent with hope so that more people may find their home in God".[25] As such, the interplay between the individual

---

[25] This vision statement is found in both Swedish and English on the church plant's web page.

formation and the formation of the community is significant in the small group. The vision statement, which is connected to the list of habits, is formulated by the church plant, and the small group practice is designed to support the formation of these common habits.

The intentional formation of virtuous habits is different from a mere cognitive comprehension of the gospel message. The habits chosen by the church plant are ways of forming virtues. They are social and cooperative, have intrinsic value, and offer the possibility of growth and formation in and through their practice. The group finds value in the habits, which could be interpreted as an active formation in the small group practice.[26]

Ideally, one signs up for the common habits by becoming a small group participant and bringing oneself into the formative process by practising the habits daily and sharing reflections and experiences with the group every (or every other) week. As evident in the description of the flow of sub-practices above, this was not always the case. Participation in the group was important for three group members, which is shown by their level of participation. One person who, when invited, responded positively never actually showed up. Another person only attended about half of the group meetings. This was a very small group, so it was impossible to retract to a non-engagement mode while participating in the meetings. Group participants are also expected to be engaged between the meetings. Practising the habits and reading the Bible texts as agreed are personal activities that could be engaged with shifting levels of engagement, which results in shifting degrees of Christian formation.

The church plant emphasises practising Christian virtues as an important part of being Christian. But the church plant identifies as part of the evangelical movement, and as such, its vision of Christian identity means conversion to and faith in Jesus Christ. Virtue formation is understood as something lived and shared with people in their neighbourhood for evangelistic reasons. For the church plant in Cathedral City, being Christian also means that one is sent into the world, forming a community in the middle of things, which is why non-Christians have a natural place in the groups.

---

[26] At this point, a comparison with MacIntyre's view on virtues is fitting. MacIntyre (2013), p 254, he describes virtues as dispositions that enable a community to achieve the goods internal to common practices and the general quest for the good through increasing self-knowledge and knowledge of the good. While I don't use MacIntyre's theory explicitly in this thesis, this is where it would be of most help, if done so. Suffice it to say that the church plant finds a formative value in common habits.

The Cathedral City church plant's small group practice uses the conventicle pattern of the free church tradition as a way to gather and form Christian lives.[27] There are similarities to the young Methodist movement's use of a list of questions in assessing one's life in community in order to form a Christian life that is both confessional and lived. In comparison, however, the small groups in Cathedral City have rather modest demands of compliance. Nevertheless, the small group practice is significant to how the church plant forms a lived Christian identity in newcomers in the community.

6.4 The Apprenticing Practice in Harbour City

As described in the previous chapter, the church plant in Harbour City has a strong emphasis on social work and a strong missional telos. Karl, one of the church's planters, says that an open and listening posture towards the city was apparent from the church's inception, but five years into the church planting endeavour, this bent is even more defined:

> [Karl]: We don't want to be a church that gathers just on Sunday. We want to see our city transformed and the kingdom of God take root in all of it, really.

Here, Karl downplays the significance of the traditional Sunday services that are usually at the centre of the church communities. Instead, he emphasises the multitude of different groups and relations that support people on their journey from social exclusion towards a life of human dignity, Christian community, and mission. The church plant is particularly concerned with fostering an apprenticeship mindset in their groups and relationships, and as such, they guide newcomers – apprentices – into a lived Christian identity and offer continual support to other members as well.

> [Karl]: [Contemporary churches] have grown up in very much of a classroom model of church, and maybe 90% of the learning has been done like that. What we're trying to do is to reduce that and have a more apprenticing mindset. So all of our leaders... we train them to apprentice others.

I interpret this apprenticing mindset as important to one of the Harbour City church plant's core practices, and in my analysis, I note that this phenomenon exists in different groups and activities. Accordingly, I call them apprenticing groups,

---

[27] Cf. Rogers (2016), p 67. Andrew Rogers, likewise, analyses how the Anglican Evangelical tradition is used in Bible reading groups in contemporary church communities.

though, in the actual community, these groups and activities have different names like "Women's group", "Beach walk", and "Missional potential".

During my field study, the pandemic restrictions hindered most groups from meeting in person. Small groups and Sunday services were held online using Zoom. Due to the format, the meetings I attended were quite similar, whether they were small groups or Sunday meetings. Unlike my fieldwork at the other church plants, I was unable to participate in person at any length in Harbour City. Therefore, I had to rely mainly on the descriptions of the participants and leaders. Since the apprenticing activities differed in focus, content, and number of persons attending, presenting a strict practice flow would not be meaningful. Instead, I will illustrate the practice by describing three examples of apprenticing arrangements. But first, we need to know more about the context of this social ministry.

The Social Ministry Context

Many people who attend the church plant come from the margins of society, and this affects how the activities and groups are arranged. Karl is encouraged by what he sees as God's presence in the margins, which he connects to the purpose of the church plant:

> [Karl]: We are often quite surprised that even in the darkest places, He shows up. That has been part of our story, that we have found God in some unlikely people, unlikely places, and unlikely situations. That is the purpose of the church. [...] We are not interested in only creating a church that invites people to an event or worship service. We are much more interested in seeing healing, restoration, and resurrection. All those key missional ideas "explode" out of the church buildings into the streets and communities.

Kristina, one of the leaders in the church plant, exemplifies this social work by describing a women's baking group and a soul hiking group that takes long walks along the sea while the participants engage in conversations. In the church's anti-trafficking work, there are some difficulties when it comes to integrating individuals in the church, and the work is performed almost entirely at locations other than the church building. This work is led by Kristina and Sara, both of whom are employed by the church plant as social workers. A handful of women whom they have met in this work come to other church activities as well. Some are very reserved about their past, while others are more open. Regardless of their willingness to share their history, the women-only groups are safe places of entry into the church community for them.

> [Kristina]: We don't want the church work to be one entity and the human trafficking work another, managed separately at the side. We need to connect things. We, as a church, work against human trafficking in the city. [...] We have examples where some

kind of basic faith has been strengthened through our involvement, and they have returned [to faith]. They have been in the process of inner healing, which is very much needed for these issues. We have seen a lot of this.

Kristina points to the centrality of providing a path forward towards personal faith for those they meet through their social ministry.

Implementations of the Practice of Apprenticeship

The three examples of the formative practice of apprenticing in this church plant are all taken from groups or relations of people who are led by church planting team members. In this analysis, I attempt to offer a broad but nuanced understanding of the practice of apprenticeship by focusing on leadership, Christian spirituality, and missional living.

Leadership

Elisabet, who is part of the planting team, has a background in social work at the municipal office. She is employed on a part-time basis by the church plant, where she is the acting leader. On this particular morning, Elisabet has an appointment with Helena, who, despite being relatively new to the church, is a co-leader of one of the women's small groups. At the last moment, Elisabet cancels the meeting because she has a minor cold and is waiting for the COVID test result. After some back-and-forth, Helena and Elisabet finally decided to meet on Skype. Helena and I connect to the video conference from the church, while Elisabet connects from home. Helena is relatively new in the church plant, and together with another woman, she leads one of the small groups.[28]

Elisabeth starts the one-to-one apprenticing session by asking: "You are good at gathering and holding the group together. How has this been for you?" Helena responds by expressing doubt about her own capability. In comparison with her co-leader, who is more outgoing, she feels like less of a leader. While she does not want to criticise the other leader, she confesses that she sometimes feels left out in leading the meetings. Elisabet turns this into a discussion about complementary roles and gifts: "You set the borders and keep the order", she says, and notes that the other leader pushes the

---

[28] Elisabet uses a course format for their apprenticing process called Calling Lab from the Underground network in Tampa, US. https://underground.teachable.com.

group onward – perhaps sometimes a bit too eagerly. An APEST[29] assessment Helena took earlier in the apprenticing course to discover her gifts and personality type supports this conclusion of their different roles in the group. As the apprenticing session continues, Elisabet encourages Helena to consider herself a valuable gift to the church community. Then, as the meeting nears its end, Elisabet asks Helena how she would like to serve the church and the surrounding community. Helena answers that she would like to help collect food from stores in Harbour City and deliver it to people in need. While the church has had to pause this social ministry because of COVID-19 restrictions, Elisabet and Helena agree to talk more about her involvement in the food ministry when the restrictions are withdrawn.

Scene: Harbour City, March 25, 2021.

Elisabet takes care to involve new people in the church plant's mission. It is so easy, she says, for the planting team to start their own little projects that no one else knows about. She tells me she is constantly looking for people to train and mentor. Faithful, available, and teachable people – which she refers to using the slightly unfortunate acronym "FAT" – who are not only signing up on paper but actually come and continue to show up. She likes working in close relationships, and her ideal church is a scalable model with smaller units, so-called "missional communities", that provide different supporting roles. The term missional, to Elisabet, relates to the less privileged in society:

> [Elisabet]: Not many in Sweden are doing what we long to do. [...] God is doing something at the fringes of society. [people who are usually not interested] come when God invites them to dinner.

When working at the social office, she found that a lot of time was spent on internal administrative procedures while hundreds of children were waiting for support and care. "More action, less order needed", she says as we conclude our interview.

---

[29] APEST stands for Apostle, Prophet, Evangelist, Shepherd, and Teacher. These gifts are referred to in Ephesians 4 and represent a way of looking at diversity that is common in the missional movement. This will be further described below.

Spirituality

Sara and Elisabet are leading a group of women who meet every other week to explore Christian spirituality. Though almost none of the women in the group have any prior experience within a free church community, they have more-or-less been handpicked to join the group:

> [Sara]: The group's purpose is to discover the relation with God more profoundly. Women who are part of the church or participate in other ways have a longing or hunger to invest in their spiritual lives. [...] We talk a lot about what it means to be a whole person and what it means to be a whole woman. It is easy to compartmentalise life and forget to care for our spiritual life. So this is a place where we challenge each other and discover together. So what does this mean, to work on your spirituality, to train these muscles? Just like when you go to the gym and shape muscles in your arms and legs, we need to train our spiritual muscles.

Sara expounds on the group's purpose by referring to the Gospel story about the Samaritan woman at the well in Sychar.[30] The woman was there to get water, but when she met Jesus, Sara explains, she received living water. Sara and Elisabet want their group to be that place where the living water is found, and when they notice a woman with a "thirst" for living, they invite her to the group, which is focused on prayer and hearing God's voice.

Their own background shapes their approach to this apprenticing practice; in fact, they started the group out of their own spiritual longing. Now they are guiding the group's women through the Alpha course material and have introduced the basics of APEST. Despite their leadership of the group, they do not see themselves as any different from the other women. This self-perception is evident in how they lead the group. They avoid teaching through talking and lecturing and instead facilitate group discussions.[31]

> [Sara]: We try to create an environment where we can discover together who God is and what God is doing through prayer exercises, both by trying to hear God's voice together and having individual exercises where you can try it yourself, perhaps a daily exercise at home for two weeks or so. Then you come back and report to the group.

The group has been meeting in this constellation for about two years, and while the participants have diverse backgrounds, trust has grown between them. This trust is very important to Sara and Elisabet, who are intent on fostering a safe

---

[30] Joh 4:1–42.
[31] Cf. Wall (2014). Philip Wall finds different pedagogies in the Fresh Expression church plants, one being the instructional paradigm leaning on a soteriology emphasising individual salvation by faith with little reference to a salvific community or embodied faith.

environment where members can be vulnerable in sharing their lives. That the group consists exclusively of women contributes to this trust, especially since some of the women come from abusive backgrounds. Sara notes that the group exists, in part, to provide a safe place to encounter inner wounds and receive healing from God.

> [Sara]: It is about discovering your own spiritual life, which often means you have to confront your own experiences and wounds, not necessarily in public, but you encounter this as you work on your inner life. Then there must be only women present.

Engagement in the group draws newcomers towards a lived Christian identity with an emphasis on Jesus' spirituality. An example of what this means can be found in a story Sara shares about a woman in the group who learns to hear God's voice:

> [Sara]: She dreamt about herself standing in the kitchen preparing food because she knew Jesus would come to visit her. She sees herself from above, and Jesus is already standing outside knocking at the door, but she doesn't hear because she is busy preparing. Then she texts me in the morning: "What do you think this means?" I answered: "What do you think?" "I think he wants me to let him in", she responds. "Then, perhaps you should" [laughter]. Then we talked about how to pray from that point. [...] If I would have said: "You should leave your heart to Jesus", then it is on my initiative. Now it was Jesus taking that initiative.

In sharing this example of how a woman with a background of abuse and vulnerability meets the church in its social ministry and comes to the women's group to explore Christian spirituality, Sara points to the importance of being sensitive to the processes in the women's lives and letting "Jesus take the initiative". To Sara, it is important to walk closely with these women in ministry and apprenticeship and to do so in a way that gives them confidence and agency. Despite the fact that the group helps people discover Christian spirituality, the leaders reach for more than spiritual experiences. They want to support the participants so that they can walk for themselves and eventually lead others. For Sara and Elisabet, this means avoiding a leadership model that always places the onus of responsibility on themselves.

Missional living

The following scene describes the final meeting of a course in missional living in the Cathedral City church plant. Karl describes the group in the following way:

> [Karl]: It is like a discipleship group where we're trying to help them to see mission through the APEST lenses. So we follow a book that a friend of mine has written. And you know, there is a practice, a missional practice, at the end of each session. [...] What

does it mean for me personally in my own prayer life, ministry life, me with others in the team. So some content and theology. But lots of practice.

During the course, they delve into the five aspects of Apostle, Prophet, Evangelist, Shepherd, and Teacher, then take a test to see how they fit into these categories and what this might mean for their lives. Between each meeting, the participants have had homework around these five aspects. They follow the book Discovering Your Missional Potential, which uses the typology of APEST found in chapter four of Ephesians.[32]

༞

Five men meet in the church facilities in the centre of the city. When I arrive, I grab a few delicious Middle Eastern-style cookies and join the group, which is gathered for the last of nine sessions in a course on missional living. Before I arrive, the group's leaders have explained to me that this time is more of a celebration to mark the conclusion of the course. These two leaders, Karl and Jan, are close friends with the three participants, though this is not immediately obvious because they are observing social distancing when I arrive. The meeting begins with worship. Since no one is comfortable playing the room's electric piano, the group plugs a phone into a speaker. This workmanlike setup does not hold us back as we begin to sing.

After the worship, we move to the adjoining room and sit down on sofas to start the course's final session, titled: "Unity, Diversity and Maturity". The men discuss how these five gifts are part of Jesus' life and how they complement each other as diversity in unity. Jan says that "for maturity, everything has to work together". God uses the way you are to show the world a facet of whom God is.

The session ends with prayer and "prophetic encouragement". Two of the men have recently received a negative decision from the Swedish migration authorities. They have lived in Sweden for a couple of years, but now they will be forced to leave. The gravity of the moment is hard to miss. We pray for God's protection and blessing over them. The final part is called ICNU, which stands for "I see in you…". This is a practice of "prophetic encouragement" where each person receives encouraging words from the others. These words can be based on what is perceived spiritually or naturally – no distinction is necessary. "You always make me laugh", one of them says as

---

[32] Daryl L Smith and Smith, Andrew B (2019), *Discovering Your Missional Potential: An Encounter with Ephesians 4 and How Jesus Lives It*, 100 Movements.

an encouragement to another. Someone else gets to hear, "You are an inspiring leader". The men are visibly affected by the good words spoken over them as they end the session and head home.

Scene: Harbour City, March 25, 2021.

༺

This scene illustrates how the church plant forms good Samaritans who are active agents in God's mission. It also shows how they use the APEST assessment tool and discourse to form a community of unity in diversity.

Practice Tool

As already mentioned, one significant tool in the church plant in Harbour City is the language of APEST, which is connected to the discourse of the missional movement.[33] APEST entails the five functions of "equipping the saints" mentioned in the book of Ephesians:

> The gifts he gave were that some would be apostles, some prophets, some evangelists, some pastors and teachers, to equip the saints for the work of ministry, for building up the body of Christ, until all of us come to the unity of the faith and of the knowledge of the Son of God, to maturity, to the measure of the full stature of Christ. (Eph 4:11–13 NRSV)

Karl is careful to point out that the church plant's use of the five functions is not directly related to individual persons but rather to the functions of the church. At the same time, he acknowledges that the functions are not distributed equally in any church community:

> [Karl]: When we talk about APEST, it's not about just… there are apostles, but rather that the church is called to be apostolic. The church is called to be evangelistic. The church is called to be shepherding and prophetic, and so forth. But some people seem to be gifted or lean heavily into that area. We don't go around with the titles. You are the apostle, the prophet… we never do that to people. But we definitely want to get people to see the church through these different lenses. So yeah, that's a… we don't want to talk too much. APEST is a big part of just helping realign the church's thinking. And so we are not just teacher-shepherd. We help people begin to play in other spaces and test out other ways of seeing the church.

---

[33] For an introduction to the APEST discourse, see Alan Hirsch (2017), *5Q: Reactivating the Original Intelligence and Capacity of the Body of Christ*, 100 Movements; Nathan Brewer (2020), *The Pulse of Christ (Revised and Expanded): A Fivefold Training Manual*, 100 Movements.

Karl refers to a renewed vision of the church, which he thinks is needed in the church in general. The church has emphasised the role of "pastor", which is mainly related to the functions of teaching and shepherding, in essence, the guarding of and caring for the already gathered and informing them about the Christian faith. As noted, the missional movement takes issue with this general emphasis on the pastoral roles and argues it has created a deficit in the areas of risk-taking and pioneering (apostle), seeking God's voice and questioning the status quo (prophet), and taking measures to recruit and call for a response to the gospel (evangelist).[34] Karl tells me how reading the missiologist Alan Hirsch and discovering the APEST understanding of church ministry was eye-opening to him. He compares it to going to the cinema and watching the movie Inception:

> [Karl]: I wasn't really prepared for it, I was on a date night, and we just went to the cinema to watch Inception. Just for a night out, I was on the edge of my seat from the beginning to the end. I have never seen anything like this, I have never seen anything like this! And [reading] The forgotten ways was really similar because I was in a moment when I was tired of all this – exploring and wondering whether I would be a church leader. I questioned my life with all those kinds of things. In my darkest moments, I was working out my exit strategy.

Hirsch's way of describing the church as a decentralised body that was not dependent on a single leader captured Karl's interest, so much so that he credits it with making it possible for him to stay in church ministry. This new way of understanding the church is also very much present in the Harbour City church plant. In two of the apprenticing practice examples cited above, APEST is used as a formative tool. It provides a common language for the community to discuss their telos and to understand themselves as individually connected to this telos. It is a language of complementary pluralism and unity in diversity that gives individuals a space to "be oneself" even while journeying together as a church community. Karl explains how he and Elisabeth reflect different giftings using the APEST language:

> [Karl]: Me and [Elisabet], for example, were working closely together when we first journeyed through this. We found ourselves really deeply connected on some issues. And that was because we were quite high on evangelism, so when it is about evangelism, it's just great. But there's real tension because she is a shepherd, and I'm an apostolic. So you know, for example, she is very much day-to-day, seeing people more clearly. It doesn't miss like when people are struggling and things like that when I could easily miss that

---

[34] Alan Hirsch and Catchim, Tim (2012), *The Permanent Revolution: Apostolic Imagination and Practice for the 21st Century Church*, Hoboken, New Jersey: Jossey-Bass. Alan Hirsch is mentioned in several discussions with the leaders of the church plant. They share his analysis and solution to the problem of the modern church.

kind of stuff. I'm very much a large picture of what we are doing. So relationally, it has really helped us not only in our strengths but also in our weaknesses.

The subject of APEST formation is, in this case, the church-planting team that is "producing" a church community with a certain culture through this tool. While the APEST tool is by no means the only formative tool at the church plant, it is clearly significant in the church's apprenticing practice. Like a sculpture's hammer and chisel, the APEST tool can help form and shape the church planter's vision – to plant a church with a culture of missional practice that encourages pluralism. The theological rationale behind this is a belief that God has created human beings to reflect the beauty of God as diversity – a beauty present only in Jesus Christ. At the same time, there are limits to diversity since it represents the unity found in the Trinity – working towards the same goal in love. There is a clear teleological sense of how APEST is employed in the context: Individuals work together to achieve the mission – expressed in terms of the kingdom of God – in Harbour City and beyond.

At this point, it warrants mentioning that the apprenticing model closely resembles Vygotsky's scaffolding model of learning. This is the involvement of a more "knowledgeable other" to build a supporting framework around the learner's development.[35] The active involvement of Elisabet, Sara, Karl, and Jan in the apprenticing arrangements provides what Vygotsky called a Zone of Proximal Development, in which the apprentices can experience formation towards the missional telos.[36]

Apprenticeship as Formation

In constructing apprenticeship as a formative practice, the church planters have emphasised their telos: forming new Christians, many of whom come from socially challenging backgrounds, towards a missionally-oriented life of dignity and action. In a way, these church planters are building on a long lineage of social activism and ministry that is historically present in Pietistic traditions like the Salvation Army. In those traditions, the leaders are sent not only to the church community but also to society as a whole.

---

[35] Raelin (2007).
[36] Lev. S. Vygotskii and Cole, Michael (1978), *Mind in Society: The Development of Higher Psychological Processes*, London: Harvard University Press. When the learner travels through the "zone of proximal development", together with a guide (who he calls "the more knowledgable other") learning happens as she stretches out of the comfortable and well-known. The guide provides "scaffolding" arrangements that help the learner to construct meaning in the social landscape.

The three examples of the apprenticeship practice are designed somewhat differently, each according to specific needs, but they share the apprenticing relationship construction and a common telos. Rather than a fixed program in which one can regulate one's engagement and participation, participation in these formative apprenticeships is a matter of meeting a more knowledgeable other who sets the pace according to the apprentice's needs, goals, and possibilities. In other words, engagement is a prerequisite rather than a response. Apprentices are chosen because they have shown up and have shown interest in being formed according to the telos of the community of practice – they are not "dragged along" but instead encouraged to go forward.

How does one become a Christian in this practice? I interpret "being Christian" in this community to mean "following Jesus", i.e., experiencing an ongoing relationship with Jesus that, in turn, motivates a desire to live missionally in community with others. In this sense, there is an emphasis on both orthopraxy (rather than orthodoxy) and activism.[37] While this emphasis might not be explicitly preached, the significance of the social ministry and the way it is implemented attest to it.

The use of the APEST tool is significant to some of the apprenticing practices in the church plant. It is also mentioned in many of the conversations I have had with the leadership team and others in the church plant. The tool represents an understanding of the Christian faith as an "outflow" from people's lives. This outflow originates in God and then takes shape through one's personality, where it is manifested through the five different personality modes that represent the ministry of Jesus. Truly following Jesus, then, must take the form of at least one or two of those five modes. APEST also brings an appreciation of diversity within the church community.

6.5 Conclusion

This chapter investigated what practices of Christian formation are present in the communities and how the formative practices are central to their respective church plants. The way the practices are designed in the local contexts is significant to understanding the underlying theological assumptions in the church plants' various approaches to Christian formation. While the three formative practices

---

[37] When using the word activism in this context, I am referring to the emphasis on social change in the lives and circumstances of less privileged people. Cf. Bebbington (1989). Bebbington describes activism as a central characteristic of modern Evangelicalism.

analysed in this chapter share the common goal of forming individuals towards a lived Christian identity as well as forming a church community, they differ both in how they perceive this identity and in how they shape the practices to achieve these objectives (Table 5).

	Revival Meeting	Small group	Apprenticeship
Telos	Self-acceptance and authenticity in Jesus	Christian virtues and close relationships	Diversity in unity, missional living
Engagement	Response to message, volunteering in team	Participation in common habits	Participation in apprenticing relationship
Tradition	Revival meeting	Conventicle	Social ministry

Table 5: A summary of the formative practices in the church plants.

The Revival Meeting Practice: People are formed to be open to the enjoyment of the love and freedom of God and to reject shame or low self-worth by receiving the good news preached, responding in worship, and surrendering themselves to Jesus. The revival meeting practice forms fishermen, who share their experience of God with others, both in person and on social media, and invite newcomers to the meeting.

The Small Group Practice: Persons are formed to be hospitable and generous, praying and bible-reading by aligning to common intentional habits in a close relational setting, in the tradition of the conventicle practice. As in the case of the revival meeting, participation in this practice leads to attitude formation – a changed appreciation of self, God and others. In addition to this, the small group practice involves the formation of behaviour: common intentional habits enacting a lived Christian identity.

The Apprenticing Practice: People are formed towards practised Christian spirituality and missional living in diversity and unity. The APEST missional tool forms the imagination of the community of practice in the different apprenticing relationships. The ecclesial context, as part of the apprenticing practice, draws on traditions of social ministry.

In quite different ways, these three formative practices are central to how the church plants engage the cities through mission. The practices are intentionally designed to perform the telos of the church plant. The three formative practices of meeting, small groups, and apprenticing all tap into the free church tradition of innovative contemporary urban missions. However, the connection between apprenticeship and social ministry is not quite straightforward. The apprenticeship practice takes advantage of the fact that the church plant meets individuals through social ministry who are empowered by apprenticeship relationships. The formative process does not necessarily start after a conversion experience but is rather described as a journey into, through, and sometimes out of the church plants. It is part of the person's whole trajectory in relation to the other practices, which is the theme in the following chapter.

7. Trajectories of Formation

In the previous chapter, the focus was on the church plants' formative practices. After describing the church plants' callings and intentions, I presented one central formative practice for each church plant: the revival meeting, the small group, and the apprenticeship. In this chapter, I use these formative practices as a starting point when I analyse peoples' trajectories within each church community in order to answer the research question: *How are people formed towards a lived Christian identity in the church plant communities?* Here, I draw on Lave and Wenger's concept of trajectories to analyse the formative trajectories not only as changing engagement and participation in the practices but also as movements into, within, and sometimes out of the communities.

7.1 Formation in Communities

Recent studies in practical theology suggest that the main reason why individuals engage in church communities is the quality of the community itself.[1] This means that an understanding of how persons come to faith needs to take social perspectives into account. Theologically, this perspective can be related to a view of salvation as a process that takes place when a person encounters God in and through

---

[1] E.g. Tangen (2012); Bryan P. Stone (2018), *Finding Faith Today*, Eugene, Oregon: Wipf and Stock. In the presentation of a large study of conversion in the United States, Stone speaks of "journeys". He finds that the primary reasons why the new believers decided to convert to the Christian faith and join a church varied across Evangelicals, Mainline Protestants, and Catholics. For Evangelicals, the main reasons were to go public with the faith they already had, to be able to grow in that faith and to respond to a loss in life or an experience with God. For Mainline Protestants, the most common reason was the congregation. They felt welcomed or accepted when meeting with it. For the Catholics, the main reason for joining was their family. While it is hard to compare the results of the present study with Stone's findings, it is interesting to note how important the congregation is across the various church traditions. Building relationships is a strong emphasis in the three church plants, as we have seen in the previous chapters. Neve (2021) finds that the evangelistic methods of emerging churches in Sweden "emphasise long-term witness and presence through service, dialogue and the possibility for people to experience God through a loving Christian community" (p 252).

the church. The community then embodies God's purposes by engaging in mission through practices such as worship, edification, and outreach. By preaching the gospel, the community provides a context of meaning that supports the individual on the journey towards repentance and faith. It helps the person to take on a new identity as a Christian and, as part of this, develop a new cognitive framework. Other practices encourage a re-formation of embodied faith (virtues and actions).[2] In the stories I have heard, God, the person, and the church community are all intertwined.

7.2 Analysing Practice Trajectories

While Wenger mainly constructs communities of practice as isolated phenomena, he acknowledges that this is an artificial model. As "shared histories of learning", these communities are "histories of articulation with the rest of the world".[3] This means that the communities of practice are dynamic and changing rather than stable and fixed. They are also shaped by circumstances outside the particular communities. When an individual participates in a community of practice, her own identity is renegotiated. In lines with this, Wenger describes identity as fundamentally temporal, ongoing, socially constructed, and complex and suggests that it is formed dynamically through participation in different communities of practice.

The concept of trajectories describes this dynamic process of participation and reflects an understanding of a person's life as a movement in a certain direction. This movement is made in relation to a community of practice, that is, as engagement towards or away from the community. Lave and Wenger speak of learning as a movement from peripheral participation towards fuller participation within the community of practice.[4] Practices are crucial in this process, and full participation in the community means the potential to master the core practices. This could also mean being a "master" in relation to others, as in the case when a long-time member guides newcomers in the practices of the community.

---

[2] Stanley J. Grenz (1994), *Theology for the Community of God*, Milton Keynes: Paternoster. The Spirit also convicts the person of their sins, and the person responds to the gospel with faith and by being baptised. A transfer of loyalty is happening as the person denounces the world to be a citizen of Christ's Kingdom. The role of the church community is to provide practices of worship, edification, and outreach, which results in the formation of a cognitive framework, identity, and an embodied faith in the new believer. See also Miroslav Volf (1998), *After Our Likeness: The Church as the Image of the Trinity*, Grand Rapids, Michigan: Eerdmans.

[3] Wenger (1999), p 103.

[4] Lave and Wenger (1991).

7.2 Analysing Practice Trajectories

According to Wenger, the dynamic process of participation results in different kinds of trajectories, which are laid out below in Figure 3. *Peripheral* trajectories refer to a situation where there is some ongoing identity formation, but the individual stays at the periphery. *Inbound* trajectories refer to the individual's intention of becoming a full participant in the practice. *Insider* trajectories refer to coping with change and renegotiating one's identity through practice. *Boundary* trajectories are those brokering identity movements that link different communities of practice. *Outbound* trajectories are movements heading away from the community of practice – and as such, they also foster a renegotiation of the person's identity.[5]

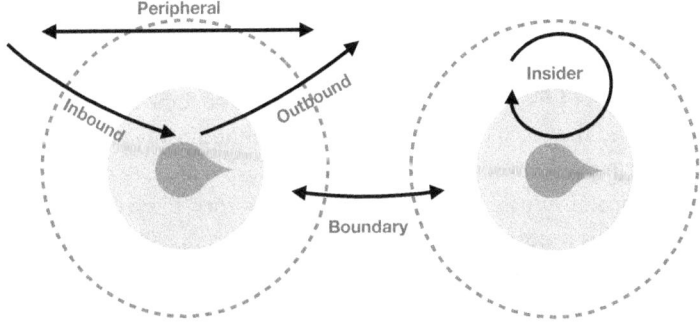

Figure 3: Wenger's different types of trajectories in the communities of practice.

Wenger delineates an individual's participation in the community of practice as belonging through imagination, alignment, and engagement – imagining together in community, aligning with the communal practice and perceptions of its meaning, and actively engaging in the community of practice.[6] While Wenger's language here does not explicitly reference the telos concept, it mirrors that kind of emphasis on a common direction and meaning of practice. In Figure 3, I illustrate the common telos through the drop-shaped centre point with a forward orientation. The circles around it represent levels of participation.

In this chapter, I will describe the trajectories of nine individuals connected to the three formative practices which I identified and analysed in Chapter 6. I will then interpret the individual's trajectories as they move towards a new identity and

---

[5] Wenger (1999), p 153.
[6] Wenger (1999), p 173.

highlight differences within the particular communities.[7] While the nine persons have unique narratives, they still participate in the same communities of practice.

The church plants are places of identity formation and meaning-making, and for this, the teleological direction of the community and its tradition are both significant.[8] I will describe the individual trajectories in order to analyse how the persons are formed as Christians in the communities of practice. For each church plant, I will start by describing a central point of identification, a practice telos that builds community through imagination within the community, alignment with the community, and engagement in the community's formative practices.

7.3 Industrial City

I have already shown that the revival meeting is vital to Christian formation in the church plant in Industrial City. Now we will meet three persons who participate in this church plant – Erik, Eva, and Dani – and analyse how the revival meeting practice has formed them as individuals within the community of practice.[9]

As discussed in previous chapters, the telos of the revival meeting practice is to provide space for individuals to make a formative journey towards a personal Christian faith. This is done by addressing common issues of life, suggesting a Christian solution to these problems, and providing practices through which the individual can respond both emotionally and physically. The emphasis on the revival meetings within the church plant is related to the planters' own experience, but the organisation of the church plant is also motivated by a trust in God's ability to move participants through the meeting practice, making them God's fishermen.

Personal Trajectories

The following three narratives from the Industrial City church plant each focus on an individual who encountered the church with a relatively vague Christian

---

[7] The individuals are selected on the grounds that they are ordinary (not main leaders), frequent participants who are involved in and knowledgeable about the church plant. I have met them in the practices described in Chapter 6, and they have, therefore, been able to provide their reflections on the practices. The persons have given their written consent to participate in the study. All names have been changed for confidentiality reasons.

[8] Cf. Joel Halldorf (2015), "Storytelling and Evangelical Identities", in Jarlert, Anders (ed.), *Spiritual and Ecclesiastical – Biographies Research, Results, and Reading* (Kungliga vitterhets historie och antikvitets akademien), 128–139.

[9] All names have been changed in order to keep confidentiality.

identity, only to have that identity activated and reoriented around the telos of the community.

Erik

Erik was invited by a friend to the church plant about two years ago. He is in his early twenties and describes his family background as Christian, by which he means that he was baptised as a child and his family celebrated Christian holidays, such as Christmas and Easter. Still, he did not call himself a Christian before entering the church plant. He was very focused on financial and material success, he says and prioritised his education planning to pursue a career in business.

> [Erik]: I got very frustrated with society in my money hunt. About taxes and... I got almost a bit racist because it was during the migration crisis. So I connected that to taxation and all that and found that I really needed to get away from here. The US was the main alternative.

While working to go abroad, he met a girl who invited him to another church in Industrial City. He accepted the invitation. He found that he enjoyed the church's community, and the community was a place where, as he puts it, "he could be himself". Then "somewhere along the way, I also opened up to God". Erik followed another girl to the church plant's revival meeting. Later, she became his girlfriend.

> [Erik]: Seeds were sown slowly in me leading to my baptism, it must have been in December 2018. Because then [my girlfriend, Einar and Margareta] asked me if I would like to be baptised. I guess they had observed my longing. [...] And I have got to know God in this process. God has really done work in me, and I have got to know him... I mean, really... how should I put it? I went from going only because of the fellowship to a personal and individual relationship with God, where He has formed me and revealed things to me.

Erik experiences how God is actively working in him, and that this paves the way for his decision to be baptised. He responds to the gospel through faith and repentance. He connects faith and baptism relationally, comparing it to a wedding:

> [Erik]: I think you welcome God to do his work in you by being baptised. After this, there comes a transformation. [The baptism] is primarily a symbol of the will to live with God. You can compare it to a marriage. You have already chosen each other, in a way at least, but at the baptism, you say your yes, as you do in the wedding ceremony.

After his baptism, he abandoned his goal to leave the country and instead went to a bible school for a few months. He says he cannot identify the occasions when he first felt God's presence; instead, he describes a continual process where God worked on him over an extended time. Today, he can perceive God's exhortations to change behaviour and ways of thinking.

> [Erik]: Not that shaming "you shouldn't do this or that". The Devil is swift in telling you that "you are bad because you have done this", while God tells you that "you will be well if you do this instead".

Today Erik is not focused on a career. Instead, he has found another purpose – his life with God. This has led to different priorities. He notes that relationships have become more important to him, and he speaks and relates differently to other people than he did in the past. He describes how he used to see others as means for achieving his ambition to become rich, whereas he now sees others as gifts from God. His engagement in the revival meeting consists of participation in the welcoming team and greeting people who walk in the door. Through his involvement in the community and this practice, he has adopted a new cognitive framework and identity, and he actively embodies faith in the community's practices.

Erik describes how his girlfriend's habit of spending time alone with God made a particular impression on him, and he points to his girlfriend, Einar, and Margareta as role models who nudge him in the right direction. Further, the sermons at the revival meetings have been important to Erik.

> [Erik]: It was kind of supernatural because when [Einar and Margareta] talked and guided me through the subjects, it was like they were talking straight to me. It was as if [the church] existed only for my sake. You just... is this for me only? If I struggled with doubt or whatever, that was the subject they preached about. If it was "the will of God", they talked about that. If it was forgiveness, they talked about that, or grace, that was the subject. That was cool!

If his initial experience in the revival meeting was rather individualised, he has come to emphasise the communal elements of the church plant. In our conversation, he points out two aspects of the church that he finds important: that the church is like a family where you do not have to perform and that the church lets him be part of something greater that makes a difference in God's kingdom. He points to a "supernatural" illumination by the Spirit, who is active in the revival meeting. According to Erik, Christian faith is about having a relationship with God and believing God wants the best for you. He is a personal God, and we get to know him by reading the Bible, praying, sitting in stillness, and listening to worship music.

Erik describes the church plant mission strategy as relational. New people arrive through an invitation to the meeting. We see how Erik embodies the fisherman ideal when he tells how he invited a university friend who had expressed interest in the church. Erik met him at the train station, brought him to church, and sat with him during the revival meeting. Afterwards, Erik and his girlfriend took a long walk with him and discussed faith. Inviting his friends feels natural for Erik. He acknowledges that while they are on their own journey, it is his job to invite and travel with them. If they show interest, he can also invite them to the introductory course in the Christian faith – which he himself has gone through twice – or a small group, though he is not presently a member of one.

Eva

Eva was born and raised in Industrial City. Her mother had an open mind with regard to religion and spirituality, but her father was an aggressive atheist, as Eva puts it. The same was true of her paternal grandfather. From an early age, Eva wanted to believe in God, but it was only later, as an adult, that she explored the Christian faith. For several years, while living in another city, she took her son to a children's choir in the Church of Sweden. In this context, faith in God grew slowly in her. When she moved back to Industrial City, she went to a church and found that most people were older than her. She heard about a new church from a colleague at work – a colleague who now has become her fiancé – and accompanied him to a revival meeting:

> [Eva]: I have always felt that I am not worthy of God's love, but everyone in the church has tried to convince me otherwise. I have always felt that I am not good enough to attend church, and I thought you must wear a long dress. [...] You get a lot of new friends, and you talk about deep stuff. And they were present at my baptism. I get more real friends that you not only meet for a casual coffee. It's family, for real!

The fellowship in the church is important to Eva, and she likes the new church because it consists of many young people. She describes it as a family, and since there are several small children in the church, it fits Eva and her son. While she feels well-received in the community, Eva still considers herself to be fairly new to faith. She participated in the introductory course and says she learnt a lot from it, including how to read the Bible and pray. Though her baptism supported the formation of her identity as a Christian, Eva does not come from a church background. Still, she finds the language used in the different gatherings easy to understand. It is not as complicated as in the church she used to attend. She experiences it as more personal and less formal, which is something Eva appreciates – along with the fact that the clergy does not "wear strange robes":

> [Eva]: Everybody welcomes you, says hi, and they are curious. When I came along, I was [the fiancé's] girlfriend, and they said: "So great you could come", "Who are you?" and things like that. I think everyone, young and old, has approached me and asked about

me. It was easy to become part [of the fellowship]. [...] And you are allowed to come as you are, even if you would say that you don't believe in God. I think people would respond, "OK, that's fine".

Dani

Dani has been a Christian all her life. She grew up attending a small, rural free church, which she describes as a small, safe community where people knew each other well and decided things together. When I ask her to describe her ideal church community, she responds with the word "family":

> [Dani]: That is the word I want to associate with church. One thing that attracted me to [the church plant] in the beginning was that I perceived that there was a longing for community and an understanding of the church as a family. And that understanding was kind of lived out.

When she moved to Industrial City, one of her old pastors recommended that she visit the new church plant. In fact, Dani was present at the very first Sunday meeting of the church plant. At that meeting, she liked how the pastors expressed their vision about spreading the gospel message and reaching out to new people, and she felt she could identify with the vision they presented in a short video. Dani felt that her old church – a traditional free church in a small city – lacked spiritual depth. There, she regularly attended a "Women's Breakfast" where she found fellowship but little in the way of prayer or devotionals. For Dani, being a part of the Industrial City church plant was not about coming to faith but rather about participating in Christian ministry and being part of a community that embodies faith.

> [Dani]: You don't have to speak about Jesus every time, or even any time, really. But you need to talk about, perhaps, how you feel when life changes or how to develop a sustainable life. Instead, we talk about flowers and sheets and... well.

Dani was "super involved" in the church plant for about ten months. She participated in Sunday meetings and small groups, helped with different gatherings, and attended team meetings. Her expectations of the new church were high, but those expectations were not entirely met. She found that the church plant was too hierarchical and that some of the members did not affirm her views of life, spirituality, and the vision of the church. She points to the church's move to a new meeting place. The decision, she feels, had already been made before the church community was involved in the process. This was a red flag for her:

> [Dani]: You need to start having church assembly meetings [församlingsmöten], perhaps I am a little stuck with this format. It could be called something else. There could be some other structure, but a kind of structure that invites more people to participate.

The negative is that it takes more time. It is easier if the pastors decide. It is faster, and then perhaps you grow faster [sarcasm].

The spirituality that Dani prefers involves nature, prayer, and meditation. In the ideal church, she thinks that lives should be shared and decisions emerge from dialogue, not just the pastors' sermons. According to Dani, a good conversational environment is helpful to discipleship, and if a diversity of views is not possible, then new people cannot be included. As she deepened her understanding of the telos of the church plant, her engagement waned, and her participation finally ceased. In the end, Dani moved on and settled in another church that shared her views on spirituality, church, and diversity.

Trajectorial Analysis

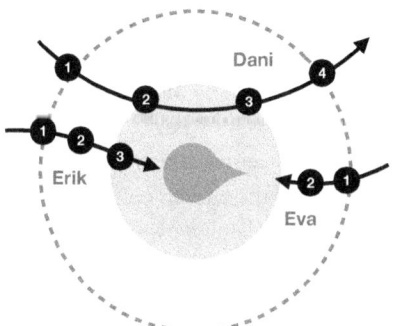

Erik:
1. Participates in the meeting
2. Introductory course, baptised
3. Voluntary group, leader team, invites people

Eva:
1. Participates in the meeting
2. Takes introductory course, gets baptised

Dani:
1. Participates in the meeting
2. Voluntary group involvement
3. Questions church culture
4. Goes to another church

Figure 4: Trajectories in participation and engagement of persons in Industrial City.

Figure 4 traces the trajectories of the three persons in Industrial City and visually describes the changes in participation and engagement in the church plant. In contrast to Dani's trajectory, Erik and Eva's trajectories are *inbound* in relation to the community of practice. In Erik's case, he is invited by his girlfriend and starts attending church meetings, (1) which increasingly aligns him with the vision and telos of the church plant. He proceeds to the introductory course on Christian faith and is baptised (2). After attending a Bible school in another city for a few months, he joins a voluntary group in the revival meeting and attends team leaders' meetings (3). He is no longer a newcomer but shares the vision. In my interview with Erik, he repeatedly uses the "we" pronoun to describe the church plant's vision and dealings. The fact that he is inviting friends and hosting them at the revival meeting also shows his clear identification with the church's vision and his personal engagement in mission. He has become just the sort of Fisherman that the church wants to foster.

Eva, too, is invited by her future life partner to the church meeting (1), then attends the introductory course and gets baptised (2). She refers to the others in the church as her family, but compared to Erik, she is less engaged in practical tasks and the inner workings of the church. (Whereas Erik uses "we" when speaking of the church, Eva refers to "they", signalling that she still views herself as somewhat outside the church.) While she learned a lot in the introductory course, she is still rather new to thinking about her faith in terms of a cognitive framework and what this might mean for her life and future.

Dani's trajectory starts as *inbound* but changes over time towards an *outbound* trajectory – a visual not unlike an inbound spacecraft that has miscalculated its re-entry and bounces off the earth's atmosphere. While this is not explicitly described in Figure 4, this change could also be framed as an *insider* trajectory. She has been identifying as a Christian since childhood and is no newcomer to the faith. When Dani moves to town, she attends the meeting and goes all in (1). She likes the vision, the fellowship and the leaders and participates in all ways possible. She actively takes part in the work of the church plant by volunteering during meetings (2). Dani's motivation declines as she learns more about the church culture (3), and when she finds another church that more closely embodies her own priorities, she aborts her current trajectory in the church plant's community of practice (4).

Summary

The main formative practice of this church plant is the Sunday revival meeting. The planters and other interviewed persons talk about the revival meeting as where the church happens. The central part of the meeting is the sermon. Erik's story confirms this image, as he mentions how the sermons not only speak to his own situation but also help him to grow cognitively in his faith, develop a Christian identity, and embody the Christian faith. All three persons emphasise the community aspect of their faith and being part of a "family"; however, in Dani's experience, a lack of affirmation and diversity in the community becomes decisive. Both Erik and Eva describe, albeit briefly, the development of a cognitive framework through the introductory course and a change in their identity through baptism. Erik mentions the ongoing process of being directly convicted of his sin by the Spirit, but generally, his formation is a function of communal practices, such as the meeting. He describes how joining a kind and generous community has allowed him to develop virtues of generosity and kindness, which have replaced the greed and selfish ambition that previously ruled him. The role of the baptismal practice as a communal practice is interesting as it marks a defining moment in Erik's faith journey and, to some extent, Eva's journey, too. Both feel that they are part of something greater than themselves. It is also interesting to note their growing sense of ownership of the church plant's vision, which is evident in how they act as Fishermen by inviting new people to the meetings. Indeed, the main arenas for self-transcending contributions are meeting-related, like inviting people and participating in different volunteering tasks.

7.4 Cathedral City

In Cathedral City, we will now meet three new persons who share their stories of how they became part of the church plant community. The church plant gathers in the local park during summertime and in homes during the cold season. Further, small groups run for most of the year, and as I have shown, these are significant in intentionally forming Christian habits and communities. Still, they are complementary to the home/park meeting.

As we have seen, the telos of the church plant is to shape an open community that fosters close relationships and a faith that involves one's whole life. Aligning with the formative practices and engaging in the life of church plant forms people into a certain kind of lived Christian identity, one that includes sharing this imagination of Christian life.

Personal Trajectories

Alex, Olof, and Ingrid are involved in both activities that are part of the church plant in Cathedral City, and their trajectories are described below.

Alex

Alex is in her early twenties and recently moved to Cathedral City for university studies. She met Anders and his wife, two church plant leaders, at the local university's Christian association. They invited her to the meeting in the park, which is how she came to join the church plant.

The Christian faith was not new to Alex. She has considered herself a Christian since she was fifteen, though the roots of her Christian identity reach deep into her childhood. She grew up in a small village where the church was a part of many people's lives, including her own and her mother's, and she remembers her grandmother telling her Bible stories and praying with her at bedtime. As a teenager, she went through the rite of confirmation in the Church of Sweden. The following year, she applied to be a student confirmation leader, a job that entails assisting the leader of the confirmation class. But despite her strong interest in faith, she was not accepted to the position. In her view, those who got the position were only there for the money:

> [Alex]: If you go to the confirmation class, it is a confirmation of the baptism. Then you are supposed to be surrounded by people who are good examples, spiritual role models who believe in God, believe in Jesus and represent the Christian life. And not only those who say: "No, I'm only here for the money". That was the sense you got.

She later began going to a local Pentecostal church that had "energy". There she found herself growing in faith. But she was critical of one of the pastors who she felt mistreated her friend, who identified as bisexual. On the whole, though, she describes the community as full of love and says she felt the presence of the Holy Spirit there:

> [Alex]: I really felt the Holy Spirit when I entered the building. Just wow! There is so much love, not only between people but also for God. It was so strong that you could almost touch it.

Before moving to Cathedral City, Alex worked for a couple of years, and her faith, as well as her engagement in a church, were put on hold. When she came to the meeting in the park, however, she felt that she had found a home. She participated in all that the church plant was organizing: the park/home meeting, small group, prayer walks, and book table by the local mall. Reflecting on her first months in the community, she says she felt very much at home. During the same time, Alex describes how she went through personal difficulties, experienced family tragedies, and saw friends fall into destructive relationships. She also struggles with low self-esteem and performance anxiety and finds it difficult to accept that God loves her. So far, she has not been sharing her faith much with friends at the university:

> [Alex]: But I feel that the more my faith is built up, [...] [the more] I will find the courage to become more missional. [...] Without [the church meeting] on Mondays via Zoom, I wouldn't have managed. It really fills me with energy, I would say. That is what is important to my faith today.

When I ask Alex about the most important activity for her in church, she points to the home/park meetings. She enjoys the focus on the Bible. Reading the Bible, she says, can become so performance-oriented, but reading the text together in the meeting makes more sense to her, especially when attendees are divided into small groups to discuss such questions as "Who is God?", "What can we learn about us as humans?", and "How is this text challenging me to live according to God's will today?". These small groups offer moments of discovery rather than showcasing achievement.

> [Alex]: It becomes so tangible and opens for curiosity, and I don't feel that performance anxiety that reading the Bible gave me before. With this Bible study as a foundation, we meet in small groups every second week.

Here, we see how the cognitive framework is discovered in the community. The practice of reading the Bible together occurs both in the home/park meetings and the small groups that gather between those meetings. For Alex, being a Christian means growing a sense of being loved by God, irrespective of her achievements. She identifies strongly with the telos of the church plant and feels that the church community is like a home where she can discover God's love. In her story, the Spirit becomes tangible in and through the community, thus affirming her Christian identity.

Ingrid

The membership status of Ingrid is not entirely clear. She grew up in another church in Cathedral City and is still somewhat active there. At the same time, she is increasingly active in the church plant. She reflects on a period of her life about ten years ago:

> [Ingrid]: Then, when I was around twenty, I was in a very active period. I was engaged in many things, and it all became a lot of activities. But when I stopped and thought about it, I felt that I didn't know why I did it. Do I really believe in this? Do I actually have any relation with God? Or why do I do all this?

It was not until she moved to another country to become a volunteer that she began to build her own faith, a faith independent of her parents' faith. This, she reflects, was done through prayer, Bible reading, and worship – a process that can be understood as a period of renegotiating her cognitive framework and developing her own identity as a Christian.

When she returned to Cathedral City, she started to attend Peter and Sofia's new church plant, though she maintained her membership in her previous church. Now, Ingrid is considering moving her membership to the church plant, but she has not yet made the decision. She says that it feels a bit like leaving your childhood home:

> [Ingrid]: When I got home, I heard that Peter and Sofia had started a new church plant in [this area], and I immediately felt in my heart that this was interesting. I would like to hear more about it. So I read on their web page about it, and I was just about to find an

apartment and ended up in [this area] partly because I like the cultural diversity and because it is cheap to live here.

When it comes to the church plant, she points to fellowship and Bible studies during the home/park meetings as particularly important for her, especially during the pandemic:

> [Ingrid]: Mainly, it is the fellowship I have with people who want to do and dream of the same things I dream of. It is those Bible studies where you can read the Bible and discover the Bible together. That is what these conversations aim at. I think this has been important for me to keep my faith alive this year.

She is part of a small group where the participants read the Bible and support each other through forming common habits. She notes that the small group has supported her Bible-reading and inspired her to pray for others more frequently. She feels that the members are struggling with similar issues, but as she puts it, "We keep an eye on each other". In general, Ingrid appreciates the church plant's tightly-knit community, which is very different from her former, much larger church. The sense of being on a mission is also much more salient in the church plant, which has a clearly articulated goal of spending time with people and building relations, for example, in the park. For Ingrid, participation in the church plant means embodying faith and engagement in common worship, edification, and outreach: "We talk to them and just be who we are with them". Here, we see the ideal of being neighbours, full of faith, showing God's love.

Olof

Olof has not always believed in God. His parents are not Christian, and as a child, he was not a Christian. But through contacts with the church in school and later through confirmation classes in the Church of Sweden, Olof found belief. Still, he would not describe his faith today as a personal relationship with God:

> [Olof]: I haven't felt the Holy Spirit directly, or what you could call it, that he has given me something… Some have these occasions where they have felt that the Holy Spirit is saying something [to them]. But I have not experienced any such occasion.

As Olof moved to Cathedral City to study at the university, he followed a friend to a church and then continued, on occasion, to attend the services there. As the pandemic hit, the friend invited him to the church plant's digital meetings, held via Zoom. Olof found that he enjoyed reading and discussing the Bible together when the meeting was divided into smaller groups, and since he lives outside Cathedral City, meeting online felt comfortable. He then joined an online small group. When comparing the small group with the larger meeting, Olof prefers the small group as it feels more personal and intimate. He sometimes finds the discussions in the larger meetings a bit formal since the groups change every meeting and not everyone knows each other. The small group, however, has been important to Olof's:

> [Olof]: Being part of the group has been a real strength. You always feel good after the group meetings. Then, praying for each other has been very good as well, I think. [...] I think the habits are helpful and important, and reading the Bible has been a good thing... because you get a better relationship with God when you read the Bible, and the conversations are very rewarding.

He sometimes finds it burdensome to read the Bible daily, as the small groups ask, because it does not give him anything of immediate value. But usually, he feels good after doing it because "after all, it is good for yourself". Still, Olof is sometimes ambivalent about dealing with matters of life in connection to what he reads in the Bible:

> [Olof]: I do want to believe, but I am pretty liberal. I look at the world in a rather liberal way, and it might not always harmonise with faith. [...] [When confronting views in the Bible that I don't agree with] I think I don't follow the Bible ...but I ignore it. Take alcohol, for example. The Bible says you shouldn't get drunk. I don't follow this [rule]. I think you should take responsibility for it if you want to get drunk.

In our later conversation about this, it becomes clear that Olof thinks that the biblical advice not to get drunk is good, but he does not always comply with it. Instead, he chooses to drink responsibly and thus does not comply blindly with how he understands the text. At other times, when he reads something strange or unreasonable, he completely disregards it. These examples show how Olof negotiates his long-term engagement through the small group's sub-practice of Bible-reading. This negotiation could be understood as synchronising his new Christian identity with a reasonable understanding of the cognitive framework he discovers through communal Bible-reading.

When I ask Olof whether he considers himself new or mature in faith, he responds that he feels rather new. Compared with the others in the small group he has been part of, he perceives himself to be the least experienced. While Olof says he will probably move back to his hometown soon, he feels positively about the prospects of joining a church there.

Trajectorial Analysis

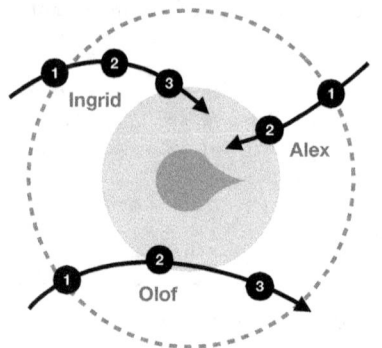

Ingrid:
1. Relationship with planters
2. Significant participation in activities
3. Moving into the area, missional engagement

Alex:
1. Participates in the meeting
2. Engages fully in the church activities

Olof:
1. Participates in the small group meeting
2. Engagement in habits and Bible reading
3. Moving to another area

Figure 5: Trajectories in participation and engagement of persons in Cathedral City.

In the lives of Alex, Ingrid, and Olof, we can see different trajectories of formation, as mapped out in Figure 5. Each person had different church experiences before coming to the Cathedral City church plant. The differences continue with Ingrid and Alex on *inbound* trajectories, while Olof's trajectory is *outbound*.

Ingrid grew up in a traditional Pentecostal church in Cathedral City and describes how she needed to go on a journey to find faith for herself, one that is independent of her family. She describes meeting with the church planters several years ago (1), which was significant for her present participation in their church plant. Today, she is engaged in most church plant activities (2) and finds that her Bible school experiences and education are welcomed. This opens new possibilities for engagement to Ingrid, who is trained in facilitating these kinds of groups, and she quickly becomes a valuable resource in the church plant. The fact that Ingrid decided to move into the area (3) was also a significant step for her. Now her home and life are linked to the mission of the church plant in everyday life. Interestingly, she is still part of her home church and claims she has not decided whether to leave it. At the same time, her engagement in the church plant is significant.

Alex has learnt Christian narratives and expressions of faith from her mother, grandmother, and her confirmation course. With that being said, she traces her own faith to a conversion experience in a local Pentecostal church. Her trajectory into the church plant community started with an invitation from Anders and his wife (1). Alex is highly engaged in the church plant and participates in meetings, small groups, and evangelistic activities (2). Bible-reading has become a formative experience for her, and the community has been supporting her through hardships during the past year. She expresses ownership of the telos of the community, and she calls it her home. Alex identifies strongly with the church plant, and her ownership of its telos grows through her engagement in ministry.

Olof, on the other hand, describes himself as a newcomer. He lives outside Cathedral City, and before the pandemic, he didn't visit the church plant. Olof has only been participating in online meetings, and his engagement has been facilitated by the church plant's adoption of digital meetings. A friend initially invited him to the meeting (1), and he has been a part of the small group that has been of great value to Olof, especially during the pandemic. Intentional habits and Bible-reading in a small community have provided Olof with material for faith formation (2). He negotiates the ethics that emerge from these conversations as he adapts them to his own life. The emotional response, seen in the calling narrative of the church planters, is limited in Olof's case. Olof says that he will leave the church plant community because he is moving from the Cathedral City area (3) and therefore takes an *outbound* trajectory.

Summary

The church plant in Cathedral City provides a community context of worship, edification, and outreach. As seen in Chapters 5 and 6, the focus on outreach and mission is strongly present in the church plant. As evidenced in the individual's stories, activities are organised in such a way as to encourage the participation of newcomers. The informants all acknowledge the role that Bible-reading plays in their formation of Christian identity: it provides the common narrative framework for understanding who God is and what following Jesus means today. The process of formation – and the establishment of a cognitive framework, a Christian identity, and an embodiment of faith –through the practice of common habits is ongoing. Interestingly, the ideal of being a faithful neighbour is mainly seen clearly in the story of Ingrid. Compared with the Industrial City church plant, the Cathedral City church plant has a much weaker emphasis on achieving cultural relevance through contemporary aesthetics and professionalism.

7.5 Harbour City

As I have shown previously, the community of practice in the Harbour City church plant engages in apprenticeship practices that foster individuals' dignity, Christian faith, and sense of mission, which I refer to as the ideal of being a good Samaritan. In the following narratives, three different trajectories will shed light on how the church plant's formative apprenticeship practice is imagined, adopted, and engaged. The telos of the formative practice draws newcomers towards a lived Christian identity – in this case, a life centred on Jesus, social ministry, and kindness.

Personal Trajectories

In following the trajectories of Helena, Anna, and Marianne, it will become clear that those who identify clearly with the telos of the church plant and its formative apprenticeship practice are characterised by their willingness to listen, let "Jesus take the initiative", and be part of a welcoming environment with empowering leadership.

Helena

I met Helena at the church premises as she had an appointment with Elisabet, one of the church plant leaders. She has been part of the church plant for about two years. She says that she always had some kind of faith in God, but before she came to the church plant, her knowledge of the Christian faith was limited, and she had no contact with the church.

> [Helena]: Before, I thought God and Jesus were two distinct persons. I didn't know you could read about them in the Bible. But I believed in God and that you get to heaven when you die. [...] Now I know more, but I still feel like a beginner.

Helena says that her faith has grown considerably since she joined the church plant. She was first introduced to the church plant when someone invited her to "Messy Church", a group where parents and their children explore faith together. "Messy Church" is held every other Thursday; on intervening Thursdays, the church hosts a faith and spirituality group for women. Helena joined both. The faith and spirituality group used the Alpha course as an introduction to the Christian faith, and Helena says she learned a great deal, including how to communicate with God.

Though Helena lives with a man who practices Asatro, the Old Norse religion, they accept each other's faith and frequently discuss matters of faith and religion. Interestingly, this dialogue with a non-Christian has helped Helena to integrate the cognitive framework of her faith:

> [Helena]: I can ask him about my faith to get new perspectives on it. I find religion and other people's faith very interesting. His brother has converted to Islam. Personally, I think other religions seem very weird. They are really out in the woods.

Elisabet is coaching Helena in her faith and leadership. In their sessions, they use the APEST[10] tool to understand better how Helena can approach her life and locate her in the church plant puzzle. Helena has found this mentorship to be very helpful. She has also become something of a mentor herself, leading a small group with another woman whom she feels complements her rather well. When the pandemic ends, Helena hopes to expand her involvement and join the church plant's social ministry.

Marianne

Marianne, who is about sixty years old, is relatively new to the Christian faith. She was raised by non-Christian parents, though she was baptised as an infant and, as a child, sometimes accompanied a neighbouring family to a large Pentecostal church – experiences she remembers as nice but a bit shallow and fake. Over the years, Marianne has sometimes visited churches for baptisms and funerals, but it is not until recently that Marianne has come to really engage with the Christian faith. It all started when Marianne and a friend attended a sewing course in another Harbour City church, where a deacon suggested that she visit this new church plant. Marianne did visit, and she enjoyed it from the very first moment she walked in the door:

> [Marianne]: You can feel it as you enter the place. First of all, everyone is welcome there, and when you come, they stand there to welcome you. You can see that they really mean it. It is not fake.

Marianne frequently tells others about the church plant and invites them to come. Her outgoing, open personality helps in this regard, as can be seen in a story she tells about a man that she once invited:

> [Marianne]: One random guy I met had experienced a psychosis that very weekend. I met him on Friday, and we started to talk. He was only thirty, but somehow he started to tell his life story. We enjoyed talking, he liked me, and I liked him, so we kept in contact. He called me from the psychiatric clinic and asked if I wanted to visit him. "Of course, I do", I said. So I asked him if he wanted to come to [the church plant], so he did. And I mean, he had a problem with drugs. He has been healed and doesn't use that stuff anymore. And they really love him. He is so sweet!

While she says she has always believed in God, she is uncomfortable calling herself a Christian, but evidently, she acts according to the good Samaritan ideal. Marianne gives me two different reasons for this. First, it is a matter of theology. She finds the story about Jesus' crucifixion problematic: Why would God crucify his

---

[10] The APEST tool is described in the previous chapter.

own son? Her way of approaching this and similar matters demonstrates that she is clearly knowledgeable about the Christian faith. The other reason has to do with the embodiment of faith. If you call yourself a Christian, she continues, you should be almost perfect – like Jesus. That is what she sees in the leaders of the church plant, whom she describes as extraordinary people. She, on the other hand, does not believe in the crucifixion and is not perfect. Thus she cannot call herself a Christian. "But somehow, God can live in me anyway", she adds. For Marianne, God is love, and being a Christian means having love in your heart. When asked why she decided to baptise her own children despite not considering herself a Christian, she responds:

> [Marianne]: I think about my children's baptism as I do about my own. All my children are baptised. My ex-husband was not happy about it, but I wanted to have them baptised and to have God's protection. So I think I have God's protection as well since I am baptised. That's how I think about it.

Interestingly, while Marianne does not explicitly identify as a Christian, she is highly engaged in the activities of the church plant. She is even co-leading a small group but seems to be ambiguous when defining what being Christian means. She has participated in "Messy church", the faith and spirituality group for women, and has frequented the Sunday services. During the pandemic, she has been to online services. She often goes to a friend's house so that they can participate on her computer together. Before the pandemic, the church plant had parties at people's homes, which she really enjoyed.

Anna

Anna lives outside Harbour City with her family. She was raised in a Christian family and, as a young adult, attended a Bible school in Stockholm and participated in several small churches in the area. Three years ago, she moved to the Harbour City area with her husband and children. From Anna's experience, small churches mean that everyone is needed and everyone can play a part. While this is often positive according to her, small churches can also place stressful demands on their members. This was the case for Anna, who sought to find a larger church when her family moved to Harbour City. While they enjoyed attending a large Pentecostal church, they eventually ended up in the church plant after becoming friends with Elisabet and Karl and visiting the church plant's Sunday meeting.

> [Anna]: It took a few months, and then we found our place there and have never left. My husband is not a Christian, but he also felt very welcome there, which was important to me. We had to go somewhere where we both felt comfortable.

Anna describes an inclusive community characterized by a "come as you are" culture and contrasts it with her experiences in Stockholm, where she felt pressure to look and behave in a certain way. The church plant in Harbour City is very diverse and open-minded and takes people in whether or not they have a Christian faith.

Anna is in the process of recovering from burnout, and as part of her recovery, she is working through issues of self-image and self-esteem – from both a general and theological perspective – with Jan, one of the church plant's leaders. Additionally, Anna has been part of the faith and spirituality group for women, which she perceives as the most important place of growth for her, not so much in terms of understanding the cognitive framework of the Christian faith but rather in terms of synchronising her faith with her identity as a Christian and experiences of the Spirit. While Sunday meetings have been important in ministering to others, she finds that the sermons lack depth.

From her childhood, she tells me, Anna brings a rather austere view of God, making her almost immune to receiving God's love. While this has been the main theme in many sermons she has heard, she has viewed God as demanding. The small and missionally-oriented churches she has been part of have usually resonated with this rather activistic understanding of faith. But in the context of this church plant, she is starting to find a God of love:

> [Anna]: [Here] it has been the opposite. God is not a judge but rather very much love. I mean, God is loving. I have read that in the Bible, but it has been hard for me to take in. [In this church] I have been able to work this through a lot with [Jan] and the other leaders that... and I am not finished yet... but I have met a much more loving God.

She points out one important condition for the possibility of this change: one is allowed to ask questions and question the given answers. This freedom has not always been a given in Anna's previous church experiences. Anna tries to read the Bible daily, but as she reads, she has so many questions about the texts and their issues, which is why she enjoys talking to Jan, who patiently tries to answer all her questions. I assess that Anna's trajectory is hindered by previous experiences of activistic culture in small churches, and while this is present to some extent in this church plant, it is tempered by a presentation and practice of Christian faith that is accepting and welcoming.

Trajectorial Analysis

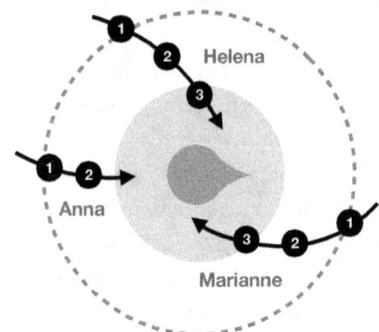

Marianne:
1. Recommended by deacon
2. Increasing participation in activities
3. Actively invites people, leader of small group

Anna:
1. Participation in meeting
2. Increased engagement and personal growth

Helena:
1. Participation in "Messy church"
2. Increasing participation in activities
3. Leader of small group, engaged in apprenticeship practice

Figure 6: Trajectories in participation and engagement of persons in Harbour City.

Marianne presents an interesting case in the Harbour City trajectories (Figure 6). She does not identify as a Christian and, as such, is unable to become a full member of a free church community, a process that usually demands a confession of the Christian faith. In the church plant, however, she is considered a full member "on a journey" within the community and is on an *inbound* trajectory. Following her participation and engagement trajectory, we see that Marianne participates in most of what is going on in the church plant. Her engagement started with a recommendation from a deacon (1) working in another church who thought Marianne and her friend would fit into the church plant's community. Marianne experienced the fellowship as warm, accepting, and inclusive. She started to engage in different activities and groups, such as the faith and spirituality group for women, Sunday meetings, and "Messy church" (2). Elisabet refers to Marianne as an evangelist because she invites and brings people to the church plant. Due to this engagement, and despite the lack of a formal confession, she is now co-leading a small group with another leader (3).

Anna and her husband also highlight the inclusivity they found in the church plant's fellowship. While she finds that sermons and worship might be stronger in other churches, the community is caring and allowing, which is important to Anna. Anna and her husband started coming to the church plant when they met two of the leaders and decided to visit the Sunday meeting (1). For health reasons, she has not engaged as much as she would like in the church plant activities. She has been to Sunday meetings, small groups, and the faith and spirituality group for women (2). Anna has an *inbound* trajectory, and the church plant has made it possible for her to re-imagine and re-form her view of who God is. While she has identified as a Christian her whole life, the implications of that identity have shifted over time. Though Anna identifies strongly with the telos of the church plant, her health condition limits her engagement, as mentioned above. Here we see a dilemma when strong social activism conflicts with the desire to provide a healing environment for vulnerable people. This is something the church plant grapples with, and the dilemma will be further developed in the following chapter. It can also be noted that the apprentice relationship with Jan is helpful for Anna's Christian formation, while the Sunday services are not.

Helena's *inbound* trajectory resembles that of Marianne's. They come from non-Christian backgrounds but have had a degree of religious faith all their lives. They were both invited to "Messy church" (1), had a positive encounter with the church plant community, and became fully engaged in the practices of the church plant (2). Today, they are both co-leading a small group (3). Helena, however, has experienced a formation that is primarily cognitive in nature; however, Marianne's formation has been a matter of socio-relational development within the community. Helena's formation is supported by the APEST tool, and as a result, she is looking for opportunities for further engagement in social ministry. Here, the apprentice relationship with Elisabet is also important to Christian formation.

Summary

The main way of doing outreach in the church plant is through social ministry, which then leads to various apprenticeship practices. To a high degree, the church plant is a ministry to the city, providing personal growth plots and self-identity development. As the focus is on people in the margin, the exposition of faith stays rather basic. Edification activities are oriented towards the embodiment of faith in practically oriented mentoring sessions and, to a lesser degree, towards an intellectual understanding of faith. The community avoids the language of difference, which makes people feel welcome, but it might diminish the momentum of the formation of Christian identity. For example, the gospel proclamation in the stories being told does not emphasise the possibility of repentance. Care and empowerment are present through the apprenticing practices in the church plant. The church plant does not want to emphasise professionalism or cultural relevancy. Instead, they prioritise giving space for everybody to contribute according to their gifts by serving in and through the community.

7.6 Conclusion

In this chapter, I used practice theory to analyse formative trajectories in the church plant communities. One advantage of this analytical angle is that formation is understood as ongoing rather than binary. In the narratives, Christian formation is described as a dynamic, continual process of forming a lived identity. Focusing on the practices also unveils the significant role of the community, both in understanding what faith means to the participants and the formation of individuals towards the practice telos.

One result from the analysis of the personal stories is that the formative trajectories emphasise the person's experience of God. The informants often identify God as an active agent in their ongoing formation, both directly and through the community. Given this result, it follows that formation leadership in church plants involves knowing when to step back to let the formation proceed uninterrupted.

In the analysis of the trajectories, I describe movements between the periphery and the centre, where the centre represents the telos of the practice. Newcomers enter the community of practice and grow through participation and engagement in the formative practices of the church plant. I have shown how participants in the practices move from the periphery of the church plants towards full participation, which entails their developing a lived Christian identity in a church plant. Hence, becoming Christian in these church plants can be described as participation in formative practices that lead people to identify with the church plant community telos.

One interesting aspect of the church plants is their openness towards newcomers. Individuals who are relatively new to the church plant or even to the Christian faith are allowed to enter into full engagement by becoming both owners of the formative practices and voluntary ministers in the central practices – sometimes without a formal confession of their own. Sociologist Grace Davies has described membership in the traditional state churches in Europe as "belonging without believing". This is often understood in contrast with evangelical and charismatic congregations, which are described as communities of believers. But here, in the church plants, we see cases of "participation without believing" – and belonging through participation.

This chapter answers the research question of *how people are formed towards a lived Christian identity in the church plant communities?* In conclusion, I find that there are different levels of formative identification in the church plants. Newcomers enter the community of practice and grow through participation and

8. Negotiating Secular Culture

The call to ecclesial re-imagination brings a re-evaluation of cultural issues. How much can the church plants adapt to the contemporary culture without losing their distinctive identity as churches? This chapter addresses those issues by answering the research question: *What cultural tensions do the church plants negotiate, and what do the negotiations mean to Christian formation?* By using the concept of negotiation, I show that the communities are still developing identities, cultures, and practices. Negotiation refers to a meaning-making process around cultural issues in the communities of practice, and this conversation is part of the Christian formation in the secular culture.[1] Naturally, my analysis involves a theological discernment in formative practice.

Generally, negotiation means that two or more parts are giving and taking, bargaining to reach an agreement on a particular issue. If negotiation is an aspect of Christian formation in the church plants, it is fair to ask what is being negotiated and who is doing the negotiating. In this chapter, the negotiation takes place between the church plants and the secular culture. These negotiations take place on two levels. The first level entails external negotiations – that is, negotiations between the church plants (subculture) and the broader (pluralist) culture. The second level of negotiations is internal – negotiations within the church plants themselves. As individuals bring secular narratives, meanings, and perspectives into the church plants, the communities form an understanding of what it means to be Christian in terms of a lived identity in conversation with a secular setting.

Analysing Formative Negotiation

According to Wenger, identity formation is a dual process of identification and negotiability. Identification is described as "an investment of the self in relations

---

[1] As pointed out in the introduction, I have chosen to view the subculture of the church plants as Christian and the culture of the surrounding society as secular. While this might be a helpful distinction when studying religion in the contemporary context, this is a simplified perspective. The reality is not as clear-cut, which will become evident in this chapter.

of association and differentiation" that "generates the social energy that sustains both our identities and our communities in their mutual constitution".[2] Negotiability "determines the degree to which we have control over the meanings in which we are invested". Wenger does not view his approach as different from identification concepts used in psychology.[3] However, he qualifies the process of forming identity using his familiar "modes of belonging": *engagement, imagination* and *alignment*.[4] As I have shown in Chapters 5, 6 and 7, I see these modes as part of forming a lived Christian identity in the church plants. Participating in a church plant means engaging through participation, investing in the social imagination, and aligning with the arrangements of the community.

8.1 Culture, Tradition, and Negotiation

As the previous chapter made clear, the communities studied here are not homogenous. The individuals who attend the church plants each come with different expectations and participate with different levels of engagement. However, by being a part of the church plants, they participate in the same practices – practices that are rooted in the particular telos of the community of practice. Indeed, when a church is planted, it is not a blank slate, as it were; rather, the negotiability of its telos is affected by, among other things, the church planters' faith tradition. My impression is that when negotiating contemporary issues, the various church planters all try to find a balance between being culturally relevant and being faithful to their ecclesial traditions. In this chapter, I will describe examples of negotiation in the communities of practice and analyse them as aspects of a sociocultural ecosystem.

Culture and Consensus

Kathryn Tanner has analysed the concept of culture and how it can be used in theological studies. In a general sense, culture can be described as a "defining mark of human life". Cultures are understood to constitute and construct human nature, and they are related to the institutions, rituals, artefacts, beliefs and values in

---

[2] Wenger (1999), pp 188, 192.
[3] Wenger (1999), p 192. E.g., Karl Inge Tangen uses identification from a more psychologically-oriented perspective.
[4] These concepts are explained on pp 98-99. In short, *engagement* means participatory trajectories in the community of practice, *alignment* means the adaptation of individuals to the common practice, and *imagination* is the social process of imagining preferred futures, which I connect with "calling".

different groups or societies.⁵ But there is also a postmodern critique which objects to the tendency to associate culture with an all-shared social consensus by the group members. These critics argue that this leads to determinism and the belief that a society shapes its members definitively. According to the postmodern position, a lack of understanding of cultural heterogeneity is "a hypothetical construction of the discipline that unself-consciously distorts the realities of lived practice", as Tanner puts it. The group boundaries and landscapes of meaning are constantly moving. They are not stable and thus not – as the modernists tended to think – able to protect the homogenous whole from disruptions:⁶

> The postmodern anthropologist can still consider culture an essentially consensus-building feature of group living. That consensus becomes, however, extremely minimalistic: it forms the basis for conflict as much as it forms the basis for shared beliefs and sentiments. Whether or not culture is a common focus of agreement, culture binds people together as a common focus for engagement.⁷

Tanner does not one-sidedly accept a postmodern understanding of culture, but she is sceptical about viewing groups as homogenous. She admits that there might be a minimalist consensus but emphasises the group's heterogeneity. Tanner's point is valid because the modernist approach of studying groups as having uniform goals and understandings of meaning easily leads to simplistic interpretations. However, I think even some minimalist consensus bears significance. In analysing the culture of communities, we need to acknowledge what is common, but at the same time, remind ourselves that this is not the whole story. Therefore, the culture is, in this sense, a moving landscape in which faith is negotiated where some things are held common, and others are not. In the communities, individuals construct the meanings through practice, and the communities and practices, in turn, shape the individuals.

Tradition

While the church plants are, in a sense, new, they still belong to a specific tradition with a long history of social habits and institutions, rituals and artefacts, and beliefs and values. The three communities of this study are in Swedish urban settings

---

⁵ Kathryn Tanner (1997), *Theories of Culture: A New Agenda for Theology*, Augsburg: Augsburg Fortress. For an engaging text on the Swedish consensus culture, see Rosenberg, G, "The Crisis of Consensus in Postwar Sweden" in N Witoszek, & L Trägårdh (eds.), *Culture and Crisis: The Case of Germany and Sweden*, Berghahn Books, New York, 2002, pp. 170–201.

⁶ Tanner (1997), p 42.

⁷ Tanner (1997), p 57.

and share a cultural heritage of the Swedish free church movement. Even though Tanner recognises a historical component, her understanding of culture is occasionally marked by an over-particularism that undermines this aspect:

> Christians in the fourteenth century did not believe what Christians believed in the fourth century, nor do African Christians believe what European Christians believe because of differences in their respective ways of life. Theological description of missions, the spread of Christianity by evangelization, becomes in this way the study of "enculturations".[8]

Of course, there is some truth to the argument that Christianity takes different forms in different historical and cultural situations.[9] However, just like in the case of the discussion about homogeneity, I think Tanner somewhat underestimates the role of tradition in Christian belief and practice. A consequence of accepting Tanner's argument would be to speak of Christianities in plural rather than a singular Christianity. I understand this as a matter of "both-and" rather than "either-or". The church and Christianity are both different and the same. There is continuity as well as change, and part of this is because churches have been adapting to different kinds of cultures. Here, we see how this discussion on homogeneity and tradition relates to the integrity of the Christian identity when negotiating secular culture in the church plants.[10]

In this chapter, I will analyse secular perceptions, cultural relevance, and how the communities deal with issues of individualism, performance culture, and power. My reference to the secular context as culture can be understood in an organic and ecological manner: It is an ecosystem to which the church plant is trying to adapt while simultaneously striving for sustainable integrity and resilience.

---

[8] Tanner (1997), p 62.

[9] Neve (2021) p 238, suggests employing a trifocal lens in assessing culture in Emerging churches that critically audit and exegete Christian tradition, Scripture, and culture. In this process, the churches' previously held positions are challenged and revised; simultaneously, the contemporary culture is challenged prophetically in the churches' practice of Scripture and Christian tradition. These processes result in (1) a more authentic local cultural expression of the Christian faith and (2) a modified Christian tradition. Church plants do not necessarily have the explicit intention of renewing the tradition. Still, this auditing is, to some degree, inevitable when building something new and practical theological choices are required. The trifocal lens is not easily distinguished, but it is still helpful in trying to understand what is involved in the formative practice.

[10] One way of dealing with this dual situation is proposed by Rowan Williams, who argues that the church is held together by the confession to the same Christ over the course of history. Rowan Williams (2005), *Why Study the Past*, Grand Rapids, Michigan: Eerdmans.

8.2 Negotiating Secular Perceptions

Before addressing the issues of negotiation within the communities, we will look at how the church plants perceive themselves to be viewed by secular society. The informants in the church plants express views on how they are perceived as Christians in society. These views are an essential ingredient in the meaning-making happening in the communities of practice since one's self-perception is affected by notions of how others perceive oneself.[11] Therefore, these perceptions give us a sense of the culture in which the church plants form Christian faith and life. These findings then serve as a background to the missional calling of the church plants and how it is negotiated in the communities.

The Spiritual Poverty of Sweden

A common theme among the study's participants concerns the perceived spiritual poverty of the broader Swedish culture. The following quotes are from leaders of the church plants:

> [Sara]: We experience a kind of spiritual poverty in Sweden [...] There are many historical explanations as to why we perceive things as we do in Sweden. This averseness towards mainly Christian faith, and religion in general... I think the church has been affected by this because we believe we need to be friends with everyone and prove that we are not stupid all the time.

> [Margareta]: In some way, we think Sweden is a spiritual wasteland. We are well off materially and have all possibilities of self-realisation and all that. Still, compared to other contexts, countries and cities, Sweden is a spiritual wasteland. So we hope to be a voice that preaches the gospel and the truth of God in our region.

In their analyses of the cultural context where their churches are planted, Sara and Margareta describe Sweden's lack of religious competence and sensitivity.[12] Sara

---

[11] Bartholomä (2015) investigates the topic of self-other differentiation in the case of free-church identity. In that case, it is about the free church in relation to the State church. In the present case, it regards the relationship between the church plants and the secular majority culture.

[12] Sara refers to a political debate about whether to allow organisations or companies to run schools with any voluntary religious activities that supplement the standard curriculum and regular schedule of classes. This discussion is highly ideological, and is often marked by an aversiveness towards religion and practitioners of religion. E.g., The Christian Council of Sweden (ed.) (2020), *Unga troende i samhället – Varannan kristen ungdom upplever sig kränkt för sin tro*, Stockholm: Christian Council of Sweden. The Christian Council of Churches in Sweden surveyed 393 individuals ages 13–25, 60% of whom belonged to the Free churches, on the question:

expresses dissatisfaction with situations when the church adapts too much to the demands of society. Margareta considers this lack of spirituality as an opportunity to preach the gospel.

The Church as Questioned or Ignored

Some respondents also perceived a hostile and demeaning view of Christians in society in Swedish secular culture.

> [Björn]: What does it mean to be a Christian today?
>
> [Lars]: Well, that is not always easy. You are considered... not a total idiot, but people think you are a bit weird.
>
> [Charlie]: [Sweden] is a secular country, like, nobody cares. Everybody says they respect their religion, but nobody believes in God in Sweden.

The experience of being seen as "weird" affects how one understands one's role and engagement in the cultural arena. People who sense that society deems their views or beliefs to be incomprehensible or invalid can either defend or renegotiate those views.[13] Charlie comes from a non-Western country where religion is very much part of everyday life, and different religious groups live side by side, sometimes in harmony, sometimes not. He thinks Sweden lacks respect for religion and that few really believe in God. Alex also has the experience of being a somewhat odd minority:

> [Alex]: The country we live in is built on Christian values, but thinking back at my late teens, me and another girl [name], who was part of the local Eritrean church, were the only confessing Christians in our class. It was pretty exciting to study natural sciences with a bunch of atheists and have had religious education during the last year. The fact that we live in a very secular country, where being Christian is a norm-breaking thing, is exciting. [...] When you ask around, you realise that most people in my generation haven't even heard about the Bible and what it says, and Jesus...

According to Alex, the norm is atheism. To not conform to the majority culture is to risk being ridiculed or questioned for one's deviating views.[14] But as someone

---

Have you been subjected to violations because of your faith? The result was disheartening: 48.7% answered yes, 39% no, and 12.2% were unsure. Even more concerning was the question about who had committed the violation: 23% answered that it was a teacher in school.

[13] Cf. Root (2017a) who uses the terms "fundamentalism" and "bourgeoise Christianity" as two paths in response to cultural change.

[14] Strhan (2015), p 198, identifies strong imaginative lines that divide the evangelical church community from the surrounding culture. She analyses this partly as a feature of the modern fragmentation of cities.

who likes to question and debate cultural assumptions, Alex thinks the secular culture's incomprehension toward religious belief is an exciting challenge rather than something that concerns her.

Lack of Knowledge and Tolerance

Alex points to a lack of knowledge among the majority, something Erik mentions, too:

> [Björn]: What hinders people from becoming Christian if you look at this society, this city or Sweden?
>
> [Erik]: I don't think you have time to reflect. In my case, it was greed and money. And then... many think that, "I'm doing fine, why would I become a Christian?" You don't see the point. And some think that this is a religious thing and you have to pray five times a day, then I have to read the Bible, I don't have time for that.

According to Erik, Swedes usually cannot see the point of faith. Religion is reduced to rules and onerous tasks. Erik, however, understands faith more as a relationship with God and fellow Christians. Anders perceives a similar lack of understanding among most Swedes and thinks that it affects the mission of the church plant:

> [Anders]: The general picture today in atheist Sweden is that you may have your faith, and that is good for you – but faith is private, just like your economy and political views. But I don't agree with this. Faith should be shared and demonstrated in public, which is part of discipleship, kind of. But that doesn't mean that people react positively. They did not do so in the Bible, either. Perhaps we modern Christians are a little bit too comfortable.

Referring to the words of Jesus about not being ashamed of him, Anders says that negative reactions to sharing faith are part of the deal when being Christian.[15]

In conclusion, the identity of Christians in the communities is, to some extent, shaped by a sense of being a questioned or ignored anomaly in a spiritual wasteland that is characterized by a lack of religious literacy and even intolerance towards religious groups. These mostly negative perceptions of how Christians are viewed in secular Sweden form an important background to the discussion about

---

[15] Cf. Maria Zackariasson (2016), *Gemenskapen*, Stockholm: Molin & Sorgenfrei; Zackariasson (2012), p 5, finds that "The religiousness associated with the free churches thus contributes to establishing them as different or diverging, in relation to the image of Sweden as a highly secularised country, at the same time as they are firmly rooted in Swedish history and tradition". My translation.

negotiability. What also emerges from the perceptions of the informants is a motive for new church plants: to challenge and ultimately transform the secular culture.

8.3 Adaptability: Negotiating Relevance

Maintaining relevancy in constantly changing cultural landscapes is a crucial issue for churches in modern societies. A common critique levelled at the established churches by the missional movement is their perceived structural and ideological rigidity.[16] The consequence of this inflexibility is the churches' inability to address contemporary challenges and engage the concerns of the culture. But even among the more flexible church plants, not everything can be adapted to the broader cultural context. This is evident in two examples from the material that illustrates how the church plants deal with pluralism.

Unique Church Expressions

One theoretical approach to pluralism can be found in Religious Market Theory (RMT), which looks at "supply" and "demand" in certain "segments" of the "religious market".[17] This theory posits that churches are offering a product in the marketplace of religion and spirituality. At times, the language of the planters reflects this market-based perspective:

> [Margareta]: We have a unique track to run, which we need to stay on. Just like all churches in this city, it has its unique track. We always try to communicate that we are not the full market supply. Some will like what we do, and others will feel that this is not my thing.
>
> [Einar]: We have a liturgy where we read Bible texts, and we have a [fancy] small light rig and so on. It's neither flashing lights nor a clerical collar. This middle way is where I

---

[16] Neve (2021) emphasises the relation-oriented nature of emerging churches. Stuart Murray (2018), *Post-Christendom: Church and Mission in a Strange New World*. Second Edition, Eugene, Oregon: Wipf and Stock. Murray consistently argues for a Post-Christendom that leaves behind religious institutional power.

[17] Eva M Hamberg (2015), "Religious Monopolies, Religious Pluralism, and Secularization: The Relationship between Religious Pluralism and Religious Participation in Sweden", *Interdisciplinary Journal of Research on Religion*, 11; Boy (2015). Boy, among others, is partly critical towards this theory since it does not question the fences of the market. It is not relevant, the critics say, to consider religion and spirituality as a clearly delimited segment. In his investigation of church-planting movements, Boy finds that the commonly assumed competition between churches is non-existent or at least overly exaggerated.

think most people feel they can be themselves the most. In the party church, I need to hype myself up to reach a level of holiness I usually don't have.

The church planters in Industrial City use an RMT discourse to emphasise the need for churches with different cultural and theological expressions. This position gives a rationale for their own project, which addresses the need for more expressions of church in the city. The planters acknowledge that the unity of the church is important. Still, while they are in contact with other local churches, they do not think that the permission or blessing of those churches is necessary to plant churches in the city.[18] The planters are independent and they form the new church according to their own views.[19]

Parts of the RMT are articulated in the missional discourse. Churches need to be different (supply) because people are different (demand) and need to hear the gospel in their own cultural language. While this view is only expressed explicitly by one of the church plants, it can also be detected in the discourse surrounding the two other church plants.[20]

Lifestyle Symbols

The following scene in Industrial City is an interesting example of how the church plant involve certain trademarks, or lifestyle symbols, into the liturgy:

The meeting in Industrial City is just about to begin. There is an unusual sense of expectation on stage as the musicians begin to lead the congregation in worship: "All that was before is now a distant past because You have made me free". But after just one song, Margareta appears on stage, and the projection of the prayerful lyrics is replaced by an image of an album cover and two familiar logos. The service has

---

[18] During spring 2022 they started to plant a new church in a neighbouring city. The week before the first meeting they advertised at the website of a major Christian newspaper about their start-up inviting people who were looking for a church in that city.

[19] Cf. Björn Asserhed (2023), "Jag ber att de alla ska bli ett, då ska världen tro", in Jaktlund, Carl-Henric, Neve, Mattias, and Rudäng, Emma (eds.), *Nya vägar för världens skull: förändringsarbete i frikyrkliga församlingar* (Bromma: Libris), 259–280. I find three different approaches to the ecumenical community among church planters: *participation* (full integration in the ecumenical community), *negotiation* (a strategic relation to other churches in order to avoid and manage conflicts), and *seeking* (positive but independent relationship). The perspectives are not mutually exclusive but often combined.

[20] This argument also aligns well with the new churches paradigm of Paas (2016).

become a release event for the church plant's new single. Margareta interviews the two musicians who wrote the song, asking about "the heart behind it". One of the songwriters tells us the story behind the new song, which she describes as a prayer of surrender to God and thankfulness over what Jesus did for us on the cross. The pair then talked about how they wrote the song and how Margareta was moved to tears when she joined them in the recording studio. As the interview ends, the crowd erupts in cheers, obviously proud of their church's new release. When the song is finally played, two logos are projected on big screens on the wall behind the stage. Apple's and Spotify's icons are watching over us as we worship. The service then continues with a collection, and Einar encourages the visitors to contribute with resources: "When you give economically, you are also behind this song. Don't give because you have to, but because you want to".

Scene: Industrial City, Sept. 6, 2020.

The worship meeting is held in a secular culture hall that was designed with concerts, not liturgy, in mind. In this worship service, however, contemporary music is a central part of the liturgy. The free church meeting tradition is open to involving popular themes, media, practices, and language.[21]

> [Margareta]: We wanted to celebrate this moment together as a church, what we had accomplished, and praying for this to be a blessing to people around the nation. We were just happy to be able to be a small part of the music world.
>
> [Einar]: Releasing this great song creates a sense of confidence in the church. We are not stuck with songs from the seventies and eighties. Giving birth to new songs strengthens the phase we are in at present. This song affected us this whole period because when we heard it, we acknowledged the theme for this season: let Your will be done.

---

[21] E.g. Joel Halldorf (2017), *Biskop Lewi Pethrus: biografi över ett ledarskap : religion och mångfald i det svenska folkhemmet*, Skellefteå: Artos. Halldorf names Pentecostal spirituality, the dominant tradition of the Industrial City church plant, as "popular religion": Sune Fahlgren (2006), *Predikantskap och församling*, Uppsala: Uppsala university. Fahlgren describes how free church liturgy incorporates new media during the twentieth century. Furthermore, Sune Fahlgren (2018), "Gudstjänst i pentekostala kyrkor", in Sundmark, Stina Fallberg (ed.), *Kristen gudstjänst: en introduktion* (Skellefteå: Artos), 169–198, argues that Neo-Pentecostal churches are cutting-edge in their use of modern media and their ability to tap into global music and fashion trends.

An interesting aspect of the scene described above is the involvement of commercial logos. Here lifestyle symbols from the secular culture become part of the liturgy. As previously noted, the leaders describe worship music as sung prayers to God. The formative act of singing prayers, confessing God and declaring truths over your life has a clear direction in line with the telos of the church plant, which is to become persons who reflect who God is to the world. But during this time of liturgical prayer, a release event is taking place. This is a different practice, bringing a different telos.

When I ask the planters about the logos and the risk of forming the participants into consumers of the contemporary culture, they find it hard to see this as a problem. They reflect on commercialising the meeting and promoting certain brands:

> [Einar]: We do that a lot. If you follow us on Instagram, suddenly, we have advertised Instagram, but consumption is always around. [...] We want to resist this consumption thing, but we won't make it a central issue because it just leads away from the focus on why you should become a Christian. Not because society is bad but because God is good. That is the focus. By showing those logos, we say we are part of and live in this world. We are not separated from it.

They acknowledge the culture of consumption as part of the world that should be resisted, but at the same time, they take advantage of the symbols and media techniques in their communication with people who are used to this cultural language and its symbols. This reflects an attitude captured by theologian Luke Bretherton when he writes that Pentecostals "points to how forms of faithful witness might be generated in and through capitalism".[22] Similarly, Halldorf argues that Lewi Pethrus, the leader of the Swedish Pentecostal movements, "built the church with the means of the market".[23] The planters in Industrial City stand in this rather pragmatic tradition. They don't find it relevant to reflect on the counter-formative power of an invasive cultural practice when placed in the context of the liturgy. I am informed that the song had around 7000 streams in the first six months on Spotify.

8.4 Integrity: Negotiating Individualism

Swedish culture's strong emphasis on individualism presents a challenge for church plants who strive to build cohesive Christian communities. To preserve

---

[22] Bretherton (2019), p 125.
[23] Joel Halldorf (2020), *Pentecostal Politics in a Secular World: The Life and Leadership of Lewi Pethrus*, New York: Palgrave MacMillan, p 153.

central values – narratives, moral guides, and theology – adaptability needs to be balanced by integrity, which entails a sense of integration, cohesion, and unified purpose. From this perspective, I understand integrity as a self-directed process of meaning-making that melds individual perspectives in common practices. Negotiating a balance between personal autonomy and community consensus becomes critical for the church plant's integrity. This process is most evident in discussions of how the church plants deal with moral issues and diversity.

Sexual Morals

The Christian church has a rich and complex history of grappling with sexual ethics in response to shifting societal attitudes.[24] This cultural negotiation can also be found in the conversations with church plant members. Sven, one of the leaders in Industrial City, reflects on this:

> [Sven]: In the church world, you shouldn't live together before marriage. Then you grow up in a world saying that you should get together with the person and try everything [sexually] before you get married.
>
> [Field study note from Cathedral City small group]: Olof found many rules in the text [1 Cor 1–8]. Today in a student's life, you are expected to have many different sexual relations. That doesn't match what Paul is writing. Anders says you can become attracted by other women, but you don't have to act on this attraction. Olof says he should get married. It seems to be easier. (No one asks what he means by that...)

Sven and Olof both experience the tension of two different cultural norms regarding sexual relations: one promiscuous, the other more chaste. The latter can be supported by references to the Bible – which is what Olof reacted to – or tradition, both of which sees sexuality as a spiritual issue. The fact that no one asks Olof to develop or clarify his comment about getting married says something about the issue's sensitivity.

A newlywed couple in one of the church plants tells me their story. They met in the church and got engaged. They started planning their wedding when the pandemic undid their plans for a summer wedding. In waiting for a new opportunity the following summer, they started to discuss how to deal with some practical issues. They had two apartments, which were very expensive, and they found it hard to resist having sex. But at the same time, they did not think it was right to move

---

[24] Steven D. Smith (2018), *Pagans and Christians in the City: Culture Wars from the Tiber to the Potomac*, Atlanta, Georgia: Emory University Studies, p 122, describes the early Christian view on sexuality (heterosexual, equal, monogamous) as "close to incomprehensible" in the surrounding ancient culture.

in together and have sex while still unmarried. They discussed this with their pastors, who advised them to get married and not wait just because they wanted to have a big party.

The young man in this couple also tells me that he left the church he grew up in because he thought that people who were devout in public ended up deviating from their professed principles. He did not want to be that person himself. This was a personal choice for the couple, and they did not want to force their way on others or cause them to feel guilt and shame. But they were quite open about their struggle in the church, which meant that others asked them about it and followed their decision to live separately until marriage.

Control in religious communities is a very sensitive issue, both in contemporary Swedish culture and Western culture in general, particularly when it comes to sexual norms that differ from those of the surrounding culture.[25] Einar expresses his disinterest in controlling people's morals:

> [Einar]: We will never act like some morality police who control that everyone lives correctly. We won't do that. But if someone comes to us and asks us, we will express our views.

There are two perspectives on this matter when it comes to Christian formation. First, the individual needs to negotiate between two cultures, either by choosing one moral over the other or by becoming culturally bi-lingual – the latter option might, however, make a person appear as a hypocrite. Second, the community needs to avoid exercising control while still teaching what they find to be a legitimate theological response to moral issues. These concerns affect the pedagogy of Christian formation in the church plants. The pedagogical approach of the Industrial City is as follows:

> [Einar]: If you have a glass of water and pour a few drops of concentrated juice, the first drops permeate the clear water and make it a bit red. A bit like that, I think the church should permeate everything.

---

[25] Strhan (2015), p 192, holds that "the small groups can be a site where church leaders police symbolic boundaries in areas that locate the church as morally distinctive from the wider culture, for example, over issues of sexual morality". Anna Strhan interestingly reflects (p 26) on her own path from being an evangelical to objectifying evangelicals with the eyes of a liberal theologian, especially taking umbrage with evangelicals' views on same-sex relationships among evangelicals. Cf. Zackariasson (2016) who identify norms about sexuality and the use of alcohol to be negotiated in and around free church youth organisations. Cf. Moberg (2013), p 183, and the discussion of inter-sex relations in a charismatic church in Stockholm.

In this image, the glass of water is a person's life, and the drop of juice is the gospel. The Christian formation is not created through boundaries and obstacles but is rather something that permeates life in a fluid, natural manner. They trust the Holy Spirit to do this work:

> [Einar]: Sometimes, it might seem that we never come to the point where we say that living together before marriage is wrong and that you shouldn't use bad language. But that is our theology. I don't know if everyone agrees that sin is no longer a problem for God. We shouldn't fight sin because Jesus did that on the cross when he said: It is finished! We should connect people to God and say to the devil: Look how generous God is!
>
> [Margareta]: And let God make us Christlike!

While this pedagogical approach actively avoids drawing firm boundaries, it holds fast to central values.[26] The planters anticipate that the newcomers will come to grow in their faith through the guidance of the Holy Spirit, eventually reorienting themselves around the church plant's central values.

Diversity

How are cultural views and values negotiated within the three church-planting communities? In my fieldwork and discussions, I encountered negotiations around diversity as it pertains to ethnicity, culture, language, and sexual orientation/identity. In the church plants studied, diversity is viewed as something fundamentally positive and human equality is theologically grounded in God's love, creativity, and communicability.

> [Margareta]: God doesn't want to make everyone exactly the same, like robots coming out of the factory. He who creates you loves you and wants you to understand how valuable you are. [Field note from worship service in Industrial City]

A sermon preached in one of the church plants emphasised that every human is unique but equal in value because God has created every human differently in love. This reflects a fundamentally positive view of diversity.

> [Karl]: I love our church. The vision is to be an inspiring intercultural expression of God's kingdom, a church that helps people grow in love for each other and our neighbours. For God, Jesus and the world or the city.

---

[26] Cf. Hiebert (1994). Hiebert suggests different sociological sets that have different approaches to borders. The planters want to avoid what Hiebert calls "the bounded set" and prefer "the centred set", which allows for change towards centred values.

8.4 Integrity: Negotiating Individualism   219

[Peter]: To me, multi-cultural has been very important. When I was twenty, I moved to [a well-known ethnically diverse area] and lived in that area for eight years. So this multi-cultural pioneering [mentality] has been there quite distinctively.

Karl (Harbour City) and Peter (Cathedral City) view the ethnic diversity in Swedish cities as something positive. They are not planting churches exclusively aimed at ethnic Swedes, and they want their church plants to reach across ethnic and cultural borders.

༉

In an online meeting with the church plant in Cathedral City, Peter, who leads the meeting, holds up a jar filled with small notes. Each note has a prayer request, and Peter encourages us to pray: "Pray in the language of your choice. Sometimes it could be in Portuguese, sometimes in Arabic". One participant prays for the requests in the jar. She uses her own language, Arabic. The prayer remains untranslated. Most of us cannot understand her words, but we leave this to God, who does.

Scene: Cathedral City, Feb. 22, 2021.

༉

Using different languages corresponds well with the ambition of being multicultural. The online meetings are often bi-lingual (Swedish and English), both in the speech and the texts presented on the screen. At the Maundy Thursday gathering outside in the neighbourhood park, one of the worship songs is sung in both Swedish and Arabic.

In a small group meeting discussing 1 Corinthians, Charlie, who is from a non-Western country, asks: "How do you in Church deal with trans people in the church?" The question arose from his reading of a passage in chapter eleven where Paul reasons about men, women, and long hair. Charlie said he finds it offensive how trans issues are discussed in Sweden. He prefers a firm, well-defined view, as is prominent in his home country. He does not explain this view in detail, but it is clear that he perceives a difference in how these issues are discussed in the two cultures. The rest of the group, three ethnically Swedish men, suggests that it is necessary to show respect, tolerance, and care when meeting LGBTQ+ persons while still maintaining one's own beliefs.

In the following quote, Alex – who believes LGBTQ+ persons should be fully included in church communities – comments on the discussion about different theological views on LGBTQ+ issues that frequently cause tension in free churches:

> [Alex]: I am fully aware that there are many different views in Christianity on this issue. I don't say one particular view is more right or wrong in general. All I am saying is that I stand for what I stand for, and I hope to be accepted and loved no matter what, kind of. That is what is most important to me.

Alex expresses hope that a strong common ground can hold the community together in spite of different opinions on the issue. While in the church plants, I spoke with two people in different communities who identified as LGBTQ+. One was hopeful about this issue in the community, but the other was less optimistic about the situation.

Summary

In my fieldwork, I found that many emphasise the necessity of individual ways and views of life being possible in a church plant. This challenges the homogeneity of the community and creates some tensions, particularly between those with progressive and traditional Christian views on sexual relationships. Navigating these sometimes-conflicting views is not easy for the individual or community. This complicates the planters' ambition to find a common approach and telos for Christian formation in the church community, and some issues are left to the individual. The risk here is a situation that becomes scattered from individualism in such a way that it undermines its integrity and the life of the community.

In the end, the church plants tend to deal with the issues pragmatically, for instance, by subordinating questions of sexual morality to more central issues. For example, they emphasise the common mission of the church and Jesus's love for the city instead of focusing on particular teachings on sexuality. This way of upholding the integrity of the church plants seems to be related to their intentionality and calling. For the Industrial City church plant, the reason for not publicly addressing issues of sexuality is to avoid alienating people who seek Jesus. The Harbour City church plant takes a similar approach because it wants to create a place of healing for the traumatised, including people from sexual minorities.

The capacity to include diversity is necessary for communities to be relevant in a secular, pluralistic culture. The church plants in this study all view diversity as something fundamentally positive and God-given. The churches – particularly those in Cathedral City and Harbour City – explicitly state that nationality and ethnicity are theologically irrelevant. They are mentioned only as important boundaries to cross in their missional outreach. However, this is not the case regarding issues of LBGTQ+ identity. While each of the church plants is engaged in discussions about what expressions of diversity are legitimate and authentic in the communities – discussions that some in the church plants might find uncomfortable – the virtues of respect and care are emphasized and fostered. It is worth noting that diversity is motivated theologically, not by using secular language.

8.5 Sustainability: Negotiating Performance Culture

Church planting demands a lot of work, and as we will see, church planters often experience pressure from denominations and other stakeholders to deliver results. The pressures are not merely external, though. During this study, I encountered many church planters who placed high demands on themselves to achieve what they felt God had called them to do. Some forces involved are more secular than sacred. The material from the interviews and observations sheds light on a noteworthy dilemma of Christian formation facing sustainable church-planting efforts.[27]

Culture of Performance

A recurring theme in interviews, sermons, and other occasions in the church plants is the need to address a widespread performance culture that springs out of instrumental rationality, namely the sense that one's value in society is based on one's achievements.[28] Church plants are themselves complex in this regard, as the planting practice is directed towards creating – or achieving – something new. The church planters operate under the assumption that their communities need to be more culturally relevant than the available alternatives, which in turn necessitates the creation of something new and noteworthy from their limited resources. (The main resource, of course, is the people in the community.) At the same time, the church plants all preach that one's value is not dependent upon one's achievement, as Sven told me:

> [Sven]: We try to stress as much as possible that all tasks are equally important, that you are a cog in the big machinery. Your job is super important. You don't have to look at

---

[27] Bebbington (1989). This might concern more than the church-planting movement. Bebbington describes activism as one general characteristic of the evangelical movement. Activism per se is not necessarily the same as a performance culture, but certainly a related feature.

[28] Tangen (2012), p 268. Tangen addresses similar observations in Neo-Pentecostal churches under the title "The Ethical Janus Face of the Performance Dynamics". The emphasis on growth occasionally creates tremendous stress on leaders as well as members of the churches.

others. My value is not dependent upon my task. What you do, and feel joy in doing, is very valuable.

On the one hand, he says that members are not valued based on achievements. What matters is the enjoyment and satisfaction a participant finds in being part of the whole and contributing what she can. On the other hand, Sven employs a machine metaphor, which – intentional or not – seems to suggest a view of people as a means to an end and a view of church as production.

Einar and Margareta have previous experience of church planting in a Neo-Pentecostal context, an experience that was not entirely positive. They describe a competitive environment where numbers are used to measure success, something that can easily lead church leaders to exaggerate attendance figures in order to project an image of success:

> [Einar]: We were compared to all the others and didn't perform as well as they did. Everyone in the [movement] family talked much about numbers and sent reports every Sunday.
>
> [Margareta]: Sometimes it was more important that things looked good than making the most of what you had.
>
> [Einar]: Even to the extent that you exaggerated and lied. A worship meeting during a campaign gathered 500 people – because someone is counting – which is fantastic. We rented a theatre and gathered 500! They send out the numbers to [the main leaders] every Sunday. But then you come to the service and suddenly hear the number 700!

Another example of the performance approach is seen in the story of Anna, who is part of the church plant in Harbour City. She describes her experiences twenty years ago when she was part of a new church near the Bible school she attended. She was a young and good worker, and because of this found herself devoting all her time to church activities. Simply put, she was a cog in the church machine. This activist spirituality took a toll on her:

> [Anna]: You were there from the morning, you had the bible school until lunch, and then you went working voluntarily the rest of the hours left of the 24 hours you got. You hit the bed for two hours and then back again.

Now, she tells me, she is trying to recover from this activist spirituality, a process that involves accepting God's love despite her inability to work endlessly in the mission field.

In one conversation at the Harbour City church plant, Karl articulated his frustration with the emphasis on numbers, which he thinks leads to bad theology and wrong practice:

8.5 Sustainability: Negotiating Performance Culture

> [Karl]: We don't want to count those kinds of numbers. Our movement is trying to get us to count members all the time. We don't want to do that. What we really want to... we want to change the scoreboard.

His church plant's denomination asks for attendance figures from Sunday services and other gatherings. Karl and his team value crossing cultural borders and partnering with others to change the city, but this kind of slow, relational work cannot be easily quantified. Even more, the way that the leaders of the church plants engage in the task of Christian formation communicates theology.

Sara, one of the Harbour City church planters, connects the church plant with its understanding of God and its mission to preach the gospel in the cultural context. Who is God, and what does it mean to become a Christian?

> [Sara]: If we, as a church, show our members and other visiting participants that everything is about doing something new and about achieving things, I think that we actually communicate an image of God as an employer or taskmaster. I think we feel an obligation to avoid doing that because it is a heavy burden to bear. But we are all affected. [in our denomination], we are activistic regarding things like social justice. We have said this many times, but action and contemplation need to go together. We must attend to the spiritual life, having retreats and sanctifying the Sabbath.

Sara speaks of finding a balance between activity and rest. She is highly engaged in social work but must regularly retreat to rest and prayer. My conversation with Sara shed light on the leadership team's struggles with this balance. Since planting the church five years ago, the leaders have experienced periods of burnout that necessitated slowing down their work. In the Industrial City church plant, Margareta preached a sermon about building on God's love, not one's own achievements:

> [Margareta]: Sometimes you hear someone say, "God's love and grace are great in the beginning, but then you need to step up and move deeper". But God's grace leads all the way every day. If you buy the lie that your own achievement is the foundation, you will miss the goodness of God. It is not based on what you do for him but on what he has done once and for all. [Field note Sunday service in Industrial City].

This shows that the church planters are aware of this dilemma. Sara reflects on resolutions to it:

> [Sara]: How do we find rhythms, and how do we use things like meditation to be both action-based and contemplative people who live as we learn and believe together and with God? [...] We work to some degree in using art to support this, selecting paintings that help reflection. We are just testing this. How can you help people rest, reflect, and be in God's presence?

How are the church plants dealing with a culture of performance? To begin with, they try to identify and verbalise it. In her sermon, Margareta addresses the basis of a Christian's value. Because of her background in other Christian environments and traditions, she understands how the church risks developing an elite Christian spirituality that understands achievement as the basis of value. To counter this, she points to God's love and acceptance as the foundation. Sara offers a slightly different strategy, emphasising that in order for a community to form a sound Christian spirituality, action and contemplation need to be balanced and integrated.

Summary

Church planting has a complicated relationship with the contemporary performance culture. If the contemporary culture uses performance and measurable achievements as a basis for personal value, church planters affirm that one's value is a matter of grace. At the same time, church planters are constantly at risk of being drawn into this meritocratic logic in part because the act of church planting sought to achieve goals that are easily quantifiable and measurable (i.e., creating converts) and require a lot of activity.

In an "activity-machine" approach, people become a means to an end: building a church. This conflicts with a theology that emphasises God's unconditional love and acceptance, which is something that the church plants want to communicate. The church plants are aware of the complexity involved in resolving this issue and are addressing it in preaching and through various formative practices.

8.6 Resilience: Negotiating Power

Internal negotiation between the different interests in the church-planting community is not always harmonious. If or when church planters are questioned, this puts stress on them, particularly since they have invested a lot in the church plant. The church planter's calling is connected to a vision of innovation of the church in a certain way.[29] As the church plant grows, there is a need to develop ways of protecting and forging this vision and, at the same time, finding structures for leadership, including decision-making that involves people beyond the original planters.

---

[29] See the presentation of the calling, pro-social action and intention embodiment in the chapter on calling (p 107).

Democratic Structures

Dani is a former member of the Industrial City community. With a background in a smaller, traditional free church in the countryside, Dani thinks that the church plant lacks democratic structures.

> [Dani]: You need to start having [formal] church assembly meetings… perhaps I am a bit stuck in that form. Maybe it doesn't have to be called an assembly meeting. There might be another structure, but some kind of structure that invites more people. The negative side is that it takes more time. It is easier if the pastors simply decide. It is much faster. Then you might grow faster, that is possible. [Sarcasm].
>
> [Björn]: Perhaps…
>
> [Dani]: But what is the cost?

When Dani became part of the church plant, it was in its initial phase, and its organisational structures were preliminary. But my perception is that the planters' vision for the church community still differs from the ideal envisioned by Dani, who finds democratic structures essential to church life and not something that can be added down the road. This might indicate differences in church traditions, but it could also reflect the fact that the church plant is young and lacks the structures of an established church. At the moment, the Industrial City community is in the process of establishing basic structures according to the vision of the planters. Eventually, the community will address how the church will be structured and governed.

In contrast, the church plant in Cathedral City drew inspiration from the Anabaptist tradition and established a decision-making process from the outset. As we saw in Chapter 5, the community's ideal democratic practice involved prayer and seeking the mind of Christ together rather than arguing for different positions and voting.[30]

Challenged Leadership

I have previously showed how the church planters have a strong intentionality through their experience of calling to plant a church in a particular place, in a particular manner, and with a particular telos of Christian formation. Such a vision is sometimes challenged. The following scene from Industrial City touches on how leadership is challenged:

---

[30] Cf. Neve (2021), p 178, who finds the Swedish Emerging Churches have a less formal decision-making process, and instead emphasise prayer and seeking the will of God.

The one-hour Bible study of women in leadership raises my curiosity. It is not explicitly stated why the online Sunday service takes this direction, but Einar refers to "questions that have been raised in the groups recently". Two and a half years into the church plant, a couple of influential persons decided to part with the community to plant their own church. They felt adamant that the leaders had "compromised with sin". Their critique focused on two particular issues: women in pastoral leadership and the fact that the church plant allowed people in the community to live together outside of marriage. This was a strong challenge to the leadership of Margareta and Einar.

Scene: Industrial City, Dec. 6, 2020.

One of the other leaders, Sven, believes that these kinds of people often show up and cause drama, especially in new church communities:

> [Sven]: They have had a lot of influence just because it is a newly started church. They wouldn't have had that in an established church. I guess that is common in new churches if you study church history, that those people come and go. It is painful experiencing it and having it so close. A lot of [conflict management] meetings just because of the drama. And being new to planting a church, we want to be humble. Perhaps we are the ones doing the wrong thing?

> [Margareta]: Four persons were loud and took a lot of energy and focus from us. Everyone else in the church was happy, and things were happening in people's lives. Positive things, but we couldn't rejoice over it because this drained us. Towards the end, we saw that if one of them attended the service, they would take notes on what we did wrong.

The planters were confronted by the men, who were leaders of one of the groups in the community. In the quotes above, Margareta and Sven describe how the church planters tried to approach this difficult situation wisely, taking time to listen to their opponents' views. When they tell me about this recent episode, it is clear that while the group has now left the community, the planters feel sad and disappointed over what happened, especially because a few new believers left with them.

> [Einar]: In that group, they nurtured radical [jargon] and started to look down upon our team leaders and small group leaders. Like: "Why should they lead, just look how they live", and so on.

[Margareta]: Our way of viewing things is that people work on their deficiencies and sins in process and dialogue to bring that person closer to Jesus, rather than just cutting it off.

This situation brings forth differing views on what lived Christian faith should look like and how the formation should be practised. Einar and Margareta prefer a softer approach, which includes dialogue and room to grow, over the inflexible approach of "the radicals".

Summary

Church plants are sensitive to competing theological ideas and visions that pull in different directions. As new people come, they bring other perspectives to the community. To some degree, being a member of the church plant means aligning with the church plant's telos, as expressed by the planters. Resilience is achieved through the planters' ability to negotiate power, at times by holding firmly to it and at times by giving it away. That being said, during the first phase of the church plant, when democratic structures have not yet been established, power is mainly negotiated relationally.

8.7 Conclusion

In this chapter, I have presented examples of the negotiation of cultural issues, both within the church plants and between the communities and the broader secular culture. When understood in the context of formation towards a lived Christian identity, the negotiation process does not begin from a neutral standpoint when it comes to cultural values or views. Rather, what it means to be a Christian is constructed through a negotiation process that involves the secular culture, free-church tradition, and the formative teloi of the church plants.

Christian formation in church plants is a matter of negotiating cultural issues to foster adaptability, integrity, sustainability, and resilience in the surrounding secular culture:

The Surrounding Culture: The material gives voice to a feeling of being questioned as Christians in Swedish society. Some take this as a challenge, while others express a sense of being exposed and being viewed as a threat to central values in Swedish culture. The church plants perceive the contemporary culture as spiritually anaemic and in need of the gospel.

Adaptability: The migration of logos and lifestyle brands into the liturgy shows how the church plants, despite certain misgivings about mainstream culture, try to use that very culture as a means of mission. The Christian formed through this liturgical renewal is a person living in the middle of the secular culture. The instinct is not to separate from culture but rather to use it missionally. The difference between adapting to culture and adapting to reach culture is partly theologically unreflected by the church planters.

Integrity: While the church plants might hold theological views deemed controversial by the surrounding culture, those views are not always emphasised since they would conflict with the telos of the church plants – to lead people to Christ. When it comes to sexual issues, for instance, church plants do not want to restrict individual members' lives but rather lead by example and only advise on these issues when asked. The church plants employ a theological language of pluralism and motivate their existence partly using a logic of supply and demand. They offer theological reasons why they view diversity as fundamentally positive while also negotiating contemporary lifestyles with the Bible and tradition.

Sustainability: Church planting risks becoming performance and activity-oriented. At the same time, church plants detect a need in contemporary culture for a gospel of God's unconditional love. This complexity is partly recognised and addressed in sermons and counteracted with contemplation practices. This is a challenge and a potential critique towards church planting. There needs to be a clear distinction between authentic missional activity and a culture of performance.

Resilience: The church plants are in the initial phase when the essential vision is carried by persons – the planters – and not structures. Demands for democratic structures are legitimate but might be premature. However, the church plants need to establish ways of negotiating power to be resilient to challenges to the teloi.

Negotiability, in this analysis, emerges as a sustainable balance between integrity and adaptability. How much room is there for adaption to secular culture? How firmly must one maintain one's cultural views and narratives? These questions reveal why discernment is so essential in church plants. Developing resilience to certain cultural issues might also cause immunity to cultural relevance.

9. Conclusions and Discussion

The aim of this dissertation has been to investigate the challenges of Christian formation in the secular landscape of Swedish culture. In order to do this, four research questions were posed to examine what Christian formation looks like in the context of advanced secularisation in missional situations. In this chapter, I will summarise the findings of the study, engage in dialogue with previous research on Christian formation, and reflect on the methods and theoretical choices made in the thesis.

Throughout the dissertation, a pattern concerning the planting of new churches and the Christian life that is formed in them emerges. Together the answers to the questions posed help us piece together a coherent and complex picture of what is going on here. To begin with, the formation of new churches often stems from a sense of calling, and embedded within this calling is a vision – an imagination – of a Christian life and community. The church plants then establish practices of Christian formation, which support newcomers and veterans alike in their journeys towards a lived Christian identity. A practice is aimed at a certain telos, and by participating in the practice, the practitioner becomes aligned with the community's vision of a Christian life. This identity is, however, not static but involves negotiations regarding what it means to live as a Christian. These negotiations take place on both a personal level – as individuals explore and develop their faith – and the community level, as the church plants try to work out what it means to be an ecclesial community in a secular culture.

9.1 Summary of Results

In this section, I summarise the results of the investigation and answer the research questions guiding it.

Callings and Intentions

The first question I posed was: *How are the callings and intentions of the church plants articulated, and what do the callings and intentions mean for Christian formation?* This was the errand of Chapter 5, which analysed the callings and intentions of the church plants as a manifestation of the clear purpose and personal mission driving action with a pro-social intention[1] This was mainly seen in the interviews with the church planters and other leaders.

The church plant in Industrial City feels called to engage the secular culture at the centre of the city. Its members create interest in social media and invite people to the church's culturally sensitive revival meeting. The church planters have a strong missional identity and intention, which includes forging a church planting model for mid-sized Swedish cities. The formative telos can be described through the ideal of forming fishermen, who "catch" people by inviting them to the revival meeting.

In Cathedral City, the church plant feels called to form faithful neighbours by creating a spiritual home for people in the neighbourhood and building close communities of diverse individuals with a shared faith. The planters want the church to be a mission station with a focus on their neighbourhood.

The Harbour City church plant feels called to form good Samaritans by establishing an equalising table of God's kingdom through a life-affirming mission that celebrates unity in diversity. This calling is manifest in the church's social work and engagement with the margins of society.

These three articulations of calling show possibilities for imagining and engaging the broader secular culture according to different teloi of Christian formation. The ideals articulated in their respective callings are present in how the church plants design their formative practices. As highlighted in Chapter 5, the church planters exhibited a remarkable level of agency in their approach and the articulation of their respective callings. Lastly, the strong connection to the place in each context emerged as a noteworthy finding.

Formative Practices

The second question addresses the issue of *what practices of Christian formation are present in the church plant communities*. In Chapter 6, I analysed one significant practice in each church plant in order to understand better their approach to Christian formation. The analyses reveal a web of sub-practices that contribute to and support the formative practices.

The revival meeting is a significant practice for the formation of fishermen in Industrial City. Here, participants are invited to accept God's love, experience

---

[1] Elangovan et al. (2010), p 430.

freedom from shame, and discover their true selves by embracing the good news proclaimed during the revival meeting. Participants are given the freedom to choose whether to observe or actively engage in worship or the call to prayer, which fosters a sense of agency in their spiritual journeys. If the revival meeting is the main practice, several sub-practices make the meeting possible, and participants can join any of the teams that perform a designated function in support of the meeting. The practice forms fishermen who invite newcomers to the meeting and share their experience of God with others, whether in person or on social media. Given the church planters' call to engage secular culture at the centre of the city, they demonstrate a strong sensitivity to contemporary culture, using language, places, and symbols that are part of the cultural world of young people.

The online small group is a practice that forms faithful neighbours in Cathedral City. In the small group's online format, necessitated by the pandemic, the neighbourhood is less present, but the intimacy is still tangible, and the practice clearly supports Christian formation. Following in the tradition of the conventicle practice, people are encouraged to cultivate hospitality, generosity, prayer, and Bible reading by embracing common intentional habits within a close-knit relational setting. As with the revival meeting practice, participation in the small group is meant to lead to a changed appreciation of self, God, and others. Furthermore, the small group practice entails the formation of behaviour – shared intentional habits that manifest a lived Christian identity. In encouraging reflection on the virtues practised between meetings, the small group practice becomes part of the fabric of participants' lives and encourages continuity in the formation process.

The apprenticeship is a practice which supports the formation of good Samaritans, people capable of building bridges and tending to wounds in Harbour City. Apprenticeship is implemented through mentoring relationships that develop qualities of leadership, spirituality, and missional living. In this way, the church plant forms participants towards both a practised Christian spirituality and a missional living that embraces diversity and unity. The missional tool APEST has shaped the imagination of the church plant and informs its different apprenticing relationships. The church plant's close link to social work, central to some free church traditions, is significant to its approach to Christian formation. The church plant is called to minister to people and places on the margins of society and, in doing so, to establish the kingdom of God in the city. The apprenticeship practices form people according to the vision of the church being a river rather than a lake; that is to say, the church wants to equip and send people on to new destinations rather than gathering them to form a single large church.

Formative Trajectories

In addressing the third research question – *How are people formed towards a lived Christian identity in the church plant communities?* – Chapter 7 examined the movement of individuals between the periphery and centre of the church plants. Newcomers enter the community of practice and grow through participation and engagement in the formative practices of the church plant. The newcomers differ in knowledge and convictions about the Christian faith.

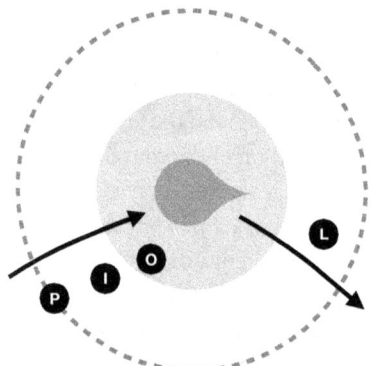

Participation: in formative practices

Identification: through baptism, gifts assessment and virtue formation through common habits

Ownership: in leadership roles, missional relocation, recruiting

Leaving: because of performance culture, alternative telos and imagination

Figure 7: Engagement modes in communities of formative practice.

A summary of the different trajectories shows four different modes of engagement (Figure 7). Being formed into a lived Christian identity, while a start, means more than mere *participation*. The continuous formation through inbound trajectories could lead to *identification* with the church plant. One interesting feature of these church plants is their openness towards newcomers, who are allowed to enter full engagement by forming *ownership* of the formative practices and church plant telos. In some cases, these newcomers even function as leaders even if they don't accept the theology of the church plant or identity as Christians. A hindered inbound trajectory could be the result of the church's demanding performance culture, which placed high pressure on individual participants. There is also a fourth mode of formative identification, namely *leaving*. This means that the formative trajectory is outbound. The individuals in this study who had left a church did so because of disagreements with the church's ecclesiology and telos of Christian formation or for other practical reasons.

Negotiation of Secular Culture

I have analysed the negotiations within the church plants as a kind of theological ecosystem. The fourth research question asked *what cultural tensions the church plants negotiate and what the negotiations mean for Christian formation*. Christian formation in church plants is a matter of negotiating cultural issues to foster adaptability, integrity, sustainability, and resilience in the secular culture. In Chapter 9, I took a step back to analyse the church plants together rather than individually. The reason for this was both that cultural tensions are shared and due to limited comparative material.

Culture: The church plants perceive contemporary Swedish culture as spiritually lacking and in need of regeneration through the Christian gospel. The attendees of the church plants note that the broader society seems to regard Christians with suspicion, bemusement, or condescension. Some take this as a positive challenge, while others express a sense of vulnerability since they are perceived as threats to some of Sweden's central cultural values.

Adaptability: The analysis shows that brands and other lifestyle symbols have migrated into the liturgical practices, which illustrates how the church plants attempt to use secular culture as a means of mission. The Christians formed in the church plants are living in the middle of the secular culture. The church plants' instinct is not to separate from culture but to strategically use aspects of it in missional work. That being said, the study found only limited theological reflection on the adaptation of secular culture in missio-liturgical practice.

Integrity: Integrity, in this context, involves the church plants' integration and internal cohesion. While the church plants might hold theological views deemed controversial by many in Swedish society, those views are infrequently emphasized since it is felt that doing so might compromise the overall telos of the church plants, which is to lead people to Christ. The leaders of the churches hold theological convictions that are often not shared by new-coming participants or even people already engaged with the church plant. To some degree, the church plants adopt pluralism and motivate their existence partly using a market logic of supply and demand.

Sustainability: Though church plants in this study seem to be doing well, many church plants close within a few years. Perhaps because of the difficulties involved with starting and maintaining a church, church planting easily becomes performance and activity-oriented, which contradicts the church plants' claim that contemporary culture needs the gospel of God's unconditional love. This tension is partly recognised and addressed in sermons and counteracted with contemplative practices, but it remains a challenge to – and potential critique of – church planting. Clearly, a stronger distinction between authentic missional activity and a culture of performance is necessary.

Resilience: The church plants are in an initial phase when the essential vision is carried by persons – the planters – and not structures. Demands for democratic structures are legitimate but might be premature. The analysis shows that the church plants must establish ways of negotiating power to be resilient to challenges to the church plant's formative telos.

In Chapter 8, the concept of negotiability emerges in the analysis as a sustainable balance between integrity and adaptability. In other words, how much room there is for adaptation to secular culture? How firmly should individuals and communities hold on to personal narratives and counter-cultural views? Developing resilience to certain cultural issues might result in diminished relevance in the culture, which is undesirable for church plants. But some degree of integrity is necessary. Here, theological discernment becomes essential with regard to identifying where the line should be drawn.

9.2 Agency: From Calling to Practice

In the following sections, I will discuss the results in terms of movements – from calling to practice, from periphery to centre, and from secular to Christian formation. I also relate the results of this study to other missional studies, particularly of church plants, and show how it both confirms, challenges and adds to patterns that have been identified by other scholars.

God, Calling, and Ecclesial Agency

The planters' calling is the catalyst for the inception of the church plants. These callings point to visions of ecclesial pro-social embodiments that provide trajectories towards a lived Christian identity. This aligns with missiologist Michael

9.2 Agency: From Calling to Practice

Moynagh's description of the missional call of church plants as a voyage of emerging identities of individuals and communities:

> Both individuals and the mission community make identity voyages, which involve a starting identity comprising ecclesial and personal identities; possible identities, which are imagined pictures of the self (or the community) helping to birth the proposed contextual church; a contextual church identity, which is the self (or the community) concretely helping to birth the church; it continues to evolve.[2]

The church planters and the emerging community embark on a shared journey of identity transformation. They are being sent. They are church planters. The community is on a mission from God. But the calling also comes from or is related to, a dissatisfaction with secular culture and the desire to introduce God and faith in people's lives. They feel a tension between what is and what should be, and they take on the task of being agents of change.

This change is accomplished by ecclesial innovation and missional action, leading to people becoming Christians. The missional vocational identity found in missiologist Richard R. Osmer's empirical study of missional leadership is clearly present in the stories of the church planters as well.[3] In describing their own journey, they identify with figures and refer to narratives from the Bible in describing this calling. But beyond that, the analysis points towards a strong relationship between calling and place. God's urging of individuals or groups to take personal responsibility for a task is directed towards people in particular places.

Furthermore, the calling is connected to certain ecclesial imagination. The planters have a clear vision of what they want to achieve: a new church. The ecclesial imagination involves a Christian formation telos. This result of my study is a significant addition to how both Moynagh and Osmer describe the callings and vocations.

The analysis of the callings of the three church plants shows different forms of ecclesial imagination. There are several similarities between my study and the models formulated by Christopher B. James based on his study of church plants in Seattle.[4] The church plant in Industrial City shares features of the Great Commission Team model, which promotes evangelism, discipleship, and proclamation. The Cathedral City church plant, which emphasises close proximity to people in the neighbourhood, resembles James's Neighbourhood Incarnation model. The strong mission patterns of community, contemplation, and advocacy in his

---

[2] Moynagh (2012), p 229.
[3] Osmer (2012).
[4] James (2018), p 63. The models are described on pp 55-57.

progressive New Community model are present, to some degree, in the Harbour City church plant.

The Harbour City church plant, however, lacks the sacramental-liturgical orientation of the New Community model. While none of the church plants in my study have this orientation, I am familiar with other church plants in Sweden that do. One interesting observation in the comparison with James's study is that none of the church plants fall into the model James calls "Household of the Spirit". Instead, all three church plants are open to a charismatic spirituality.

Re-inventing Practices of Christian Formation

Formative practices are central to how the church plants engage the places to which they are called. How the practices are designed in the local contexts is significant to understanding the underlying theological assumptions in the churches' approaches to Christian formation.

The descriptions of the church plants' respective visions point to strong intentionality. The practices are intentionally designed around the formative ideal of each church plant. The three formative practices of the revival meeting, small groups, and apprenticing are rooted in free church traditions but have been adapted in innovative ways to suit contemporary urban missions.

The church plants' use of traditional free church formation practices is not simply a matter of repeating what has historically worked. Rather, it is a creative re-contextualisation of theological convictions connected to ecclesiological imaginations. Church planting is an innovative practice.[5] However, this innovation can be based on practices gathered from tradition while reshaping them to fit contemporary urban settings. For instance, the social ministry in the city from a kingdom of God perspective could be reinterpreted in a culture that invokes activism around equality and climate issues. Revival meetings connect social media to events in a way that fits the contemporary cultural environment. The conventicle tradition offers a context for developing close relationships that satisfy a contemporary longing for authenticity and human connection.

In her ethnographic study of a church in Stockholm, Jessica Moberg identifies an inward turn and a therapeutic culture where individuals "open up" to God and others. Interestingly, the words of her informants are almost identical to those of one of the planters in this study. They both emphasize that they want people to "take off their masks" and "be themselves". These expressions are part of the jargon

---

[5] Selvaratnam (2020), p 190.

that builds the contemporary narrative, both within and outside the churches. Therapeutic authenticity is especially present in the practices of the meeting and the small group, where individuals open their private sphere and publicly share it with others and God.[6] In encouraging the participants to have their journey through the practices, the church plants can create pathways within the community culture that acknowledge individualism while at the same time offering a narrative that is based on an understanding of the gospel that eschews the individualism and the perceived self-centeredness of contemporary culture.

9.3 Participation: From Periphery to Centre

One critique towards situated learning theory is that it tends to describe the community as homogenous.[7] But Etienne Wenger explicitly advises against a homogeneous reading of communities.[8] It is obvious that none of the study's three church plants are closed-off to newcomers and people from different religious or cultural backgrounds. They have all found some balance between adapting to the cultural context and preserving integrity as an alternative community. As seen in the analysis of trajectories, people are at very different places on their formative journeys, and they travel in different directions. This variation is a part of the heterogeneity found in the church plants. The formative process does not begin after a conversion experience; instead, it is described as a journey towards (and occasionally away from) the centre of the church plants.

Modes of Participation

I find missiologist Paul G. Hiebert's descriptions of social mindsets helpful in understanding their heterogeneity.[9] As described in Chapter 2, Hiebert uses mindsets as sociological types and argues that different mindsets characterise different kinds

---

[6] Moberg (2013).
[7] Roberts (2006); Fenwick (2012), p 68.
[8] Wenger (1999), p 76.
[9] Hiebert (1994). A *bounded* mindset defines Christian faith from correct belief (orthodoxy) and behaviour (orthopraxy), with a clear distinction between being Christian and non-Christian. A *centred* set instead defines a Christian as a person who is moving towards Christ and emphasises growth. *Fuzzy*-set Christianity means that there is some relation to a loosely defined Christ, which leads to a community without much in common. Michael Lee (2007), p 62, assesses the value of Hiebert's theology when applying a centred set to what it means to be Christian. He finds that this application "rightfully shifts the emphasis from intrinsic, humanly observable characteristics to relatedness or allegiance to the person of Christ".

of communities (Figure 8).[10] The communities in this study are heterogeneous, while the core group of leaders is homogeneous. Both newcomers and veterans participate in the communities, thus resembling what Hiebert calls centred-set communities. This is evident in the clearly defined centre, and the use of relationship-building is a key evangelism strategy within these groups.

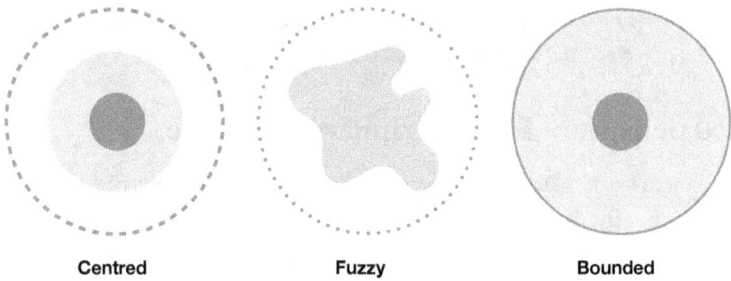

Centred   **Fuzzy**   **Bounded**

Figure 8: Paul G. Hiebert's centred, fuzzy and bounded sets.

A relatively high degree of negotiability should not be taken as evidence for a fuzzy set (rather than a centred set.) Clearly, the church plants were engaged in negotiation with the surrounding secular culture. However, when analysing the callings and formative practices, I discovered strong intentionality and clear teloi. Acknowledging the need for cultural adaptability, the church plants have adapted their practices to resonate with newcomers. This is reflected in their choice of meeting venues, gathering formats, and communication styles. I also discovered a tendency to identify potential barriers to newcomer participation, which were then removed or toned down so as not to interfere with the mission. As centred-set churches, they have a clear and focused idea of what it means to be a Christian within their communities: following Jesus Christ by participating in the formative practices with the church plant.

Hiebert sees potential problematic tendencies in all types of communities, including centred set ones: "If secularism is the cardinal danger of bounded sets, idolatry is the greatest evil in centred sets".[11] A strong centre represented by certain

---

[10] Cf. Mark D. Baker (2022), *Centered-Set Church: Discipleship and Community Without Judgmentalism*, Downers Grove, Illinois: InterVarsity Press.

[11] Hiebert (1994), p 129. The fuzzy community risks becoming syncretistic, picking up beliefs and practices that threaten the integrity of the Christian community. The bounded set risks drawing a too strict line between life inside the community and outside of it, with different rules applying.

leaders might lead to a cult-like situation. While this has not been the case in the church plants I have studied, the communities depend on the planters, and they influence the participants in the church plants. Power is relational rather than institutional.

Levels of Formative Engagement

In the analysis of trajectories, I saw movements between the periphery and the centre, where the centre represents the telos of the community of practice. This can be described as different modes of formative engagement. In his dissertation, Karl Inge Tangen presents ten themes that might explain why individuals become part of and identify with new churches. These themes can be related to different formative practices (Table 6).

Theme	Resource	Practice
1. Vision	Connection to a meaningful and action orientated vision	Preaching
2. Theo-dramatic horizon	Everyday life connection to the biblical narrative	
3. Connection with God	Rituals and Spirit encounters	Culturally sensitive worship
4. Churches of relevance	Contemporary aesthetic and professionalism	
5. Growing organisation	Living its story through dynamic practices	Small groups
6. Community	Friendships with family qualities	
7. Role models	Trustworthy and empowering leaders	
8. Metaphorical Home	A place for self-identity development	Spiritual practices
9. Path for personal growth	Ground for a personal "growth plot"	
10. Arenas for self-transcendent contributions	Callings by God to serve in the world	Ministry

Table 6: Tangen's identification themes with related practices.

The first group of themes are connected to the practice of preaching. These are vision and Theo-dramatic horizon, which connect the individual with a meaningful, action-oriented vision connected to the Biblical narrative. The themes that are connected to the practice of worship offer a connection with God through rituals and spirit encounters in culturally relevant meetings with contemporary aesthetics and professionalism. The third part of the list concerns how the community is organised and formed to grow close relationships. The church provides the individual with the sense of being part of a growing organisation or movement, thereby making it possible for a person to live her story through dynamic practices and, simultaneously, be part of a "metaphorical home" with friendships that have family-like qualities. In addition, there are supportive leaders who are trustworthy role models. The fourth part regards spiritual practices that make the church a place for the development of self-identity and personal "growth plots". The final theme in Tangen's list has to do with the ministry of the church. The community offers arenas for self-transcendent contributions, identifying personal callings by God to serve in the world.[12]

In relating Tangen's results with the findings of this study, it is clear that certain themes are more prominent in certain types of church plants, which offers a deeper understanding of the church plants as environments for Christian formation. The Industrial City church plant, similar in many respects to the two Neo-Pentecostal churches in Tangen's study, embodied all but the last of the themes. While the theme of ministerial arenas for self-transcending contributions is not entirely absent, it is mainly directed inward to invitation and participation in meeting-related task teams. In the church plant in Cathedral City, the small group and spirituality-related themes aimed at building community and self-identity development are at the centre, along with vision and Theo-dramatic Bible practices. Professionalism and finding a culturally relevant aesthetic are less prominent. The Harbour City church plant emphasises an action-oriented vision for self-transcendent contributions through small groups with apprenticeship relations with empowering leaders.

According to theologian Andrew Root, one of the main problems with the church in secular culture is that it no longer offers language and practices for divine action.[13] In her dissertation, Anne Mie Arndt Skak Johanson, likewise, points to the importance of spiritual experiences in shaping people's engagement with the Danish Lutheran Church:

> The Danish context is characterized by a rationalistic perception of the world in all its aspects. A rational worldview does not operate with a transcendent reality. The new missional axiom indicates that the rational mind needs a spiritual encounter to shake and penetrate the rational foundation, in order to open up to a transcendent reality.[14]

---

[12] Tangen (2012).
[13] Root (2017a), p 116.
[14] Johanson (2020), p 150.

The findings of this study confirm the significance of personal spiritual experience to inbound trajectories. Among the individuals I interviewed, several point to how meeting God through worship, baptism, personal prayer, and Bible reading made a decisive difference to their faith. There are recurring formulations such as "have a longing or hunger for Jesus", "It felt like a heavy stone had been lifted off", "he wants me to let him in", "at the baptism, you say your yes, as you do in the wedding ceremony", "[the sermons] were talking straight to me" It is also clear how these experiences have guided the participants towards a deeper Christian commitment or an engagement in the church plant.

I identify four distinct modes of engagement: *participation, identification, ownership* and *leaving*. These modes capture the range of engagement in the church plants. Ruth Perrin points to different levels of church engagement and the reasons for them. Her main interest lies in the motives for non-engagement. She mentions relationship issues involving failing leaders, church conflicts, and feeling exploited or undervalued in the church. The church's resistance to change could also be an issue. Some individuals preferred to channel their ministerial aspirations through secular service rather than church involvement. Some people who were involved in churches while growing up found faith to be insufficient as they entered adulthood. Others who were involved in churches while growing up found faith to be insufficient as they entered adulthood. Yet other people found family life too demanding for church engagement. Those who leave the church plants do so, in part, for other reasons.[15] The church plants are the results of callings to particular places in contemporary culture and address and negotiate issues that established churches might fail to deal with. One case of the leaving mode found in the study regards differences in the Christian formation telos – how Christian life is imagined.

9.4 Telos: From Secular to Christian Formation

Sweden is a highly individualistic and culturally progressive society, which is why the Christian communities' negotiation of secular culture is significant in Swedish church plants. As evident in the fieldwork materials, being a practising Christian is not the norm in Sweden. People in these church plants feel that they are far from the cultural norm and that their identity as Christians is challenged by the secular culture.

---

[15] Perrin (2022), p 169.

James K.A. Smith argues that the secular challenge is related to practices in particular since Western societies offer practices of secular formation. The shopping mall and the football arena form people toward identities as consumers and tribal nationalists.[16] Smith argues that the Christian liturgy forms the person towards a different telos. Christian formation is "a formation of desires and imagination that creates a certain kind of person who is part of a certain kind of people".[17]

In the Swedish setting, we can observe similar practices that form people in various ways. Anne-Christine Hornborg, professor of the History of Religions, takes the neo-spiritualism of secular Swedes as an example of practices that grow between religion and secularism. Practitioners can maintain their secular identity, holding on to some scientific rationalism, and yet be spiritual beings without the need for a congregation (or biblical morality).[18]

Practices shape the culture in society, including for those who are Christian and part of the church plants. This turns them into participators in the practices of communities with different ideals. While the church plants want to form fishermen, faithful neighbours, or good Samaritans, the shopping mall wants to create consumers, while parades shape conformism. This is something the church plants need to negotiate, and to some extent, they become involved in a counter-formation to offset what they perceive as problematic tendencies in the secular formation practices. But attempts to become relevant or attractive in the broader secular culture run the risk of eroding the churches' language, narratives, and practices in the public sphere.[19] The churches can inadvertently be shaped by practices of secular formation, as when they approach potential new members as customers of their lifestyle-related products.[20]

A pluralist society needs to provide space for religious minorities to form identities from their own traditions and resources. The formative practices investigated in this thesis are shaped in contemporary culture to form lived Christian identities in persons and communities in secular settings. Even though practices can use contemporary culture creatively, they are rooted in their church plant's own tradition

---

[16] Smith (2009).

[17] Smith (2009), p 29.

[18] E.g. Anne-Christine Hornborg (2012), "Secular Spirituality in Contemporary Sweden", *Swedish Missiological Themes*, 100 (3), 203–320.

[19] Dandelion (2019); Woodhead and Heelas (2000).

[20] Per Ewert (2022), *Moving Reality Closer to the Ideal: The Process towards Autonomy and Secularism during the Social Democratic Hegemony in 20th Century Sweden*, Oslo: VID. The author describes how Swedish Social democracy had a vision of domesticating the state church to being an integral part of the ideological formation of citizens.

9.4 Telos: From Secular to Christian Formation

and resources. By forming new church communities, the church planters claim the agency to address secular culture and its formative goals, including privatisation, pluralisation, and rationalisation.

While their free church traditions ground the church plants' formative practices, they intentionally and forcefully depart from those traditions in some instances. For instance, evangelicals' tendency to cordon themselves off from the majority culture – described by, among others, Anna Strhan – is not as clearly visible in the church plants I have studied.[21] Rather, they describe the secular challenge both as a problem and a motivator. All three formative practices take this condition into account – sometimes by confronting the culture, sometimes by taking advantage of it. Pluralism motivates the church plants to boldly raise their voices.

I find that differentiation, which causes the disappearance of Christian faith in the public sphere, pushes the churches to find an agency in Christian formation. In the church plants, this is articulated around a calling narrative. Just as the churches are no longer invited to play a part in shaping society's common narratives, the church plants do not primarily aim to construct these narratives. In this way, they operate according to market logic, becoming one of the many options in the religious life-making market.[22]

Free churches and, to an even greater degree, church plants have accepted pluralisation – yes, historically, they have even been drivers of it since it has meant the voluntary association and the possibility to form communities outside the state church. The free church tradition is negotiated in the church plants through innovative contemporary expressions of being church. Privatisation and individualism are negotiated in the church's handling of issues like sexual norms and different forms of internal diversity, and this negotiation challenges the individual-community relationship.[23] Rationalisation is seen, at least partly, in how cultural issues are pragmatically subordinated to a missional telos in the church planting communities. However, I find that the church plants avoid rationalising faith by reducing the language or practices to a Moral Therapeutic Deism that does not allow room for divine action.[24] Rather, divine action is a central feature, both of how the church plans are initiated – through a divine calling – and for the trajectories of

---

[21] Strhan (2015), p 201.
[22] Boy (2015).
[23] Cf. Moberg (2013). Moberg identifies a cultural negotiation around issues related to relations with the opposite sex and the use of material objects in prayer.
[24] Root (2017a).

many individuals who reference some kind of spiritual experience as crucial for them.

Missional Contextualisation

Heterogeneous Christian communities engage in negotiations around their formative practices, and through those negotiations, the meaning of the practices develops and is clarified. In my analysis of these negotiations, I described how the church plants are balancing adaptability, integrity, sustainability, and resilience in the secular culture. I concluded that negotiability emerges through a sustainable balance between integrity and adaptability – between adapting to secular culture and maintaining one's personal narratives and cultural views. I will return to this ecosystem analogy below.

I previously argued that Christianity maintains an interplay of continuity and discontinuity with its tradition.[25] Missiologist Mattias Neve has found that emerging church communities cultivate a mindset of offering alternative expressions of church. These communities' emphasis on innovation and deconstruction of boundaries could be understood as consequences of the core values of this kind of Christianity, which Neve describes as "a protest against what is perceived as either unhelpful or downright destructive elements of evangelical Protestant doctrine, ecclesial forms, and culture".[26] Along with tradition and culture, he points to the importance of the Bible in the trifocal exegesis of ecclesial practice. Bible reading is essential to formative practices, but the role of Scripture in the process of innovation in the discernment is unclear in the church plants in this study. I find that an active engagement in the cultural contexts involves reading culture in the light of personal experience with God. As seen in the analysis, calling involves vision. The church planters embody missional imagination in a deeply secular culture, but something resembling the trifocal process of contextual discernment does not seem to be a communal effort in the church plants.

In the analysis, I identify the need for a balance between adaptability and integrity. Richard R. Osmer discusses a two-pole scale between what he calls identity and relevance. I find that an excessive pursuit of cultural relevance risks turning the community into something other than ecclesia.[27] Likewise, excessive integrity

---

[25] See pp 207-08. Rowan Williams argues that the church is held together by the confession to the same Christ over the course of history. Williams (2005).

[26] Neve (2021), p 177. For an explanation of Neve's trifocal lens, see p 260 in his book.

[27] Fahlgren (2006) argues for a strong connection between what the church does and what the church is, the fundamental practices and ecclesial identity.

9.4 Telos: From Secular to Christian Formation

means erecting borders towards society – maintaining what sociologists of religion Pink Dandelion describes as a "hedge" between the clean community and the unclean culture. A church cannot easily be built on individualism, which is deeply ingrained in Swedish society. Swedish culture's unspoken mandate to relegate religion to the private sphere does not remove the need for community.[28] The church plants deal with individualism through a centre mindset. So as not to compromise their missional goals, the church planters only address issues like sexuality and aspects of diversity when asked directly about them. Otherwise, they trust the Holy Spirit to lead the church members along a journey to the church's core moral and theological centre.

Being culturally relevant is important to the church plants but in different ways. This is most clearly seen in the revival meeting practice. Language, place of meeting, and music are carefully selected to remove cultural obstacles for newcomers. Other ways of being culturally relevant include a strong emphasis on activism, as seen in the context of the apprenticeship practice, and building a church on close relationships rather than "prefabricated" religious markers like clerical clothing or church buildings. These examples point to a kind of religious minimalism in the missional strategy of the church plants.

This kind of minimalism is characteristic of the missional movement. It seeks a return to the original core of Christianity, often in the early church, as described in the Book of Acts and the Gospels. The argument is that when Constantine made Christianity a state religion in the late fourth century, it led to a shift from a community-based faith to an institutionalized religion, potentially compromising the church's original focus on spreading the message of Christ. After a long period of "Christendom", the church must now be reformed to its original design.[29] This perspective offers a critique of the institutionalisation of the church while offering valuable lessons for contemporary churches, particularly those with a missional focus. The core principles of "what Jesus started" are ways of putting words to the church's integrity in times of change. Missiologist Allan Hirsch describes how a renewed focus on core principles can shift the focus from ecclesiology to missiology – an outflow of Christology – leading to ecclesiology.[30] In other words, the

---

[28] Berggren and Trägårdh (2009); Dandelion (2019)

[29] E.g. Murray (2018); Steve Addison (2012), *What Jesus Started: Joining the Movement, Changing the World*, Downers Grove, Illinois: IVP Books; Steve Addison (2011), *Movements That Change the World: Five Keys to Spreading the Gospel*, Downers Grove, Illinois: InterVarsity Press; Alan Hirsch and Frost, Michael (2013), *The Shaping of Things to Come: Innovation and Mission for the 21st-Century Church*, Ada, Michigan: Baker.

[30] Hirsch (2006), p 143.

early church can provide a model for returning to church communities where the concern is doing what Jesus did rather than building an institution occupied with itself.

Ecclesiologist John Fitzmaurice raises concerns about an overly minimalist approach.[31] Like practical theologian William McAlpine, he finds the tradition to be part of the valuable heritage of the church rather than unnecessary baggage.[32] I find that minimalism, for minimalism's sake, is unhelpful. The main reason for this is missional – for whom is the church's core message important? To communicate in the contemporary context, it is necessary to be not only relevant in terms of being approachable but also seen as an authentic church.

Fitzmaurice is right in suggesting using authentic core practices like the Eucharist and baptism for Christian formation. When speaking of the free church tradition – I would add the meeting, conventicle and social ministry. Core practises such as these have the potential to speak authentically in secular contexts. There is an advantage to understanding missional strategies from a practice perspective (as opposed to a singular cognitive perspective) since it gives a holistic perspective of the lived. Sometimes church plants are said to reject tradition, but in this study, we can see a creative rethinking of methods and approaches.[33]

9.5 Reflections on Theory and Methodology

This research has been conducted using ethnographic methods and employed situated learning theory with an abductive approach. One important aspect of this project is that the fieldwork was carried out during a pandemic. In this section, I will comment briefly on these research choices and conditions.

Ethnography, Situated Learning, and Theological Discernment

I initially stated how I use the term "ethnographic" to refer to both methods and a tradition of research practice. I have used ethnographic methods, field studies with participatory observations and interviews to achieve "thick descriptions" of contextual practices "in living colour".[34] But more importantly, from the beginning, the research has been guided by both the practice orientation and attention

---

[31] Fitzmaurice (2016).

[32] McAlpine (2011).

[33] An example of this is Karl who discusses the need for ecclesial re-innovation for the sake of mission (p 138).

[34] Ward (2012b), p 6. Agar (1996), p 10.

to what goes on in practice. The abductive approach has led me to start and stay in the contexts while at the same time continuously engaging with theories and research.

The ethnographic methods of field studies and interviews used in the thesis project have served the aim well. However, one could argue that the thesis, and its constructions and presentations of the gathered material, are rather modest in their ethnographic modus. My journey started with a more "purist ambition" as an ethnographer than how I ended up finishing the text. A more radical ethnographic approach would have involved the writer being more present in the texts by continuously reflecting on things like my own position in relation to the informants, my interpretations of situations, and the practices in which I have been a participant.[35] While not trying to hide such conditions, I have gravitated towards a modest approach to avoid "overcharging" the texts with meta-reflections. However, as emphasised in the introduction and the chapter on methodology, the researcher, as a game-maker, is always present in the research and results.[36]

I turned to situated learning theory as the theoretical point of departure because it brings relevant tools when analysing Christian formation. By using concepts from this theory, I was able to analyse pathways between the centre and periphery, as well as the negotiation of secular culture in the church plants. I made modifications by adding complementary concepts and perspectives – calling and telos, in particular. It is fair to ask whether the thesis needs situated learning theory and whether it would have been better without it. I find that having this theoretical foundation has helped me considerably in my analysis. And while modifications have been necessary, that is part of the abductive way of working.

Theological discernment needs more than ethnographic descriptions of human actions and socio-cultural theory. Andrew Root encourages the theologian to keep an open door for divine action in empirical descriptions while at the same time acknowledging the limits to the claims of such descriptions.[37] This is the approach I have had in the field studies and the presentations of the analyses. For the church, it is of utmost importance to retain and develop a theological discourse involving divine action and God's presence. A church that conforms to secular understandings of its own practice might find itself to be something other than ecclesia.

---

[35] E.g. Selka (2022); Ghodsee (2016).
[36] Ideström and Stangeland Kaufman (2018).
[37] Root (2016), p 52.

Research in the Pandemic

As mentioned in the methodology chapter, I received ethical approval for the field studies at almost the same time as the first pandemic restrictions were announced in Sweden. I had early contact with the church plant in Industrial City and was able to start immediately. Additional restrictions were introduced gradually, which made it possible for the relatively small church plant to operate almost unaffected during my stay. I could attend all gatherings and meet individuals to interview. Only later, this church plant had to move entirely to meeting digitally.

While the field studies in the different church plants overlapped, I stayed for about six months in each church. Field studies in the second church plant, in Cathedral City, started during the autumn of 2020. Meeting outside meant fewer restrictions at the time, so the church plant met in a public park. The leaders postponed the start of home-based meetings and eventually cancelled them. Instead, the church plant started meeting digitally on Zoom. At this time, my field studies were increasingly forced to move to digital platforms and small gatherings.

The first few months of the pandemic meant a partial lockdown in Sweden, and being relatively small communities, they were not much affected by the restrictions. At this time, no one thought the pandemic would last very long. But when the restrictions were increasingly harder, they affected the church plants more. Church planting is, first and foremost, about building relationships with new people, which wasn't possible then.

As has been described earlier, the field study of the church plant in Harbour City was notably more limited than the first two. The winter and spring of 2021 were difficult times for the church plants. Very few groups gathered onsite. Those who did gather didn't allow visitors to avoid the risks involved in contacts outside a very closed circle. In addition to this, visiting Harbour City involved long trips, which meant higher risks of being affected by COVID-19. This meant that I only had a few days to meet the church planters and participate in a few groups' onsite gatherings. Most of the observations were done during digital meetings.[38] This is a limitation of the study. However, the material I was able to gather in total was very rich.

It follows that the majority of the material was gathered during the pandemic. Almost half of the participative observations and interviews have been done using

---

[38] Frida Mannerfelt (2023), *Co-preaching: The Practice of Preaching in Digital Culture and Spaces*, Stockholm: Enskilda Högskolan Stockholm. Mannerfelt studies preaching in digital spaces. She argues that the deep relationality of the practice of preaching involves not just humans and texts but also material arrangements. This feature is amplified in digital spaces.

digital tools such as Zoom. Therefore, it is fair to ask whether the study is a traditional field study or a study of digital practices. I would argue that the study is a field study done during a pandemic where practices are partly onsite and partly online. I have followed the practices of the church plants as they have migrated between these locations. My intention has been to give thick descriptions of the practices and contexts in which the practices have been located. I consider this a feature that is unique to this thesis in relation to earlier studies and something that might provide a window into how church plants will function in the future. In these adaptable groups, it is likely that digital tools will play an increasingly important role.

9.6 Conclusion

This chapter summarises the thesis findings and discusses them in relation to other Christian formation studies. I have investigated Christian formation in the context of advanced secularisation in missional situations. Using the concepts of trajectories and negotiation, I have analysed pathways between the centre and periphery and the negotiation of secular culture in church plant communities. I presented this as three movements: Christian formation in Swedish church plants involves an intentional movement from calling to practice, a movement of participation from periphery to centre, and a movement of telos from secular to Christian formation.

Reflecting on the methodological and theoretical choices of the thesis, I concluded that the ethnographic methods are well-suited to a study of practices of Christian formation, while the situated learning theory provides helpful tools – even more so when complemented with theological concepts and perspectives.

In the final chapter, I will point to the implications of the study and what can be learnt from the reflection on Christian formation in Swedish church plants.

10. Theology for New Gardens in the Wasteland

In this final chapter, I will examine a few theological issues regarding the formation of Christians in a secular culture. Five themes emerge as particularly significant from the study: the role of experience in faith formation, the role of digital media, missional ecclesiology, church planting as a Christian formation ministry, and the role of discernment in practical theology.

10.1 Experiential Faith

Theological knowledge among newcomers is relatively limited in the church plants, which is something the church plants seek to address in various ways.[1] In Industrial City, the church plant has introduced a six-week introductory course to the Christian faith for newcomers to understand why the Bible is central to the Christian faith and how it can speak into the lives of Christians. This provides a foundational introduction for newcomers by delving into themes such as the importance of the Bible in the lives of Christians. The Harbour City church plant has a women's group for Christian spirituality. The group reads the Bible and investigates faith by addressing the participants' questions, but the emphasis is on experiential faith: How can a relationship with God become a part of one's everyday life?

Experience of God

Here, we delve into a component in the formation of faith that is not given enough attention in Christian formation research and which might be difficult to interpret within the framework of learning theories – the experience of God in Christian formation. Andrew Root is among those scholars who have pointed to the

---

[1] My general impression is that those who are more knowledgeable about the Christian faith are immigrants.

importance of experiencing the divine in Christian formation.[2] In their respective research, Anne Mie Arndt Skak Johanson and Karl Inge Tangen find that experiences of God are necessary for the individual to identify with the church:

> A spiritual experience reveals a transcendent reality and starts a change in the mind from an exclusively rational mindset to a mindset including the transcendent realm.[3]

> [P]eople identify with these churches because they facilitate rituals and Spirit encounters that mediate experiences in which God is engaged as a caring father and as the dynamic Lord of history.[4]

According to these scholars, faith is primarily received through experience rather than cognition. In my material, it is also evident that experiences of the divine play an important role. Such experiences provide guidance and direction. They also shape people's spiritual trajectories – and provide a kind of spiritual inertia that moves people along those trajectories. And yet, in Root's view, the church often shies away from discussing experiential faith in order to be accepted in secular society.[5]

This is not the case in the church plants I have studied. Instead, they foster a culture that facilitates these encounters and encourages people to openly discuss and share them. For example, Peter, the Cathedral City church planter, describes how he met Jesus through Bible reading, which kindled his desire for God. Einar, the church planter in Industrial City, describes shaking and crying when a pastor prayed for him. This profound emotional experience revealed to him that Jesus is a graceful God and that the Bible is true, propelling him into his calling as a church planter. Testimonies from Alex in Cathedral City and Marianne in Harbour City underscore the shared experience of God's love in the church community. Erik says that while he initially went to the Industrial City church plant to meet people, he continued attending because he discovered his own longing for God and saw how God was working in him.

As discussed in the previous chapter, none of the church plants fit the description of "Households of the Spirit", as Christopher James calls church plants, with a particular emphasis on charismatic spirituality. Still, all the church plants embody a spirituality that welcomes charismatic experiences, such as perceiving God's voice, seeking prayer through healing or seeking guidance from God. When they describe their formative trajectories, many informants speak specifically

---

[2] Root (2017a).
[3] Johanson (2020), p 144.
[4] Tangen (2012), p 312.
[5] Root (2017a), p 116.

about experiences of God in and through individual and shared Bible reading, listening to sermons, singing worship, baptism, and prayer ministry. These experiences are more grounded in feeling God's presence in everyday life than ecstatic experiences. What we see here could be described as a kind of everyday mysticism. It is neither characterised by the peak experiences of charismatic Christianity nor by highly advanced spiritual exercises of a monastic type. Rather, regular practices both lead to and are nurtured by a felt everyday experience of the presence of God.

In the church plants, the members expect to encounter a present and active God. This emphasis on an experiential faith and a personal encounter with God stands in contrast to the larger church planting movement's occasional tendency to focus primarily on organisational matters, worship style, finances, and numerical growth. However, the formative practices in these church plants are centred around the development of a spirituality infused by a present, active, and loving God.

10.2 Modern Technology and Practices of Christian Formation

The development of learning theories during the 21st century has been shaped by several trends in academia. Traditionally, the behaviouristic perspective on learning has focused on right behaviour, the constructivist on correct cognition, and socio-cultural perspectives on the importance of the social context for learning. Faith formation, in particular, has been primarily associated with cognitive processes, but recently there has been a growing emphasis on practice perspectives, especially within the field of practical theology.

The thesis findings align with the development of learning theory in late modernity. And the development of technology. Social media prioritises images and videos over text, which is the predominant communication medium in the late modern era.[6] While texts allow for precise details and comprehensive information, social media prioritises short, readily accessible messages. The church planters recognise the significance of this medium and use it to both reach new audiences and foster a sense of community.

---

[6] Cf. Walter J. Ong and Hartley, John (2012), *Orality and Literacy: The Technologizing of the Word*, Oxfordshire: Routledge; Joel Halldorf (2023), *Bokens folk: En civilisationshistoria från papyrus till pixel*, Stockholm: Fri Tanke. For a study of how digital technology shapes ecclesial practices, see Mannerfelt (2023).

The Cathedral City church plant's Bible reading groups provide another instance of learning but with a socio-cultural orientation. One might argue that the strong focus on the text reflects a modernist cognitive emphasis characteristic of the free church tradition. However, the church plant emphasises reading and conversation as a shared spiritual practice rather than an individual habit. This practice conjoins the socio-cultural understanding of shared practice with the cognitive approach to the text and thus contributes to the formation of the community as much as the formation of the individual. This is not new to the practice itself, but the renewed interest in social practice has brought theoretical perspectives, such as formative trajectories and negotiation of secular culture, to the foreground.

What is new, however, is the online conventicle. The church plants innovated on the conventicle tradition by moving the practice online when onsite gatherings were no longer possible during the COVID-19 pandemic. One striking feature is how easily and naturally the group members use digital media for these intimate gatherings, even when discussing quite personal matters. Another is the scant critical reflection on the possible drawbacks of using digital technology for spiritual practices.

10.3 Ecclesiology

Church planting is a response to a calling from God and a reaction to the lack of effective ecclesial models in the context. A classic understanding of ecclesiology starts with a set of the church's defining elements, such as the administration of sacraments and the preaching of the word. As a response to secularisation (and the institutionalised church's inability to offer an effective response of its own), the missional movement has underlined the sent nature of the church. However, church plants occasionally fail to care for the church's unity.[7] Part of missional theology is the apostolic sentness and the acknowledgement of the West as both post-Christian and in urgent need of evangelistic action. These churches are sent to cultures and places where Christianity once was the majority narrative but these contexts now seem to be without an ecclesial life relevant to most people.

---

[7] Paul B Coulter (2016), *Church and Mission in Four Aspects: Church Planting Within a Missionary Ecclesiology for the One, Holy, Catholic and Apostolic Church in Contemporary Northern Ireland*, Aberdeen: University of Aberdeen. Coulter shows that while the Apostolic confession identifies the church as one, holy, catholic, and apostolic, the church plants tend to overemphasise apostolic ($\dot{\alpha}\pi o\sigma\tau\acute{\epsilon}\lambda\lambda\omega$, to send away) at the expense of the church's unity. See also Asserhed (2023).

The Significance of Calling

Practical theology has mainly studied Christian formation in liturgy, which emphasises the sending at the end of the worship service. A notable theological finding in this study is that church planters feel called. There is, it can be argued, a difference between being sent at the end of the liturgy in a church and being called to missions. The church planters that I meet in my field study imagine church differently, and they feel called to areas where traditional structures have diminished or disappeared. This reverses the order. The life of the church plants begins with a calling to form Christians in a particular manner and context. This movement, which I have described as a movement from calling to practice, is significant for three reasons:

- *The calling fosters strong intentionality:* The church planters are sent by their denominations, but even more, they feel called by God. Thus, they don't depend first and foremost on the institution but on God's provision and blessing. The personal experience of a calling outweighs the institutional confirmation from the denomination. Calling can foster perseverance, patience, and other virtues necessary when working with church plants.
- *The calling carries the formative genome:* In all three church plants, it was evident how important spiritual experiences in the lives of the planters were manifested in the formative practices that embodied the church plants' teloi. This indicates that the calling carries a formative telos for what it means to be Christian and to be church, including visions of new ecclesial expressions.
- *The calling is place-bound:* Closely linked to the ecclesial imagination is a particular place. The place informs how the ecclesial practices form Christians through church planting towards its telos.

Liquid Ecclesiology

A missional ecclesiology is more liquid than solid. Pete Ward, in delineating the marks of what he calls a liquid ecclesiology, argues that the ground has shifted in late modernity. He refers to sociologist Zygmunt Baumann, who describes late modernity as "liquid". The church in the present era is better understood as an organic body than an institution. The image of a "solid church" holds to the understanding of the Christian community as "gathering in one place, at one time, with the purpose of performing a shared ritual".[8] This understanding, Ward says, is shared by both Catholics and Protestants (including those by Evangelical and Pentecostal denominations). In contrast, the concept of a Liquid Church suggests a positive appraisal of fluidity. A church that is flexible and without clear borders is able to interact with and engage the liquid culture of late modernity; as such, it might actually be more equipped to follow Christ into the world.[9] Ward notes that if that is the case, it has consequences for how the church imagine and interact with contemporary culture in missions:

> Christ comes to the Church and the world in and through cultural forms of expression. This presence is not inevitable, nor does a particular form of words or ideas ensure it. Christ is present because of the freedom of the Spirit to reflect in and through the cultural expression of Christians, such that the light of Christ shines as presence, encounter, and transformation. The freedom of the Spirit does not nullify or negate the cultural form of the expression of the faith as message, however; it animates it, giving it life and making it young.[10]

But culture is material and semiotic and, therefore, brings all kinds of meanings into everyday things and matters. Ward uses the example of the introduction of the guitar as an instrument for worship. In some contexts, it has become the primary worship instrument, while in others, it is not accepted. The meanings that have been attributed to both the instrument and the new cultural expressions that it brings make the guitar a watershed in ecclesial culture.[11]

In this study, the fluidity of the church plants can be seen in their attitudes to traditional forms of church. One example is how Peter, the main leader in Cathedral City, calls himself a "project leader" rather than the more traditional "pastor". The reason for this, he explains, is that he does not want to be a "professional Christian". Instead, he focuses on meeting people. His step away from a traditional ecclesial role is motivated by an identity centred on missional engagement. Another example of fluidity can be seen in the Harbour City church's move from a traditional church building to a storefront facility. This move was motivated by the planters' desire to be closer to the marginalised, but it also functions as a critique of the established church as both preoccupied with itself and insulated and aloof from ordinary people. Thirdly, the use of culture and worship songs as cultural artefacts in Industrial City shows how the planters view spirituality as

---

[8] Ward (2017a), p 11.
[9] Ward (2008), p 103.
[10] Ward (2017a), p 81.
[11] Ward (2017a), p 72.

something that migrates from the liturgical context of the Sunday meeting to the phones and earbuds of people in and beyond their church plant.

Liquid ecclesiology is missional because it assumes that God is working outside and independent of the gathered church community. The rejection of traditional, solid structures allows for invention and creativity regarding forms, practices, and places. Because as Wards says, "The Holy Spirit appears to have been quite content to use what is limited and perhaps flawed forms of communication to bring people to faith and into the Church".[12] This fits well with church planting since it is an innovative missional strategy that creatively uses culture to form lived Christian identities in secular people. In that sense, church planting presupposes liquid ecclesial forms. However, liquid ecclesiology needs to be accompanied by theological discernment. When the borders are blurred, some central ecclesial characteristics may need to be strengthened. Otherwise, church might be anything and meaning nothing. The ministry of church planting means taking this risk for the sake of the world – intentionally participating in God's mission and life in the wasteland.[13]

10.4 Ministry

In this thesis, a broad image of what Christian formation means in missional situations emerges through the narratives. Clearly, the three church plants foster different ecclesial imaginations, possess different formative teloi, and seek to create different kinds of disciples – fishermen, faithful neighbours, and good Samaritans. Despite these foundational differences, the church plants have much in common, not the least the calling to be church communities with the mission to form people towards a lived Christian identity in what they perceive as the secular wasteland of Sweden.

I have already pointed out how Andrew Root, in framing the challenges for faith formation in a secular age, advises the churches to avoid the temptation of idealising the young and youthful. Root argues that this entails adjusting too much to the demands of secular culture. Instead, he wants the churches to open the door to the possibility of divine action in and through church ministry. This, however, challenges secular rationality, a rationality that, to some degree, has infiltrated both churches and theological reflection.

---

[12] Ward (2017a), p 123.
[13] Ward (2008), p 103.

Serving the Neighbour

The ministry of church planting means the balancing act of living for God and living for others. For the church planter, taking God's calling seriously demands taking responsibility for the innovation of the ecclesia to reach those outside the church. Creative pro-social action becomes a necessary outflow of faith. Faith, in Root's theology, means union with Christ, which is not only received as a gift for oneself but as Christ's kenosis *in and through* your own life – for the neighbour.

> We can have faith only as the gift of Jesus's own faith because Jesus has experienced the fullness of God's ministry, tasting the completeness of God's faithfulness in resurrection. [...] You live in union with the resurrected Christ, who calls you to embrace the gift of faith by sharing in his person, forming your life to the song of kenosis by being your neighbour's minister. [...] And theosis is to share In God, not in power and might, but as a minister who shares in the glory of God by experiencing the fusion of the divine with the human through a hypostatic union – by sharing in and ministering to persons.[14]

Ministry, according to Root, is understood as a kenotic outflow towards the neighbour in close cooperation with God. Planting churches adds a dimension to the Christian formation ministry – the building of the body of Christ. As Stefan Paas and Hans Schaeffer put it, "building community and making disciples are two sides of the same coin".[15] In addition, as we have seen in the three church plants of this study, planting churches includes a strong contextual element. Part of the church planter's calling entails developing an ecclesial imagination, which is not abstract but comes from being present in a particular place, walking the streets and meeting real people.

Being Holy

In this study, we have seen that the church plants have different approaches to holiness as an end goal for Christian formation. But none of the communities want to have a bounded-set of church community in which they live holy lives separated from a depraved world.[16]

The history of the free church movement and changes in holiness theology are important backgrounds to understanding contemporary church planting in

---

[14] Root (2017a), p 191. Similarly, Stefan Paas (2019), *Pilgrims and Priests*, London: SCM, proposes that Christians have a calling to be priests in a strange culture, carrying their families and neighbourhoods before the Lord in prayer.

[15] Stefan Paas and Schaeffer, Hans (2021), "Reconciled Community", *Ecclesiology*, 17 (3), 325–347, p 340.

[16] Hiebert (1994), p 114.

Sweden.[17] The free churches in Sweden are historically rooted in the Evangelical revival, where a call to conversion and a holy life was central. By emphasizing the purity of the Christian community, pietism in Sweden deviated from the teaching and praxis of the Church of Sweden. Pietists reimagined the church and the Christian life as they thought it should be and initiated practices with diverging teloi. If they initially thought of themselves as the true and pure church, consisting of members who were orthodox in faith and characterised by a high moral standing during the 19th century, these churches later felt a need to reflect on and adjust some of their attitudes since they were seen as judgemental and narrow.

The clearest example of conscious adjustment is found in the example from Industrial City. The church planters have an ideal of living a morally pure life when it comes to relationships, an ideal guided by God's will as they find it expressed in the Bible. However, this expectation is not emphasised in the church plant. The expectation is instead on the Holy Spirit to do the work of sanctification. The ethics of the church is something that new converts are supposed to discover by other means than sermons on hot topics and moral reproachment. This demands patience and faith from leaders that God forms people without their direct involvement. They are not, they say, interested in controlling people's lives, and they are aware that a strong emphasis on morals might repel people who would otherwise be interested in the spiritual life with Christ that is at the centre of the community. Thus, a too-strong emphasis on living a holy life is to the detriment of the goal of being culturally relevant and an attractive community.

The three church plants have not abandoned the ideal of a morally pure life. But what they have lost – or adjusted – is their faith in the pure community. Therefore, the terminology of participation in a church community is more relevant than formal membership. The latter represents an insider/outsider, pure/impure, converted/unconverted ecclesial imagination. In contrast, participation

---

[17] Halldorf (2012), p 159. The concept of holiness in the Bible and the Christian tradition is often referred to as a quality of God. Objects, places, and people become holy as they belong to God. Here lies a calling to be set apart for God by living according to God's instructions. Identity as a Christian, thus, means making God the guide to a morally impeccable lifestyle. The early church emphasised *theosis* – being transformed into God's likeness. The Medieval church in the West offered holiness through institutions and sacraments. In Martin Luther's critique of the strong role of the institutional church, God was given a more prominent role in the sanctification of believers. This, in turn, laid the ground for the Evangelical revival, which instead emphasised the individual's conversion and moral life. Cf. Alister E. McGrath (2016), *Christian Theology: An Introduction*, Hoboken, New Jersey: John Wiley & Sons; Lenhammar (1999); Jarlert (2001).

conveys an image of movement from/towards Christ, which may result in purity, conversion, and mission.

10.5 Discernment

I have described Sweden as a culture of advanced secularity. However, while the Christian faith is sometimes seen as irrational, a majority of the population – over 5 million people – still belongs to the Church of Sweden. Whatever the reasons for their membership might be, it may seem unfair to describe Swedish culture as overwhelmingly secular. Christian narratives can still be found in many places and be picked up and used in new ways. In this mixed situation, it can be a challenge to discern between embracing contemporary secular culture and seizing real missional opportunities for the church. Finding themselves planted in the wasteland, the gardens, and the life these churches want to bring is dependent on discerning between *operating in* the secular versus being *operated by* the secular.

Missional Discernment

In the introduction, I referred to Richard Osmer's articulation of the tension between the poles of relevance and identity.[18] To help the church constructively balance relevance and identity, Mattias Neve suggests a trifocal lens to critically audit Christian tradition, Scripture, and culture.[19] In order to be authentic churches in mission – avoiding becoming museums of past times or mirrors of contemporary culture – churches need their missional discernment to include theological reflection.

Discernment can only be practised from a position of normativity. In other words, we are no longer merely describing but making judgements on what is more or less important or adequate. Pete Ward discusses theological discernment in relation to the claim that the presence of Christ in the church and the world is real. While this claim might be ontologically true, the expressions of it in the life of the church are always relative, he argues.[20] This is a theological statement acknowledging the fact that the church can confess but never control the divine. It highlights the tentative nature of the epistemological descriptions in an ethnographic study,

---

[18] Osmer (2012), pp 50–51.

[19] Neve (2021), p 240. I describe Neve's model on p 69 in Chapter 2 and p 208 note 9 in Chapter 8.

[20] This is in line with critical realism methodology, which is the tradition I draw on in this thesis.

10.5 Discernment

which in turn opens the door for reflection, different interpretations, and discussion. Ward describes this discernment as a spiritual practice that involves reading the scriptures with prayerful reflection:

> Discerning the body [of Christ in the lived], i.e., reflection, rests on the revelation of Christ seen in the scriptures and in particular the gospels. So while reflection demands the attention and discipline that is required to draw close to the complexities of the lived experience of believing, it finds its life and energy in Jesus Christ the Light of the world, the image of God, reflected in the gospel as it is made alive and vivified by the Holy Spirit in the Christian community.[21]

Theological discernment is an essential concern for the churches engaging in mission. Stefan Paas and Hans Schaeffer note this in discussing how the forming of church communities involves discernment. The communities are hermeneutical spaces in which people can discover and explore God's salvation. This is because the communities are simultaneously fellowships of people and reflections of the community of the Trinity. Furthermore, Paas and Schaeffer argue that since the boundaries of church communities are porous, they are also missional – open to invite, include, connect, and learn.[22] Discernment, seen in this way, becomes both contextual and concrete:

> [Christian missionary community formation] as a contextual practice begins with the discernment of God working towards community in concrete settings where isolation, self-centeredness, illness and various forms of injustice hinder the realization of community.[23]

As we have seen, participating in the ministry of church planting is contextual. It means engaging with real people and cultural issues. It also means taking part in the eschatological kingdom ministry of Jesus, building communities of hope.

The Garden as a Discernment Model

I have proposed the garden as a model for discernment, partly because it is an image where cultural issues can be held in tension. When planting a church, there needs to be a missional discernment that sees possibilities for engagement with those non-Christian people who are frequently overlooked by already established churches. This means discerning a calling to join Him in planting in a particular place or among a particular group of people and planting with a particular vision

---

[21] Ward (2017a), p 186.
[22] Paas and Schaeffer (2021), p 335.
[23] Paas and Schaeffer (2021), p 334.

of how to form people towards a lived Christian identity – Where is Christ, and what is He doing?

The results of this thesis highlight many challenges faced by new churches in a secular society. Planting a church involves risking exposure to secular teloi. It also risks advancing the internal secularisation of the church rather than opening new possibilities for Christian formation. It should be said that there is no inherent contraposition between Christian and secular, generally speaking. The risk, however, lies in conflicting teloi leading to Christian faith and practice that amounts to little more than "exclusive humanism", as Charles Taylor names the social imaginary that "accounts for meaning and significance without any appeal to divine or transcendence".[24] Privatisation, especially, is a secular challenge to churches and church plants since it undermines the common life. Further, pluralisation challenges the unity in a church community. As we have seen, diversity is negotiated in church plants. Sometimes successfully, sometimes less so.

The garden as discernment model involves the four concepts of *adaptability, integrity, sustainability,* and *resilience*. These are characteristics necessary for a seed to grow into a plant and, eventually, a garden. In order to offer formative practices that foster a Christian telos, church plants need both *adaptability* and *integrity*. They must possess both the ability to adapt to changing and uncertain circumstances and the capacity to remain one integrated ecclesia. Without the *integrity*, the church plants might be conformed or deformed rather than formed. Without some *adaptability*, the church plants would soon become irrelevant. Christ's call to mission, therefore, presupposes holding adaptability and integrity in tension. Formative practices need to find ways to use this tension creatively.

Christian formation also needs a degree of *sustainability* – the capacity to remain healthy. Free church Christianity often possesses a stroke of activism that needs to be balanced by grace and acceptance. This is particularly the case in church plants, which are very much entrepreneurial ventures with reaching people as their main focus. One reason why church plants often fail and need to close – why they wither – lies in the fact that the formative practices are not sustainable over time. Another reason is the lack of *resilience* – the ability to endure challenges. Planting a church is the choice to walk towards the unforeseen. Not all people engaging in the practices of the community will align with the telos of the church planters. This can cause conflict. At the same time, negotiating diversity can be

---

[24] Taylor (2007); Smith (2014), p 141.

essential to the process of refining formative practices. *Resilience*, therefore, demands responsiveness and flexibility.

I suggest that these four concepts – adaptability, integrity, sustainability, and resilience – are helpful to the ministry of church planting in a secular society. More specifically, finding balance in the tensions between these concepts requires discernment between *operating in* secularity versus being *operated by* the secular.

10.6 Epilogue: Growing Gardens of Christian Formation

This thesis's metaphor of an ecosystem of Christian formation in a barren wasteland is helpful in interpreting and reflecting on the results. Furthermore, it develops the language and metaphors of other researchers whose work I have drawn on. After leaving the "community of practice" concept behind, Etienne Wenger uses the language of "landscapes" of practice.[25] Stephen Kemmis suggests that practices might be understood as "species in an ecosystem" and "as living things connected to one another in "ecologies of practices".[26] Christopher B. James describes the post-Christian culture of Seattle as poor soil.[27] The thesis's descriptions of the cultivation of culture, the planting of church communities, and the organic life of these communities show that this metaphor is more than a catchy slogan. Formative practices are better imagined as organic life than schematics of frameworks or machines.

Describing Swedish culture as a lifeless wasteland is obviously a bit one-sided. Many would consider, and in many aspects rightly so, Sweden a flourishing, well-ordered, highly developed, democratic country with all the possibilities for cultural diversity one could wish for. But do those possibilities extend to religious groups such as Christian communities? "Detraditionalisation" and internal secularisation challenge Christian communities' narratives, theology, and moral groundings.[28] Secularisation removes the institutional scaffolding of a common Christian narrative and demands changes to the formative practices of Christian communities. The challenges are not first and foremost political or judicial, but cultural. The secular wasteland is both a concern and a motivator for church planters in Sweden.

---

[25] Wenger-Trayner et al. (2014).
[26] Kemmis et al. (2012), p 36.
[27] James (2018).
[28] Woodhead and Heelas (2000); Dandelion (2019).

The garden is the life space where an organism grows. The soil can be rich or poor, and the location can be exposed to climate and weather, both good and bad. God's calling to church planters has a missional telos and a cultural locus. It is an urge from God to individuals or groups to take personal responsibility for growing Christian communities in a particular culture. Different gardens hold different species, need different cultivation, and provoke different imaginations of Christian formation. What kind of life flourishes in a wasteland?

Church plants can offer Christian formation through formative, God-saturated practices that shape secularised people towards a self-perception of being Christian. Cultivating these gardens means shaping a life-affirming culture that can exploit the possibilities of the culture while at the same time being something other than the surrounding wasteland. This involves negotiating a sustainable balance between missional activism and contemplative spirituality. Resilient structures for leadership are needed, as well as a healthy balance between adaptability to contemporary culture and integrity of lived Christian identity.

In this thesis, gardens represent a spiritually rich life lived in community with others. This stands in contrast to the perceived wasteland, which gives little room for religious life. I have described the church plants as heterogeneous communities that possess both a degree of resilience to the wasteland's secular culture and the strength to protect the integrity of the lived formative practices. While the church planters believe the reigning secular culture is incapable of providing either the good news of God's love or a changed appreciation of self and others, they feel that they have something valuable: an invitation to live a real life and embrace the love of God.

Appendix I: Interview Guide: Participant

1. Berätta lite kort om din bakgrund?
(Tell me a little about your background?)

2. Hur fick du kontakt med <församlingsplantering>?
(How did you get into contact with <church plant>?)

3. Hur kom du med i <praktik>?
(How did you join <practice>)

4. Om du beskriver för någon som inte varit med, vad gör man i <praktik>?
(How would you explain <practice> to someone who hasn't been there, what do you do?)

5. Hur har det varit att vara med i gruppen från din synvinkel?
(From your perspective, how has it been to part of this group?)

6. Kan du nämna något särskilt som varit viktigt för dig?
(Can you name something that has been especially valuable to you?)

7. Vad är det att vara kristen?
(What does it mean to be a Christian?)

8. Hur har du och din tro förändrats sedan du kom med?
(How have you, and your faith, changed since you joined?)

9. Har du andra växtplatser?
(Are there other places of growth you attend?)

10. Hur har Covid påverkat <praktik> för dig?
(How has Covid affected your participation in <practice>?)

Appendix II: Interview Guide: Leader

1. Berätta lite kort om er bakgrund.
(Tell me a little about your background.)

2. Hur kom det sig att ni planterade denna församling här?
(How did you end up planting this church at this place?)

3. Vad är målet med församlingsplanteringen och hur jobbar ni för att uppnå det?
(What is the purpose of the church plant and how do you work to achieve this?)

4. Om du beskriver för någon som inte varit med, hur ser det ut och vad gör ni i planteringen?
(How would you explain the church plant to someone who hasn't been there, what does i t look like and what do you do?)

5. Vilka utmaningar har ni mött, så långt?
(What challenges have you encountered so far?)

6. Kan du nämna någon särskild händelse som varit viktigt för er så långt?
(Can you name a special occasion that has been important to you so far?)

7. Vad är det att vara kristen/lärjunge och hur blir man det?
(What does it mean to be a Christian/disciple and how do you become one?)

8. Hur har Covid påverkat er som församlingsplantering?
(How has Covid affected you as a church plant?)

Appendix III: Group Interview Guide

Maximalt 90 min. Temat är "Mission i staden",
Fokus är staden som plats för ert arbete.
(Maximum 90 minutes. Theme: "Mission in the city"
The focus is on the city as the place of your work)

Poängen med gruppsamtalet är att höra era olika perspektiv på samma fråga, olika röster och tankar uppmuntras
(The goal of the group conversation is to hear different perspectives on the question, different voices and views are encouraged)

1.
a) Staden, vad kännetecknar den? Vad är er vision för den?
(What charachterises the city? What is your vision for it?)

b) Människor Vem vill ni nå? Var finns dom?
(People: who do you want to reach? Where can they be found?)

2.
a) Olika lokaler (motiv, resultat)
(Different facilities, the motives and results)

b) Flytt (motiv, dröm, resultat)
(Moving, motives, dreams and result)

3.
a) Arbete/kallelse, hur vill ni arbeta? Vilka svårigheter ser ni med ert arbetssätt?
(Work/calling, how do you want to work? Are there difficulties with this way of working?)

b) Corona vs arbetssätt, hur har ni arbetat? Vad har ni vunnit/förlorat?
(Corona vs way of working, how have you dealt with this? What have you gained/lost?)

Bibliography

Addison, Steve (2011), *Movements That Change the World: Five Keys to Spreading the Gospel*, Downers Grove, Illinois: InterVarsity Press.
— (2012), *What Jesus Started: Joining the Movement, Changing the World*, Downers Grove, Illinois: IVP Books.
Afdal, Geir (2013), *Religion som bevegelse*, Oslo: Universitetsforlaget.
— (2021), "Two Concepts of Practice and Theology", *Studia Theologica – Nordic Journal of Theology*, 75 (1), 6–29.
Agar, Michael H. (1996), *The Professional Stranger*, Amsterdam: Academic Press Incorporated.
Ammerman, Nancy Tatom (2021), *Studying Lived Religion: Contexts and Practices*, New York: NYU Press.
Andersson, Greger, Roland Spjuth, and Fredrik Wenell (2017), Unga i karismatiska och evangelikala kyrkor resonerar om sin tro", *Scandinavian Journal for Leadership & Theology*, (4), 1–22.
Anker, Trine (2020), *Analyse i praksis: en håndbok for masterstudenter*, Oslo: Cappelen Damm Akademisk.
Appelfeldt, Joel (2023), *Dopet som hantverk*, Skellefteå: Artos & Norma bokförlag.
Asserhed, Björn (2013), *Discipleship in Community – Learning Trajectories of Church Community Leaders in the Discipleship Enterprise*. Linköping: Linköping University.
— (2020), *Församling som mission*, Stockholm: Vidare.
— (2023), "Jag ber att de alla ska bli ett, då ska världen tro", in Jaktlund, Carl-Henric, Mattias Neve, and Emma Rudäng (eds.), *Nya vägar för världens skull: förändringsarbete i frikyrkliga församlingar*. Bromma: Libris, 259–280.
Astley, Jeff (2017), "The Naming of Parts: Faith, Formation, Development and Education", in Stuart-Buttle, Ros and John Shortt (eds.), *Christian Faith, Formation and Education*. New York: Springer, 13–28.
Baker, Mark D. (2022), *Centered-Set Church: Discipleship and Community Without Judgmentalism*, Downers Grove, Illinois: InterVarsity Press.
Bartholomä, Philipp (2015), "The Ecclesiological Self and the Other: Concepts of Social Identity and Their Implications for Free Churches in Secular Europe", *Ecclesial Practices*, 2 156–176.
Bass, Dorothy C. and Craig Dykstra (2008), *For Life Abundant: Practical Theology, Theological Education, and Christian Ministry*, Grand Rapids, Michigan: Eerdmans.
Beard, Christopher (2015), "Missional Discipleship: Discerning Spiritual-formation Practices and Goals within the Missional Movement", *Missiology: An International Review*, 43 (2), 175–194.
Bebbington, David W. (1989), *Evangelicalism in Modern Britain*, London: Psychology Press.
Berger, Peter L. (2014), *The Many Altars of Modernity*, Berlin: De Gruyter.

Berggren, Henrik and Lars Trägårdh (2009), *Är svensken människa? Gemenskap och oberoende i det moderna Sverige*, Stockholm: Norstedts.
Bielo, James S. (2009), *Words upon the Word*, New York: New York University Press.
— (2013), "Urban Christianities: Place-making in Late Modernity", *Religion*, 43 (3), 301–311.
Blomberg, Frances Fulling (2014), *Forming and Sustaining Christian Community in a Consumer Culture: An Analysis of and Search for Appropriate Models*. Cardiff, UK: University of Wales.
Bolton, Ruth N., et al. (2013), "Understanding Generation Y and Their Use of Social Media: A Review and Research Agenda", *Journal of Service Management*, 24 (3), 245–267.
Bosch, David J. (2011), *Transforming Mission*, New York: Orbis Books.
Boy, John D. (2015), *Blessed Disruption: Culture and Urban Space in a European Church Planting Network*. New York: City University of New York.
Bramer, Paul D.G. (2007), "Christian Formation: Tweaking the Paradigm", *Christian Education Journal*, 4 (2), 352–363.
Bretherton, Luke (2019), *Christ and the Common Life*, Grand Rapids, Michigan: Eerdmans.
Brewer, Nathan (2020), *The Pulse of Christ (Revised and Expanded): A Fivefold Training Manual*, 100 Movements.
Brodd, Sven-Erik (2015), "Ecclesiology under Construction", in Fahlgren, Sune and Jonas Idestrom (eds.), *Ecclesiology in the Trenches*. Eugene, Oregon: Wipf and Stock, 1–28.
Bryman, Alan (2016), *Social Research Methods*, Oxford: Oxford University Press.
Cahalan, Kathleen A. (2005), "Three Approaches to Practical Theology, Theological Education, and the Church's Ministry", *International Journal of Practical Theology*, 9 (1), 63–94.
Cameron, Helen, et al. (2010), *Talking about God in Practice*, Norwich: Hymns Ancient and Modern Ltd.
Casanova, José (1994), *Public Religions in the Modern World*, Chicago: University of Chicago Press.
Sweden, The Christian Council of (ed.) (2020), *Unga troende i samhället – Varannan kristen ungdom upplever sig kränkt för sin tro*, Stockholm: Christian Council of Sweden.
Cornou, María Eugenia (2016), *Worship as a Formative Practice: The Worship Practices of Methodists, Baptists, and Free Brethren in Emerging Protestantism in Argentina (1867–1930)*. Amsterdam: Vrije Universitet.
Coulter, Paul B. (2016), *Church and Mission in Four Aspects: Church Planting Within a Missionary Ecclesiology for the One, Holy, Catholic and Apostolic Church in Contemporary Northern Ireland*. Aberdeen: University of Aberdeen.
Cox, Harvey (2010), *The Future of Faith*, New York: Harper Collins.
Dandelion, Pink (2019), *The Cultivation of Conformity*, Oxfordshire: Routledge.
Danermark, Berth, Mats Ekström, and Jan Ch. Karlsson (2019), *Explaining Society: Critical Realism in the Social Sciences*, Oxfordshire: Routledge.
Davie, Grace (2007), *The Sociology of Religion*, Thousand Oaks, California: sage.
— (2014), "Managing Pluralism: The European Case", *Society*, 51 (6), 613–622.
Dreier, Ole (1999), "Personal Trajectories of Participation across Contexts of Social Practice", *Outlines. Critical Practice Studies*, 1 5–32.
Eckerdal, Jan (2012), *Folkkyrkans kropp: Einar Billings ecklesiologi i postsekulär belysning*, Skellefteå: Artos.
Elangovan, A.R., Craig C. Pinder, and Murdith McLean (2010), "Callings and Organizational Behavior", *Journal of Vocational Behavior*, 76 (3), 428–440.

Eliot, T.S. (2021), *The Waste Land*, Berkeley, California: Mint Editions.
Ellström, Per-Erik (2010), "Organizational Learning", in Peterson, Penelope, Eva Baker, and Barry McGaw (eds.), *International Encyclopedia of Education, Vol 1*. London: Elsevier Science, 47–52.
Engeström, Yrjö (2001), "Expansive Learning at Work: Toward an Activity Theoretical Reconceptualization", *Journal of Education and Work*, 14 (1), 133–156.
Ewert, Per (2022), *Moving Reality Closer to the Ideal: The Process towards Autonomy and Secularism during the Social Democratic Hegemony in 20th century Sweden*. Oslo: VID.
Fahlgren, Sune (2006), *Predikantskap och församling*. Uppsala: Uppsala university.
— (2015), "Studying Fundamental Ecclesial Practices", in Fahlgren, Sune and Jonas Idestrom (eds.), *Ecclesiology in the Trenches*. Eugene, Oregon: Wipf and Stock, 87–105.
— (2018), "Gudstjänst i pentekostala kyrkor", in Sundmark, Stina Fallberg (ed.), *Kristen gudstjänst: en introduktion*. Skellefteå: Artos, 169–198.
Fenwick, Tara (2012), "Matterings of Knowing and Doing: Sociomaterial Approaches to Understanding Practice", in Hager, Paul, Alison Lee, and Ann Reich (eds.), *Practice, Learning and Change*. Berlin: Springer, 67–84.
Fitzmaurice, John (2016), *Virtue Ecclesiology: An Exploration in the Good Church*, London: Routledge.
Frost, Michael (2015), *Surprise the World: The Five Habits of Highly Missional People*, Carol Stream, Illinois: Tyndale House.
Ghodsee, Kristen (2016), *From Notes to Narrative: Writing Ethnographies That Everyone Can Read*, Chicago: University of Chicago Press.
Grenz, Stanley J. (1994), *Theology for the Community of God*, Milton Keynes: Paternoster.
Guder, Daniel L. and Lois Barrett (1998), *Missional Church: A Vision for the Sending of the Church in North America*, Grand Rapids, Michigan: Eerdmans.
Hager, Paul, Alison Lee, and Ann Reich (2012), "Problematising Practice, Reconceptualising Learning and Imagining Change", in Hager, Paul, Alison Lee, and Ann Reich (eds.), *Practice, Learning and Change*. New York: Springer, 1–16.
Halldorf, Joel (2012), *Av denna världen?: Emil Gustafson, moderniteten och den evangelikala väckelsen*, Skellefteå: Artos.
— (2015), "'En församling i varje stad' – Ideal för lokal församlingsverksamhet i 1900-talets svenska pingströrelse", in Josefsson, Ulrik and Magnus Wahlström (eds.), *Församlingsplantering i Pingst – Rapport från ett forskningsprojekt på IPS 2015* Forskningsrapporter från Institutet för Pentekostala Studier, Nr 6. Institutet för Pentekostala Studier, 39–62.
— (2015), "Storytelling and Evangelical Identities", in Jarlert, Anders (ed.), *Spiritual and Ecclesiastical – Biographies Research, Results, and Reading*. Kungliga vitterhets historie och antikvitets akademien, 128–139.
— (2017), *Biskop Lewi Pethrus: biografi över ett ledarskap: religion och mångfald i det svenska folkhemmet*, Skellefteå: Artos.
— (2018), "Mötet i frikyrklighet och väckelse", in Sundmark, Stina Fallberg (ed.), *Kristen gudstjänst: en introduktion*. Skellefteå: Artos, 137–168.
— (2020), *Pentecostal Politics in a Secular World: The Life and Leadership of Lewi Pethrus*, New York: Palgrave MacMillan.
— (2023), *Bokens folk: En civilisationshistoria från papyrus till pixel*, Stockholm: Fri Tanke.

Hallingberg, Gunnar (2010), *Läsarna: 1800-talet folkväckelse och det moderna genombrottet*, Stockholm: Atlantis.
Hamberg, Eva M. (2015), "Religious Monopolies, Religious Pluralism, and Secularization: The Relationship between Religious Pluralism and Religious Participation in Sweden", *Interdisciplinary Journal of Research on Religion*, 11.
Heelas, Paul and Linda Woodhead (2005), *The Spiritual Revolution*, Hoboken, New Jersey: Wiley-Blackwell.
Hiebert, Paul G. (1978), "Conversion, Culture and Cognitive Categories", *Gospel in Context*, 1 (4), 24-29.
— (1994), *Anthropological Reflections on Missiological Issues*, Ada, Michigan: Baker Academic.
Hirsch, Alan (2006), *The Forgotten Ways*, Grand Rapids, Michigan: Brazos Press.
— (2017), *5Q: Reactivating the Original Intelligence and Capacity of the Body of Christ*, 100 Movements.
Hirsch, Alan and Tim Catchim (2012), *The Permanent Revolution: Apostolic Imagination and Practice for the 21st Century Church*, Hoboken, New Jersey: Jossey-Bass.
Hirsch, Alan and Michael Frost (2013), *The Shaping of Things to Come: Innovation and Mission for the 21st-Century Church*, Ada, Michigan: Baker.
Hopwood, Nick (2016), "Sociomaterialism, Practice Theory, and Workplace Learning", in Hopwood, Nick (ed.), *Professional Practice and Learning: Professional and Practice-based Learning*. Cham: Springer International, 53-115.
Hornborg, Anne-Christine (2012), "Secular Spirituality in Contemporary Sweden", *Swedish Missiological Themes*, 100 (3), 203-320.
Ideström, Jonas and Tone Stangeland Kaufman (eds.) (2018), *What Really Matters*, Eugene, Oregon: Pickwick Publications.
— (2018), "The Researcher as Gamemaker – Response", in Ideström, Jonas and Tone Stangeland Kaufman (eds.), *What Really Matters*. Eugene, OR: Pickwick Publications, 173-182.
Illeris, Knud (2016), *How We Learn*, Oxfordshire: Routledge.
Internetstiftelsen (2021), *Svenskarna och internet 2021*, Stockholm: Internetstiftelsen.
Jamal Thornton, Brendan (2022), "Fieldwork", *Fieldwork in Religion*, 17 (1), 13-25.
James, Christopher B. (2018), *Church Planting in Post-Christian Soil*, Oxford: Oxford University Press.
Jarlert, Anders (2001), *Sveriges kyrkohistoria: Romantikens och liberalismens tid*, eds. Jarlert, Anders and Inga Wernolf, Stockholm: Verbum.
Jasiński, Karol (2021), "The Internal Secularisation of Religion", *Collectanea Theologica*, 91 (4), 95-111.
Lave, Jean (2018), "The Practice of Learning", in Illeris, Knud (ed.), *Contemporary Theories of Learning*. Oxfordshire, UK: Routledge, 200-208.
Johanson, Anne Mie Arndt Skak (2020), *When What We Know Is Not Enough: Exploring Danish Contemporary Faith Development in the Local Congregation*. Pasadena, California: Fuller Theological Seminary.
Johnsen, Elisabeth Tveito (2014), *Religiøs læring i sosiale praksiser. En etnografisk studie av mediering, identifisering og forhandlingsprosesser i Den norske kirkes trosopplæring*. Oslo: Universitetet i Oslo.
Josefsson, Ulrik (2005), *Liv och över nog: den tidiga pingströrelsens spiritualitet*, Skellefteå: Artos.
Kemmis, Stephen, et al. (2012), "Ecologies of Practices", in Hager, Paul, Alison Lee, and Ann Reich (eds.), *Practice, Learning and Change*. Berlin: Springer, 33-50.

Kittelmann Flensner, Karin (2015), *Religious Education in Contemporary Pluralistic Sweden*. Göteborg: Götebrog University.
Knoblauch, Hubert (2005), "Focused Ethnography", *Forum: Qualitative Social Research*, 6 (3), 1–14.
Larsson, Staffan (2006), *Didaktik för vuxna – tankelinjer i internationell litteratur*, Stockholm: Vetenskapsrådet.
Lave, Jean and Etienne Wenger (1991), *Situated Learning*, Cambridge: Cambridge University Press.
Lee, Michael H. (2007), *Assessment Of Paul Hiebert's Centered-Set Approach To The Category "Christian"*. Dallas: Dallas Theological Seminary.
Lenhammar, Harry (1999), *Sveriges kyrkohistoria: Individualismens och upplysningens tid*, eds. Lenhammar, Harry and Inga Wernolf, Stockholm: Verbum.
Leve, Lauren (2022), "Interlocutors", *Fieldwork in Religion*, 17 (1), 47–61.
Lockneus, Elin (2023), *Kyrkbänksteologi*, Skellefteå: Artos Norma Bokförlag.
Lundåsen, Susanne Wallman and Lars Trägårdh (2013), "Social Trust and Religion in Sweden: Theological Belief Versus Social Organization", *Religion and Civil Society in Europe*. Dordrecht: Springer Netherlands, 109–124.
Lundgren, Linnea (2021), *A Risk or a Resource?: A Study of the Swedish State's Shifting Perception and Handling of Minority Religious Communities between 1952–2019*. Ersta Sköndal Bräcke Högskola.
Lövgren, Johan (2017), *The Reflective Community: Learning Processes in Norwegian Folk High Schools*. Oslo: MF Norwegian School of Theology.
Lövheim, Mia and Heidi A Campbell (2017), "Considering Critical Methods and Theoretical Lenses in Digital Religion Studies", *New Media & Society*, 19 (1), 5–14.
Macintyre, Alasdair C. (2013), *After Virtue*, London: A&C Black.
Malphurs, Aubrey (2004), *Planting Growing Churches for the 21st Century: A Comprehensive Guide for New Churches and Those Desiring Renewal*, Ada, MI, US: Baker Books.
Mannerfelt, Frida (2023), *Co-preaching: The Practice of Preaching in Digital Culture and Spaces*. Stockholm: Enskilda Högskolan Stockholm.
Mcalpine, William R. (2011), *Sacred Space for the Missional Church*, Eugene, Oregon: Wipf and Stock.
Mcgavran, Donald A. (1990), *Understanding Church Growth*, Grand Rapids, Michigan: Eerdmans.
Mcgrath, Alister E. (2016), *Christian Theology: An Introduction*, Hoboken, New Jersey: John Wiley & Sons.
Mcguire, Meredith B. (2008), *Lived Religion: Faith and Practice in Everyday Life*, Oxford: Oxford University Press.
Melin, Jonas, Peter Svanberg, and Julia Wellstam (2020), *Vi planterar nya församlingar*, Evangelie förlag.
Miller-McLemore, Bonnie J. (2012), "Five Misunderstandings about Practical Theology", *International Journal of Practical Theology*, 16 (1), 5–26.
— (2014), *The Wiley Blackwell Companion to Practical Theology*, London: John Wiley & Sons.
— (2016), "The Theory-Practice Binary and the Politics of Practical Knowledge", in Mercer, Joyce A. and Bonnie J. Miller-McLemore (eds.), *Conundrums in Practical Theology*. Leiden: Brill, 190–218.

— (2022), "Understanding Lived Theology: Is Qualitative Research the Best or Only Way?", in Ward, Pete and Knut Tveitereid (eds.), *The Wiley Blackwell Companion to Theology and Qualitative Research*. London: John Wiley & Sons, 461–470.
Mills, C. Wright (1959), *The Sociological Imagination*, Oxford: Oxford University Press.
Mission And Public Affairs Council, Church Of England (2004), *Mission-shaped Church*, London: Church House.
Moberg, Jessica (2013), *Piety, Intimacy and Mobility*. Huddinge: Södertörns högskola.
Moynagh, Michael (2012), *Church for Every Context: An Introduction to Theology and Practice*, Norwich: Hymns Ancient and Modern Ltd.
Mowat, Harriet (2022), "Interviews and Observation", in Ward, Pete and Knut Tveitereid (eds.), *The Wiley Blackwell Companion to Theology and Qualitative Research*. Hoboken, New Jersey: John Wiley & Sons, 382–392.
Murphy, Debra Dean (2001), "Worship as Catechesis: Knowledge, Desire, and Christian Formation", *Theology Today*, 58 (3), 321–332.
Murphy, Nancey C., Brad J. Kallenberg, and Mark Nation (2003), *Virtues & Practices in the Christian Tradition*, Notre Dame, Indiana: University of Notre Dame Press.
Murray, Stuart (2018), *Post-Christendom: Church and Mission in a Strange New World. Second Edition*, Eugene, Oregon: Wipf and Stock.
Mutch, Alistair (2003), "Communities of Practice and Habitus: A Critique", *Organization Studies*, 24 (3), 383–401.
Neve, Mattias (2021), *In Pursuit of Proximity: A Missiological Study of Four 'Emerging church' Communities in Sweden*. Amsterdam: Vrije Universitet.
Nicholson, Steve and Jeff Bailey (1999), *Coaching Church Planters*, Association of Vineyard Churches.
Nicolini, Davide (2012), *Practice Theory, Work, and Organization*, Oxford: Oxford University Press.
Niemandt, Cornelius J.P. (2012), "Trends in Missional Ecclesiology", *HTS Teologiese Studies / Theological Studies*, 68 (1), 1–9.
Nilsson, Per-Erik and Victoria Enkvist (2016), "Techniques of Religion-making in Sweden: The Case of the Missionary Church of Kopimism", *Critical Research on Religion*, 4 (2), 141–155.
Nordbäck, Carola (2014), "Trons mötesplatser – Ett kyrko- och väckelsehistoriskt perspektiv", in Amundsen, Arne Bugge (ed.), *Vekkelsens møtesteder*. Lund: Lunds universitet, 9–52.
Norris, Pippa and Ronald Inglehart (2011), *Sacred and Secular: Religion and Politics Worldwide*, Cambridge: Cambridge University Press.
Ong, Walter J. and John Hartley (2012), *Orality and Literacy: The Technologizing of the Word*, Oxfordshire: Routledge.
Osmer, Richard R. (2008), *Practical Theology: An Introduction*, Grand Rapids, Michigan: Eerdmans.
— (2012), "Formation in the Missional Church: Building Deep Connections between Ministries of Upbuilding and Sending", in Zscheile, Dwight (ed.), *Cultivating Sent Communities: Missional Spiritual Formation*. Grand Rapids, Michigan: Eerdmans, 29–55.
Ott, Craig and Gene Wilson (2011), *Global Church Planting*, Ada, Michigan: Baker Academic.
Paas, Stefan (2011), "Post-Christian, Post-Christendom, and Post-Modern Europe: Towards the Interaction of Missiology and the Social Sciences", *Mission Studies*, 28 (1), 3–25.
— (2016), *Church Planting in the Secular West*, Grand Rapids, Michigan: Eerdmans.

— (2018), "A Case Study of Church Growth by Church Planting in Germany: Are They Connected", *International Bulletin of Mission Research*, 42 (1), 40–54.
— (2019), *Pilgrims and Priests*, London: SCM.
Paas, Stefan and Alrik Vos (2016), "Church Planting and Church Growth in Western Europe: An Analysis", *International Bulletin of Mission Research*, 40 (3), 243–252.
Paas, Stefan and Marry Schoemaker (2018), "Crisis and Resilience Among Church Planters in Europe", *Mission Studies*, 35 (3), 366–388.
Paas, Stefan and Philipp Bartholomä (2020), "The Missional Future of Free Churches in a Secular Context: A German Case Study", *Journal of Empirical Theology*, 33 (2), 157–177.
Paas, Stefan and Hans Schaeffer (2021), "Reconciled Community", *Ecclesiology*, 17 (3), 325–347.
Palmer, Michael D. (2016), "Ethical Formation: The Theological Virtues", in Chandler, Diane J. (ed.), *The Holy Spirit and Christian Formation: Multidisciplinary Perspectives*. London: Palgrave Macmillan, 107–127.
Perrin, Ruth (2022), "Qualitative Research and Young Adult Faith", in Ward, Pete and Knut Tveitereid (eds.), *The Wiley Blackwell Companion to Theology and Qualitative Research*. Wiley Online Library, 162–172.
Raelin, Joseph A (2007), "Toward an Epistemology of Practice", *Academy of Management Learning & Education*, 6 (4), 495–519.
Reckwitz, Andreas (2017), *The Invention of Creativity: Modern Society and the Culture of the New*, Cambridge: Polity.
Reite, Ingrid Christine (2014), *Between Settling and Unsettling in a Changing Knowledge Society: The Professional Learning Trajectories of Pastors*. Oslo: MF Norwegian School of Theology.
Roberts, Joanne (2006), "Limits to Communities of Practice", *Journal of Management Studies*, 43 (3), 623–639.
Rogers, Andrew P. (2016), *Congregational Hermeneutics: How Do We Read*, Oxfordshire: Routledge.
Root, Andrew (2016), "Regulating the Empirical in Practical Theology", *Journal of Youth and Theology*, 15 (1), 44–64.
— (2017a), *Faith Formation in a Secular Age*, Ada, Michigan: Baker Academic.
— (2017b), "Faith Formation in a Secular Age", *Word & World*, 37 (2), 128–141.
Rosenberg, G (2002), "The Crisis of Consensus in Postwar Sweden" in N Witoszek, & L Trägårdh (eds.), *Culture and Crisis: The Case of Germany and Sweden*, Berghahn Books, New York, 170–201.
Rutba-House (ed.) (2005), *School(s) for Conversion: 12 Marks of a New Monasticism*, Eugene, Oregon: Cascade Books.
Sargeant, Wendi Anne (2011), *Christian Education and the Emerging Church*, New York: Pickwick Publications.
Schaeffer, Hans (2022), "Concrete Church: Qualitative Research and Ecclesial Practices", in Ward, Pete and Knut Tveitereid (eds.), *The Wiley Blackwell Companion to Theology and Qualitative Research*. London: John Wiley & Sons, 151–162.
Schatzki, Theodore R. (2001), "Practice Theory", in Schatzki, Theodore R., Karin Knorr-Cetina, and Eike von Savigny (eds.), *The Practice Turn in Contemporary Theory*. New York: Psychology Press, 1–14.
Schmidt, Ulla (2021), "Practicing as Knowing", *Studia Theologica - Nordic Journal of Theology*, 75 (1), 30–51.
Selka, Stephen (2022), "Positionality", *Fieldwork in Religion*, 17 (1), 92–100.

Selvaratnam, Christian Nathan (2020), *The Craft of Church Planting: Guild Training Models for Apprenticing Church Planters*. Wilmore, Kentucky: Asbury Theological Seminary.

Serpa, Sandro and Carlos Miguel Ferreira (2019), "Micro, Meso and Macro Levels of Social Analysis", *International Journal of Social Science Studies*, 7 (3), 120–124.

Sfard, Anna (1998), "On Two Metaphors for Learning and the Dangers of Choosing Just One", *Educational Researcher*, 27 (2), 4–13.

Sigurdson, Ola (2009), *Det postsekulära tillståndet – religion, modernitet, politik*, Göteborg: Glänta.

Smith, Christian and Melinda Lundquist Denton (2009), *Soul Searching: The Religious and Spiritual Lives of American Teenagers*, Oxford: Oxford University Press.

Smith, Daryl L and Andrew B Smith (2019), *Discovering Your Missional Potential: An Encounter with Ephesians 4 and How Jesus Lives It*, 100 Movements.

Smith, James K. A. (2009), *Desiring the Kingdom: Worship, Worldview and Cultural Formation*, Grand Rapids, Michigan: Baker Academic.

— (2013), *Imagining the Kingdom: How Worship Works*, Grand Rapids, Michigan: Baker Academic.

— (2014), *How (Not) to Be Secular*, Grand Rapids, Michigan: Eerdmans.

Smith, Steven D. (2018), *Pagans and Christians in the City: Culture Wars from the Tiber to the Potomac*, Atlanta, Georgia: Emory University Studies.

Stangeland Kaufman, Tone (2018), "Mapping the Landscape of Scandinavian Research in Ecclesiology and Ethnography – Contributions and Challenges", in Ideström, Jonas and Tone Stangeland Kaufman (eds.), *What Really Matters*. Eugene, OR: Pickwick Publications, 15–37.

Stone, Bryan P. (2018), *Finding Faith Today*, Eugene, Oregon: Wipf and Stock.

Strandenæs, Thor (2010), "Missionally Relevant Rituals for the Secular City: A Quest for Christian Rituals which Adequately Interact with Citizens' Lives and Needs", *Swedish Missiological Themes*, 98,3 341–360.

Strhan, Anna (2015), *Aliens and Strangers*, Oxford: Oxford University Press.

Svanberg, Peter (1999), *Church Planting in Sweden in the 21st century: A Model for New Methodist Churches*. Asbury Seminary.

Swinton, John (2012), "'Where Is Your Church?' Moving towards a Hospitable and Sanctified Ethnography", in Ward, Pete (ed.), *Perspectives on Ecclesiology and Ethnography*. Grand Rapids, Michigan: Eerdmans, 71–94.

Swinton, John and Harriet Mowat (2016), *Practical Theology and Qualitative Research – second edition*, London: SCM.

Tangen, Karl Inge (2012), *Ecclesial Identification Beyond Late Modern Individualism*, Leiden: Brill.

Tanner, Kathryn (1997), *Theories of Culture: A New Agenda for Theology*, Augsburg: Augsburg Fortress.

Taylor, Charles (2007), *A Secular Age*, Cambridge, Massachusetts: Harvard University Press.

Tholvsen, Øyvind (2021), *Frikyrkoundersökningen – En rapport om frikyrkornas utveckling i Sverige 2000–2020*, Sveriges Frikyrkosamråd.

Thurfjell, David (2015), *Det gudlösa folket*, Stockholm: Norstedts.

Timmermans, Stefan and Iddo Tavory (2012), "Theory Construction in Qualitative Research: From Grounded Theory to Abductive Analysis", *Sociological Theory*, 30 (3), 167–186.

Index of Biblical Literature

Psalms	136	Acts	245
107:4–9	17		
		Romans	162
Matthew	161		
5:44	129	First Corinthians	162
6	153	1–8	216
7:3	163	2:1–5	109
19:19	129	6:12–20	163
20:17–19	164		
		Galatians	162
Mark	162	5:13–26	163
1:6	112		
		Ephesians	162
Luke		4:11–13	135, 169, 170, 173, 197
10:33–34	134		
		First John	
John	162	1:1	77
3:16	126		
4:1–42	170		

Index of Authors

Addison, Steve 245
Afdal, Geir 58, 89, 90, 93, 97
Agar, Michael H. 75, 79, 246
Ammerman, Nancy T. 46, 48
Andersson, Greger 38, 39
Anker, Trine 74
Appelfeldt, Joel 68
Asserhed, Björn 42, 93, 213, 254
Astley, Jeff 21, 26, 89–90

Baker, Mark D. 238
Barrett, Lois 29
Bartholomä, Philipp 21, 39, 68, 209
Bass, Dorothy C. 57
Beard, Christopher 26, 29
Bebbington, David W. 148, 178, 221
Bailey, Jeff 42
Berger, Peter L. 36, 81
Berggren, Henrik 33, 245
Bielo, James S. 50, 104, 105, 108
Blomberg, Frances Fulling 159
Bolton, Ruth N. 119
Bosch, David J. 148
Boy, John D. 19, 20, 68, 113, 212, 243
Bramer, Paul D.G. 57
Bretherton, Luke 37, 215
Brewer, Nathan 173
Brodd, Sven–Erik 44
Bryman, Alan 82, 84

Cahalan, Kathleen A. 58
Cameron, Helen 44, 92
Campbell, Heidi A. 119
Casanova, José 18, 35
Catchim, Tim 174
The Christian Council of Sweden 209
Cole, Michael 94, 175
Cornou, María Eugenia 58, 59

Coulter, Paul B. 254
Cox, Harvey 65

Dandelion, (Ben) Pink 19, 66, 68, 242, 245, 263
Danermark, Berth 73
Davie, Grace 18, 31, 35, 36
Dreier, Ole 99
Dykstra, Craig 57

Eckerdal, Jan 44
Ekström, Mats 73
Elangovan, A. R. 25, 53, 104, 105, 107, 230
Eliot, T.S. 17
Ellström, Per–Erik 90
Engeström, Yrjö 94, 98
Enkvist, Victoria 34
Ewert, Per 242

Fahlgren, Sune 44, 92, 146, 214, 244
Fenwick, Tara 94, 96, 237
Fitzmaurice, John 68, 246
Frost, Michael 135, 159, 245

Ghodsee, Kristen 85, 247
Grenz, Stanley J. 180
Guder, Daniel L. 29

Hager, Paul 44, 92, 94, 146
Halldorf, Joel 32, 37, 40, 147, 215
Hallingberg, Gunnar 147
Hamberg, Eva M. 212
Hartley, John 253
Heelas, Paul 19, 58, 66, 68, 242, 263
Hiebert, Paul G. 63, 237, 238
Hirsch, Alan 29, 30, 107, 135, 173, 174, 245
Hopwood, Nick 94

Hornborg, Anne-Christine 242

Ideström, Jonas 50, 51, 79, 94, 247
Illeris, Knud 95
Inglehart, Ronald 36
Internetstiftelsen 119

Jamal Thornton, Brendan 78
James, Christopher B. 55–57, 109, 126, 140, 141, 235, 263
Jarlert, Anders 32
Jasiński, Karol 19
Johanson, Anne Mie Arndt Skak 63, 64, 70, 240, 252
Johnsen, Elisabeth Tveito 59, 93
Josefsson, Ulrik 147

Kallenberg, Brad J. 95
Karlsson, Jan Ch. 73
Kemmis, Stephen 146, 263
Kittelmann Flensner, Karin 34
Knoblauch, Hubert 76,

Larsson, Staffan 90
Lauren, Leve 79
Lave, Jean 48, 74, 93–103, 145, 179–180
Lee, Alison 44, 92, 94, 146
Lee, Michael H. 64, 237
Lenhammar, Harry 32, 259
Lockneus, Elin 59
Lundåsen, Susanne Wallman 33, 34
Lundgren, Linnea 32, 33
Lundquist Denton, Melinda 38, 54
Lövgren, Johan 93
Lövheim, Mia 119

Macintyre, Alasdair C. 93–95, 103, 165
Malphurs, Aubrey 42
Mannerfelt, Frida 248, 253
Mcalpine, William R. 29, 246
Mcgavran, Donald A. 43
Mcgrath, Alister E. 259
Mcguire, Meredith B. 48
McLean, Murdith 25, 53, 104, 105, 107, 230
Melin, Jonas 41

Miguel Ferreira, Carlos 74
Miller-McLemore, Bonnie J. 44, 46, 47
Mills, C. Wright 36
Mission And Public Affairs Council 23, 41
Moberg, Jessica 21, 22, 67, 149, 152, 217, 237, 243
Moynagh, Michael 42, 62, 108, 117, 139, 235, 236
Mowat, Harriet 46, 47, 84
Murphy, Debra Dean 25, 27, 45
Murphy, Nancey C. 95
Murray, Stuart 212, 245
Mutch, Alistair 96

Nation, Mark 95
Neve, Mattias 22, 68–69, 71, 244, 260
Nicholson, Steve 42
Nicolini, Davide 91, 93, 94
Niemandt, Cornelius J.P. 29, 47
Nilsson, Per-Erik 34
Nordbäck, Carola 40,
Norris, Pippa 36

Ong, Walter J. 253
Osmer, Richard R. 21, 54, 70, 235, 244, 260
Ott, Craig 41

Paas, Stefan 21, 22, 40, 41, 42, 43, 61, 66, 258, 261
Palmer, Michael D. 95
Perrin, Ruth 62, 241
Pinder, Craig C. 25, 53, 104, 105, 107, 230

Raelin, Joseph A. 44, 175
Reckwitz, Andreas 43
Reich, Ann 44, 92, 94, 146
Reite, Ingrid Christine 93
Roberts, Joanne 96, 101, 237
Rogers, Andrew P. 102, 166
Root, Andrew 21, 27, 36, 37, 48, 49, 55, 65, 77, 111, 210, 240, 243, 247, 252, 258
Rutba-House 28

Sargeant, Wendi Anne 26, 27, 89
Schaeffer, Hans 258, 261
Schatzki, Theodore R. 94
Schmidt, Ulla 45
Schoemaker, Marry 41
Selka, Stephen 80, 247
Selvaratnam, Christian Nathan 61, 236
Serpa, Sandro 74
Sfard, Anna 91
Sigurdson, Ola 36
Smith, Andrew B. 172
Smith, Christian 38, 54
Smith, Daryl L. 172
Smith, James K. A. 25, 27, 28, 30, 37, 44, 45, 46, 55, 58, 242
Smith, Steven D. 216
Spjuth, Roland 38, 39
Stangeland Kaufman, Tone 50, 51, 79, 94, 247
Stone, Bryan P. 179
Strandenæs, Thor 59, 70
Strhan, Anna 21, 22, 67, 156, 210, 217, 243
Svanberg, Peter 23, 41, 61
Swinton, John 46–47, 80

Tangen, Karl Inge 20, 22, 65, 70, 239, 240, 252
Tanner, Kathryn 206, 207, 208
Tavory, Iddo 73
Taylor, Charles 36, 38, 55, 262
Tholvsen, Øyvind 31, 41, 81
Thurfjell, David 31, 32, 34, 35
Timmermans, Stefan 73

Trägårdh, Lars 33, 34, 245
Tveitereid, Knut 26, 47–48, 63, 77, 84, 94
Tveito Johnsen, Elisabeth 59, 93

Vålandsmyr, Johannes 22
Volf, Miroslav 180
Vos, Alrik 22
Vygotskii, Lev S. 94, 98, 175

Wall, Philip Roger 20, 23, 60, 156, 170
Ward, Pete 20, 45, 46, 48, 49, 75, 76, 246, 256, 261
Weissenbilder, Marcus 31
Wellstam, Julia 41
Wenell, Fredrik 38, 39
Wenger(-Trayner), Etienne 46, 59, 89, 90, 93, 95–105, 146, 180, 181, 206, 237, 263
Westerlund, Katarina 30, 31, 93
Wigg-Stevenson, Natalie 76
Williams, Rowan 208, 244
Wilson, Bryan R. 18, 35
Wilson, Gene 41
Winn, Christian T. Collins 148
Woodhead, Linda 19, 58, 66, 68, 242, 263
Woodhead, Linda 19, 58, 66, 68, 242, 263

Zackariasson, Maria 34, 35, 93, 211, 217
Zscheile, Dwight 20, 29

Index of Subjects

Abductive approach 73–74, 246–247
Activism 148, 175, 176, 201, 236, 245, 262, 264
Alpha course 131, 170
Al Massira course 131
Anonymity
    Cultural 138
    Methodological 85, 148, 182
Authenticity 18, 22, 36, 47, 65, 69, 236, 237

Bible reading 39, 56, 118, 124, 125, 128, 131, 142, 158, 159, 160, 162, 165, 166, 185, 189, 190, 192, 199

Calling definition 104
Church planting
    Definitions 41
    Paradigms 22, 43, 61,
Christian formation definition 18, 26, 30
Conventicle 148–149, 166, 177, 236, 246, 254
Contextualisation 20, 47, 69, 106, 206, 209, 233, 234, 236, 244, 260
Covid-19 78, 86, 131, 150, 158, 162, 168, 248, 249
Critical realism 48, 49, 73, 77, 260
Culture 111, 112, 115–117, 159, 205–212, 25–217, 227–228

Democracy 32, 186, 225, 228, 234
Discernment 46, 47, 69, 205, 228, 234, 244, 247, 260–263
Diversity 101, 132, 134, 143, 172, 174, 175, 187, 218–221

Experiential faith 27, 28, 30, 49, 54, 58, 64, 65, 69, 71, 77, 118, 124, 129, 140, 147, 148, 164, 171, 177, 179, 183, 192, 194, 199, 202, 230, 241, 244, 251–253
Ecclesial imagination 61, 107, 235, 255–260
Ecumenism 212, 254

Faithful neighbours 122, 129, 131, 132, 143, 195, 230, 231
Fishermen 117, 121, 143, 182, 189, 230
Free church tradition 20, 31, 32, 35, 39, 40, 81, 103, 136, 147–148, 177, 214, 236, 243, 254

Good Samaritans 134, 139, 142, 143, 170, 173, 195, 197, 230, 231

Invitation evangelism 110, 117, 127, 133, 157, 167, 169, 183, 185, 189, 192, 196, 200

Leadership 22, 54, 85, 123, 124, 149, 161, 168, 171, 196, 202, 224–227, 231, 235,
Liquid ecclesiology 255–257
Lived identity definition 24, 90, 102

MyLife workshop 131

Neighbourhood missiology 56–57, 122, 125, 126, 128, 131, 230

Online meetings 79, 86, 126, 128, 131, 158, 167, 192, 195, 198, 219, 226, 231, 249

Practice theory 92, 93, 94, 146,

Prayer 116, 124, 126–129, 133, 139, 152, 153, 155, 159, 162, 164, 170, 172, 187, 191, 214, 215, 219, 252

Religious Market Theory 68, 212, 213

Secularisation
    And formation 30, 39
    Internal 19, 66, 205, 233, 262
    And minorities 32–34, 209–211
    As motive for mission 115, 243
    Swedish context 20, 30–34

    Theories of 18, 35, 36
Social media 110, 118, 121, 126, 142, 149, 156, 177, 230, 253

Virtue formation 33, 67, 95, 143, 159–160, 163, 165, 177, 180, 188, 192, 195, 221, 231, 232, 255
Vulnerability 109, 170, 201, 233

Worship singing 28, 67, 116, 127, 147, 152, 156, 157, 215, 219, 253

Dissertationes Theologicae Holmienses

1. Eurell, John-Christian. *Peter's Legacy in Early Christianity: The Appropriation and Use of Peter's Authority in the First Three Centuries.* DTH 1. Stockholm: Enskilda Högskolan Stockholm, 2021.
2. Mannerfelt, Frida. *Co-preaching: The Practice of Preaching in Digital Culture and Spaces.* DTH 2. Stockholm: Enskilda Högskolan Stockholm, 2023.
3. Appelfeldt, Joel. *Dopet som hantverk: Gudstjänstkreativitet och liturgisk taktik i Svenska kyrkan och Equmeniakyrkan.* DTH 3. Skellefteå: Artos Academic, 2023.
4. Gobena, Abate. *Sanctity and Environment in Ethiopian Hagiography: The Case of Gedle Gebre Menfes Qiddus.* DTH 4. Stockholm: Enskilda Högskolan Stockholm, 2023.
5. Lockneus, Elin. *Kyrkbänksteologi.* DTH 5. Skellefteå: Artos Academic, 2023.
6. Asserhed, Björn. *Gardens in the Wasteland: Christian Formation in Three Swedish Church Plants.* DTH 6. Stockholm: Enskilda Högskolan Stockholm, 2024.

www.ingramcontent.com/pod-product-compliance
Lightning Source LLC
Chambersburg PA
CBHW070238230426
43664CB00014B/2350